A HEART  ON FIRE

CATHERINE MARTIN

A HEART ♡ ON FIRE

QuietTime
MINISTRIES

PALM DESERT, CALIFORNIA

A Heart On Fire—Discover The Priceless Privilege Of Knowing Christ
Copyright © 2002 by Catherine Martin
Published by Quiet Time Ministries
Palm Desert, California 92255
www.quiettime.org

ISBN-13: 978-0-9766886-3-1

Second Edition published by Quiet Time Ministries 2012

Printed in the United States of America
12 13 14 15 16 17 18 19 20 / ACS/ 11 10 9 8 7 6 5 4 3 2

Dedicated to…
the Lord Jesus Christ
who daily gives me a burning heart of love for Him.

My Professors at Bethel Theological Seminary
who inspired me to run the race set before me with excellence.

As I wrote this book of quiet times, I thanked the Lord again and again...

For Dr. Wessel, my New Testament professor who challenged me
to give my very best and who gave me such a love for intense and detailed study,
who taught me to rightly divide the Word of God,
who gave me a love for the Greek language,
who introduced me to great authors including F.F. Bruce,
and who is now in the presence of the Lord.

For Dr. Youngblood, my Old Testament professor, who challenged me
to be specific, detailed, and complete in everything I study and write,
who taught me to work hard to complete and assignment,
who, by example, as one of the translators of the New International Version
taught me that the work of study and writing can influence thousands.

For Dr. Al Glenn, my Theology professor who gave me such a love for doctrine
and taught me not to be afraid to go outside the box as a woman in ministry.

For Dr. James Smith, my Christian History professor, who passed on to me
a love of studying the lives and hearts of saints like Polycarp and Martin Luther.

I could never have written this book of quiet times without all of you!

— ⚬⚬⚬ —

Didn't we feel on fire as he conversed with us on the road,
as he opened up the Scriptures for us?

LUKE 24:32 THE MESSAGE

I certainly do count everything as loss
compared with the priceless privilege
of knowing Christ Jesus my Lord.

PHILIPPIANS 3:8 WILLIAMS TRANSLATION

Turn your eyes upon Jesus,
Look full in His wonderful face,
And the things of earth
Will grow strangely dim
In the light of His glory and grace.

HELEN H. LEMMEL 1922

CONTENTS

❧ FOREWORD ❧

They say that you form an opinion of a person the first time you meet them. I don't know whether that's always true, but it was surely the case when I first met Catherine Martin almost twenty years ago. She had matriculated at Bethel Seminary San Diego and had enrolled in one of my courses. Although it was a large class (the course was required of all entering students), she stood out primarily because of her glowing smile. She was always perky ("cheerful and lively," according to the definition of "perky" in my dictionary), like Katie Couric of NBC-TV's morning show "Today." Come to think of it, I can't remember ever seeing Catherine when she didn't have a smile on her face.

As it turned out, however, Catherine was much more than just a pretty face. She quickly demonstrated the diligent and systematically determined side of her nature as she waltzed through the challenge of all three of my courses in which she had enrolled: Biblical Prolegomena in the fall of 1987, Old Testament 101-102 in the winter of 1988, and Old Testament 102-103 in the spring of that year. Those who know Catherine will not be surprised to learn that she earned an A grade in each of them -- effortlessly, as nearly as I could gauge. It soon became clear that she was an exceptional student, concluding her formal education at Bethel with a straight-A grade-point average of 4.0 and graduating in 1993 with the degree of Master of Arts in Theological Studies, summa cum laude.

Catherine's future ministry in the service of Christ had already begun long before she came to Bethel. She had worked for Josh McDowell and Bill Bright for several years beginning in 1978, and she served as a women's Bible-study leader for more than a decade, including her time as a seminary student. So it was only natural that she should found and direct an organization such as Quiet Time Ministries soon after graduation. 1994 thus became a pivotal year in the life and ministry of Catherine Martin.

Growing up in Chicago as a young Christian, I was advised by my spiritual mentors to spend a "quiet time" every day with my Lord. That meant that I was to read my Bible and pray every day -- a worthy and important spiritual exercise. Recently I discovered that the phrases "quiet time" and "Catherine Martin" are virtual synonyms -- or at least they are closely associated with each other in the minds of many people. I typed "quiet time" in the appropriate box of the Google search engine, and in less than a second I gained access to more than 2,000,000 references to that phrase. Reference number 3 on the first page was totally about Catherine Martin's Quiet Time Ministries. She is obviously making a deep and lasting spiritual impact on a wide audience throughout the world.

A Heart On Fire, by Catherine's own admission, draws its title from the story of Cleopas and his friend on the road to Emmaus shortly after Jesus' resurrection. Jesus joined them on their journey and entered into a lively discussion with them: "Beginning with Moses and all the prophets, He explained to them the things concerning Himself in all the Scriptures" (Luke 24:27). Later, after they finally became aware of who he was, they said to each other, "Were not our hearts burning within us while He was speaking to us on the road, while He was explaining the Scriptures to us?" The Emmaus travelers were not the first to experience that fiery sensation, of course; they were part of a continuing company of believers that numbered, among others, the prophet Jeremiah, who declared that "the word of the Lord . . . in my heart becomes like a burning fire shut up in my bones" (Jeremiah 20:8-9).

The great evangelist and founder of Methodism, John Wesley, relates concerning his encounter with the living Christ at Aldersgate on May 24, 1738: "I felt my heart strangely warmed. I felt I did trust in Christ, Christ alone for salvation, and an assurance was given me that He had taken away my sins, even mine, and saved me from the law of sin and death." For your part, I hope that you will carefully and prayerfully read through A Heart On Fire under the patient and expert guidance of Catherine Martin. And, from time to time, may you experience the way of the burning heart as you and Jesus walk along your Emmaus road together.

RONALD YOUNGBLOOD
Emeritus Professor of Old Testament
Bethel Seminary, San Diego

❧ INTRODUCTION ❧

When I was a little girl, my brother and I used to go with my mother to a park in Phoenix. She would sit and study for her master's degree and my brother and I would play. One of the things we loved to do was pick up rocks and throw them in the middle of the pond. We would stand there for hours and do it again and again, fascinated by the series of ripples, one wave after another, created by the splash. The higher the rock went into the air, the more force it created when it hit the water, and the more ripples occurred as a result. That's the ripple effect.

The ripple effect is all about impact and influence. When something impacts another with an incredible force, then the influence is incremental in its magnitude. Two thousand years ago something happened with such great force that it created a ripple effect that has continued to this day and will continue on into eternity. A man named Jesus Christ entered the dimension of time and space and His Presence on earth for a brief thirty-three years was of such force that His influence has multiplied to this day. Jesus was no ordinary man. He did things that no man has ever done. He raised people from the dead. He gave sight to someone who was blind from birth. He made a paralyzed man walk. He fed thousands with just a few loaves of bread and some fish. He made the wind and rain stop with just a few words. He made outrageous claims. The greatest claim of all was that He was God. He said in the presence of many: "I am the way, the truth, and the life. No one comes to the Father but through Me" (John 14:6).

People everywhere were faced with a choice whenever He spoke. He did not just talk in platitudes. He asked for decisions about life and a commitment to God. People had to decide if He was who He claimed to be. Was He really the only way to God? Was His exclusive claim true? After hearing Him speak and watching Him do miracles, things that no other earthly person could do, many left their former way of life and believed in Him. They followed Him wherever He went. They listened to Him teach about the kingdom of God, captivated by His words. Lives were turned upside down.

And then, the unthinkable happened. The same words and life that drew many to God also confronted others with truths they did not want to accept. And those enemies arrested Jesus and put Him to death. They figured that if they could just erase Him off the face of the earth, then this wave of newfound excitement about a Person would immediately end. There was one thing they did not calculate into their devious plan. What if this Jesus really was who He claimed to be? What if He indeed was God visiting earth? What if His death really did accomplish the ultimate result—forgiveness of sins for all who would come to Him and believe in Him. And what if death could not keep Him in a grave? What if indeed He did come back to life after three days just like He said He would?

Three days after His crucifixion two women went to His tomb. As they approached the tomb they saw something that changed their lives forever. There was a violent earthquake, an angel came down from heaven, went to the tomb, and rolled the stone away from the entrance of the tomb. The guards, shaking with fear, ran away. The angel told the women to look inside the tomb. When they did, they found it empty. Jesus had risen from the dead. The angel told them to go tell all of Jesus' disciples. The women hurried away from the tomb. They were afraid yet excited at the same time. Could it be true? While on their way, all of a sudden, Jesus appeared to them. There He stood, right before their very eyes. They fell at His feet and worshipped Him. Jesus was alive. Not even death could have the ultimate power over Him. He is indeed who He claimed to be! He is God. His words are true. He is the way, the truth, and the life. No one comes to the Father, but through Him.

Those words are simultaneously life-changing and arresting. Why? Because no one can ignore them. They call for a decision. Either decide that He is who He claimed to be or He is not. There is no middle ground. To not decide is to decide against. And so, the best thing, the most brilliant thing that any one person can do is to consider the words of Jesus and make a decision for Him. "Yes He is who He claimed to be. I will give my life to Him."

The words of Jesus will turn your life upside down. His words always call for decisions about how you live and ask for your wholehearted surrender and commitment. If you will truly listen to Jesus and what He says, your heart will be ignited in such a way as to burn forever. You will have a heart on fire — on fire for Jesus Christ. And your burning heart will create such waves that it will generate the ripple effect.

When you meet Jesus Christ and begin to spend time with Him your heart will begin to burn from within. That is the way it always is. Knowing Him is what life is all about and it is the greatest pursuit you can have in life. Paul the Apostle said: "I certainly do count everything as loss compared with the priceless privilege of knowing Christ Jesus my Lord" (Philippians 3:8 WMS). Before he met Jesus, Paul was zealously committed to destroying Christians because he thought they were enemies of God.

Jesus met Paul and personally revealed Himself to him. Paul discovered that Jesus was indeed who He claimed to be, and he gave his heart, his allegiance, and his life to Jesus. He determined to follow Him wherever He led, completely sold out to Him. There was nothing as important to him as knowing Christ. He sacrificed all for this one thing: knowing Christ. As he engaged in this pursuit, he discovered that knowing Christ was a priceless privilege. The result was a heart on fire for Jesus Christ. Thousands of lives were transformed as a result. Paul wrote most of the letters in the New Testament. And the ripple effect continues on.

I remember when I first began spending time alone with the Lord Jesus Christ, my excitement about knowing Him grew beyond anything I could have imagined. I became passionate for Him and loved to tell others about Him. I was at a convenience store one day. I started talking to the man at the counter about Christ. The man said, "Don't talk to me about Christ. The one who needs to hear about it is that kid over there." He pointed to a kid with long hair who was twirling a basketball on one finger. I walked over to him and began talking to him about Christ. We sat on the curb outside that store for over an hour as I explained to him the importance of surrendering his life to Christ. Then I left and never really gave that experience much thought after that.

About a year later I was leading a time of sharing at a conference in Prescott, Arizona. One young man in the back of the room raised his hand indicating his desire to share a few words with the group. I called on him. He spoke directly to me: "Do you remember me?" I replied, "No." He said, "You spoke to me at a convenience store a year ago. As a result of what you said, I gave my life to Christ, and I'm now attending Moody Bible Institute." I could hardly believe that one brief encounter could have such an astounding result. That is what happens when Jesus Christ is part of the encounter, no matter how brief or seemingly insignificant. That's the ripple effect. It goes on and on and on. And oh, what an adventure it is!

In *A Heart On Fire*, you will spend time with this One I have been talking about: Jesus Christ. You will begin by walking with Him on the Road to Emmaus where He met two discouraged disciples who had witnessed His crucifixion. They did not recognize Him at first, but He explained to them from the Scriptures who He was and what His purpose was. When He finally revealed Himself to them, they said: "Didn't we feel on fire as he conversed with us on the road, as he opened up the Scriptures for us" (Luke 24:32 The Message). Day by day, you will listen to the words of Jesus, He will open up the Scriptures for you, and you will discover that your heart will begin to feel as though it is on fire. It is a burning, all-consuming love for Jesus Christ.

Together we will embark on a devotional journey with Jesus in the form of quiet times alone with Him. Each quiet time is organized according to the PRAYER™ Quiet Time Plan™:

Prepare Your Heart

Read and Study God's Word

Adore God in Prayer

Yield Yourself to God

Enjoy His Presence

Rest in His Love

Each week consists of five days of quiet times and then a devotional reading on Days 6-7. Each quiet time includes devotional reading, devotional Bible study, journaling, prayer, worship, hymns, and application of God's Word. Journal Pages and Prayer Pages (adapted from The Quiet Time Notebook™) to record your thoughts and prayers are in the back of this book. With *A Heart On Fire* and your Bible you have everything you need for quiet time with the Lord. Because schedules vary, you can be flexible and may choose to take more than one day for each quiet time. You may complete each quiet time at your own pace, taking as little or as much time as you can give to spend alone with the Lord.

There are optional studies in some of the quiet times included for those with more time. Additionally, in the Yield Yourself to God section of your quiet times, I have included a large and diverse amount of devotional reading written by some of the greatest authors of all time on the subject of Jesus. Many times, I made the decision to include more than one excerpt because I didn't want you to miss the opportunity to read the rich thoughts of these great authors. If you are short on time, you may choose one or more of the devotional excerpts and return later to read more.

I encourage you to interact with the ideas and Scripture in each quiet time by underlining what is significant to you and writing your comments in the margins and thoughts in the provided space throughout the study. Mark it up and make it yours! Oh what an adventure you will experience as you discover the priceless privilege of knowing Christ.

If you desire to learn more about how to have a quiet time, I encourage you to get my book *Six Secrets to a Powerful Quiet Time.* To learn more about different kinds of devotional Bible studies for your quiet time, I encourage you to read my book *Knowing and Loving the Bible.*

As you begin *A Heart On Fire*, I would like to ask you, "Who or what are you living for?" In this postmodern era many people believe that there is nothing worth living for or dying for. Sadly, many Christians fall into this same quiet desperation and aimlessness. What if the words of Jesus are really true? What if He is the way, the truth, and the life? What if He is the only way to God? If so, then you can get truly excited. It means that there is something so great, priceless in fact, that it is worth fighting for to your very last breath. What is that one thing? Knowing Christ. The result? You will be who you have never been. You will do what you have never done. And you will dream what you have never dreamed.

Will you ask God to ignite your heart as you draw near to Him? Will you ask Him to give you that priceless privilege of knowing Christ that Paul talked so much about? Will you ask Him to do something so great that you will never be the same? I invite you now to pray that all-powerful prayer: Father give me…A Heart On Fire.

VIEWER GUIDES

At the end of each week you will find your Viewer Guide to take notes from the video message. In each message, Catherine teaches from God's Word, and challenges you to draw near to the Lord. These messages are especially designed to accompany your studies each week. These videos messages are available on the companion *A Heart On Fire* DVDs or as Downloadable M4V Video messages. These messages are also available on Audio CDs and as Downloadable MP3 Audio messages. Search the Quiet Time Ministries Online Store at www.quiettime.org or call Quiet Time Ministries at 1-800-925-6458.

FOR LEADERS

A Heart On Fire is a powerful resource for group study including a complete Leader's Guide with Discussion Questions in the Appendix. *A Heart On Fire* DVD Leader's Kits are available at the Quiet Time Ministries Online Store at www.quiettime.org. You may also call Quiet Time Ministries at 1-800-925-6458. *A Heart On Fire* is available as a 1-book Leader's Kit or a 10-book Leader's Kit. The kit includes the *A Heart On Fire* book(s), *A Heart On Fire* DVDs with 9 video messages, *The Quiet Time Journal*, and the Quiet Time Ministries Signature Tote. Each *A Heart On Fire* book is organized into 8 weeks with 5 days of quiet time per week and Days 6-7 for review and meditation. The book also includes 9 Viewer Guides for the group video sessions, Leader's Guide and Discussion Questions, and Journal and Prayer Pages.

QUIET TIME MINISTRIES ONLINE

Quiet Time Ministries Online at www.quiettime.org is a place where you can deepen your devotion to God and His Word. Cath's Blog is where Catherine shares about life, about the Lord, and just about everything else. A Walk In Grace™ is Catherine's devotional photojournal, highlighting her own photography, where you can grow deep in the garden of His grace. Quiet Time Ministries proudly sponsors Ministry For Women at www.ministryforwomen.com—a social network community for women worldwide to grow in their relationship with Jesus Christ. Connect, study, and grow at Ministry For Women.

LETTER TO THE LORD

The goal of *A Heart On Fire* is to take you on a journey through the Bible to see the priceless privilege of knowing Christ, to grow in your intimate relationship with Him, and to give you a heart on fire for Him. When you have completed these quiet times you will have read and studied many of the most important passages of Scripture about Christ and will have meditated on many devotional readings by some of the great classic Christian authors.

As you begin these quiet times, will you stop now to think about your own life? Where are you? How is your relationship with the Lord? Are you intimate with Him? How well do you know God's Word? Are you standing at a crossroads? Are you in need of a defining moment that will move you to a new purpose and direction in your life? Write a letter to the Lord, expressing your desire for Him to work in your life in a powerful way as you spend quiet time alone with Him in this study. Pour out your heart to the Lord and be sure to include the following prayer: *Lord, give me a heart on fire.*

My Letter To The Lord

Face To Face With Jesus

Welcome to *A Heart On Fire*, a quiet time study all about the priceless privilege of knowing Christ. In this study in God's Word, you are going to discover truths that will grow your intimate relationship with Christ and give you a heart on fire for the Lord. These Viewer Guides are designed to give you a place to write notes from my *A Heart On Fire* messages available on DVD, Audio CD, or Downloadable M4V Video and Downloadable MP3 Audio for your computer or mobile device. In our time together today, we want to look at the kind of relationship the Lord Jesus desires with you.

"If anyone really loves me, he will observe my teaching, and my Father will love him, and both of us will come into face-to-face fellowship with him; yes, we will make our special dwelling place with him" (John 14:23 wms).

What can you learn from Jesus' promise in John 14:23?

1. The Lord wants to spend face-to-face _____with you.

2. The Lord wants to make His special _____in your heart.

3. The secret to intimacy with Jesus is to cultivate a _____ of spending time with Him and hearing Him speak to you.

How can you cultivate this love of hearing the Lord Jesus speak to you? The best place is in your _____.

4. Intimacy with Jesus means that you fall in love with Him. Your heart will _____ on fire with love for Him and that love will spread everywhere.

   a. Cultivate the sense of _____ together with the Lord Jesus.

b. Cultivate times of _____ with Him.

c. You and the Lord will _____ together.

d. You and the Lord will _____ and grieve together.

e. You and the Lord will _____ together in ministry.

f. Cultivate a time of _____with the Lord.

What is the result when you cultivate an intimate relationship with the Lord?

1. You will experience the _____of Christ.

2. You will _____Jesus.

3. You will see His _____. You will know Him.
2 Corinthians 3:18, 4:6

≫ℰ   *Video messages are available on DVDs or as Downloadable M4V Video. Audio messages are available on Audio CDs or as Downloadable MP3 Audio. Visit the Quiet Time Ministries Online Store at www.quiettime.org.*

Week One

THE BURNING HEART

Luke 24:32

Were not our hearts burning within us while he talked with us on the
road and opened the Scriptures to us?

Luke 24:32 NIV

THE DEFINING MOMENT

It was now about the sixth hour, and darkness came over the whole land until the ninth hour, for the sun stopped shining. And the curtain of the temple was torn in two...

LUKE 23:44-45 NIV

PREPARE YOUR HEART

It appeared that they had finally won. This man who had plagued their conscience with His words was dead. They nailed him to a cross. It was the most horrifying way they could think to kill a man. Crucifixion. These religious leaders smiled with satisfaction knowing that this man could no longer challenge their authority in the moral arena of everyday life. While these leaders were smiling at their success, the friends of the dead man wept uncontrollably at their loss. In fact, those closest to Him could not bring themselves to leave the place of the cross. They stood at a distance in shock and grief. They were overwhelmed by the events of the past week. For three years they had followed this man Jesus wherever He went. They listened to His words filled with love and promise of eternal life. They believed. Their lives were transformed. Not only did they watch in horror one day as Jesus was arrested. Their worst fears were realized. Now He was dead. What did His death mean? Did it mean that everything He had said was a lie? Did they have to rethink everything they had believed? It was a defining moment in their lives.

What they did not understand is that it was not only their defining moment, but it was a defining moment for all of mankind. What is a defining moment? It is the moment when you make a move in a direction, step up to the plate, and resolve to do something you know is right. All of us have defining moments that shape the course of our lives. If we have gone in a disastrous direction, the defining moment moves us to a new place. If we have undergone a severe loss, the defining moment carries us to a new purpose. If we experience change, the defining moment gives us a new position. It has been said that the bend in the road is not the end of the road unless you fail to take the turn. There are times in life when we find ourselves standing at a crossroads. There is a bend in the road. It may be either self-imposed or has come in the form of uncontrollable and sometimes cataclysmic circumstances. Either way, we stand at that crossroads. And just ahead—a defining moment.

The world stood still that day when Jesus died on the cross. And there are times in your life when it is as though your world stands still. You are standing at a crossroad. There has been a bend in the road for you. What do you do when the world stands still for you? The friends of Jesus had no idea what was around the corner for them. Just three days later He would rise from the dead and greet them face to face. Their mourning would be turned to joy.

Today, as you begin *A Heart On Fire*, think about where you are, and ask God to speak to you in the crossroads of life, the bends in the road, and give you a heart on fire.

READ AND STUDY GOD'S WORD

1. What was it like in those last days of Jesus on earth? Luke, the physician, gives an account of this time in Luke 22:39-71 and Luke 23:1-56. Turn to these chapters and read them with thought and care. Imagine that you are there. Describe what it must have been like to be one of the disciples during this time.

2. What is most significant to you about Jesus from your reading in Luke?

3. What did that day when the world stood still and Jesus was crucified on the cross really mean? Look at the following verses and record your insights.

John 3:16-17

Optional Verses: (If you have more time, write your insights in your journal pages in back of this book): Psalm 25:15, Psalm 121:1, Isaiah 42:18-23, Matthew 6:22-24, Mark 8:16-21, Romans 4:25, 5:8-11, Ephesians 1:18-21, Hebrews 9:26-28, 1 John 4:9

4. What is your most significant insight from your time in God's Word today?

ADORE GOD IN PRAYER

O God, renew us in Thy love today,

For our tomorrow we have not a care,

Who blessed our yesterday

Will meet us there.

But our today is all athirst for Thee,

Come in the stillness, O Thou heavenly Dew,

Come Thou to us—to me—

Revive, renew.[1]

AMY CARMICHAEL IN TOWARDS JERUSALEM

YIELD YOURSELF TO GOD

By the sacrifice of Himself He put away sin. And now He offers us Himself to take the place of sin. He gives Himself, the sacrificed One, who has finished redemption, to us to put away sin within us, too. It is as the Son, the living One, that He is High Priest; it is in eternal life power, by a life working in us, that He brings us to God. And so, by His Spirit, He, in His self-sacrifice, lives in us, and makes it true in the experience of each true disciple—sin put away by the sacrifice of self. The law for the Head is the law for every member. And now the alternative is put before us: Which shall it be? Sin and myself or Christ and His Self? Christ has opened for us a heavenly life-sphere, out of which sin has been put away—the sanctuary of God's presence. Which shall it be—self-pleasing or self-sacrifice—a life in self or a life in Christ. Though we may not always be able to see fully all that Christ's work means, or realize all the riches of blessing it brings, there is one word not difficult to carry in which all is centered. That word is Himself. He gave Himself a sacrifice for sin; He gives Himself the putter away, the conqueror of sin; He is Himself all that we can desire or need. Blessed the soul that rests in nothing less than HIMSELF.[2]

ANDREW MURRAY IN THE HOLIEST OF ALL

All highways of biblical truth lead to the Cross. The whole emphasis of the Gospel records is upon his death and not upon his life—the latter was ever leading to the former. All through Scripture God is pointing to Calvary: the Passover, the Temple worship, the Old Testament offerings and sacrifices. The Cross was no afterthought in God's mind, as 1 Peter 1:18-20 makes clear. From before the foundation of the world Calvary was planned. As Jesus walked and taught for three years, he was on a steady march to the great climax where every sin of man would be healed and forgiven, and the last enemy, death overcome. Jesus was the great and final Passover Lamb. Since the destruction of the Temple and the scattering of the Jews, while Passover is observed there is no sacrificial Lamb. When we look at Calvary, can we ever make light of sin? Nothing so reveals the depths of our lostness and the dreadful disease of sin which ravages all mankind, and shows there is no hope for anyone until we can say, Nothing in my hand I bring, simply to thy cross I cling. That is the whole emphasis of the Gospel. Get on your knees in thankfulness, adoration and praise.[3]

ALAN REDPATH IN THE LIFE OF VICTORY

ENJOY HIS PRESENCE

There is always a moment, a point in time, when a spark is created and a fire is ignited. In the same way, as you stand at the crossroads in life, there is that defining moment when you turn to the Lord. Have you made that decision? If not, pray the following prayer and invite Him into your life today: *Lord Jesus, I need You. Thank you for dying on the cross for my sins. I invite you now to come into my life, forgive my sins, and make me the person You want me to be. Amen.*

Maybe you have already prayed a prayer similar to the one you just read, but you have not really been living for Jesus. You want to be on fire for Him, but the cares of the world have pressed in on you. Take this bend in the road as an invitation from the Lord to draw near to Him. And as you begin to understand the priceless privilege of knowing Him, your love for Him will grow, and your heart will catch on fire. Take some time now and ask Him to give you a heart on fire for Him.

REST IN HIS LOVE

"For Christ died for sins once for all, the righteous for the unrighteous, to bring you to God" (1 Peter 3:18 NIV).

THE ROAD TO EMMAUS

As they talked and discussed these things with each other, Jesus
Himself came up and walked along with them…

LUKE 24:14-15

PREPARE YOUR HEART

They were confused, heartbroken, and bewildered. Two followers of Jesus headed back home. They had a seven mile journey ahead of them on a winding, dusty road. And yet, they could hardly put one foot in front of the other. They talked about everything that had happened. They did not just talk about events. They discussed and reasoned together about the meaning of these things. Who was Jesus of Nazareth? Surely He was a prophet. He worked miracles and His words were powerful. And yet, if He really was who He claimed to be, how could He be sentenced to death and crucified on a cross? It did not make sense. Their hearts were heavy. As they were walking and reasoning, a stranger came up and walked along with them on the road. He began questioning them, and asked them what they were talking about. What they did not realize was that this stranger was Jesus Himself.

When you are confused and downcast, where do you go and what do you do? When you are curious about events in your life, what is your response? There is a road waiting for you to travel, and a walk that you can take in every circumstance. It is the road to Emmaus. It is the road where Jesus walks with you.

Every man and woman of God down through the centuries has walked on the road to Emmaus. They have known His Presence in their lives. What does that mean? It is more than a feeling. It is the result of acting on the fact of His Presence in spite of the absence sometimes of any feeling whatsoever. It may be better understood as a confident certainty that He is there. How can you know? Because of the certainty of His Word. You bank your life on what He says.

Corrie Ten Boom walked on the road to Emmaus when she was a prisoner in a Nazi concentration camp. She describes her experience: "We were surrounded by people who had behind them a training in cruelties, but we had moments when we were conscious that we were walking with the Lord. Often we had to go too early to roll call, which started at 3:30 AM. Betsie and I would walk through the camp, and there were three of us present. Betsie said something, I said something, and the Lord said something. I can't tell you how, but both Betsie and I understood clearly what He said. These walks were a bit of heaven in the midst of hell. Everything around us was black and dark, but in us there was a light that belonged to eternity. Jesus said: *All who listen to my instructions and follow them are wise, like a man who builds his house on solid rock. Though the rain comes in torrents, and the floods rise and the storm winds beat against his house, it won't collapse, for it is built on rock* (Matthew 7:24-25)."[4]

As you begin your time with the Lord today, turn to Psalm 1 and think about the words. Ask God to give you a delight in His Word as you draw near to Him today.

READ AND STUDY GOD'S WORD

1. It was three days after the crucifixion of Jesus. Some of those who loved Jesus went to the tomb where His body had been laid. Describe what they witnessed and experienced.

Matthew 28:1-10

John 20:1-18

2. Following His resurrection, Jesus appeared to two of His disciples on the road back to their home in Emmaus. Read this account in Luke 24:13-35 and record your insights about the following:

What were these two disciples doing when Jesus began walking with them?

What is most significant to you about the conversation between Jesus and His two followers?

What caused their hearts to burn?

Why do you think they did not recognize Jesus at first?

3. What is your most significant insight from this event on the road to Emmaus?

ADORE GOD IN PRAYER

Where in your life do you really need the Lord to meet you today? Will you talk with Him about those heart concerns right now? Turn to your prayer pages and record your needs as you bring them to the Lord. Be sure to put the date so that you can see how He specifically answers you in the days to come. Notice that there is a place to record those specific answers to your prayers

YIELD YOURSELF TO GOD

The two friends who journeyed to Emmaus did not notice any resemblance between the stranger who joined their company and their beloved Lord, of whom they had been thinking and speaking…The main cause of this, we believe was sheer heaviness of heart. Sorrow made them unobserving. They were so engrossed with their own sad thoughts that they had no eyes for outward things. They did not take the trouble to realize who it was that had come up with them; it would have made no difference though the stranger had been their own father. It is obvious how men in such a mood must be dealt with. They can get outward vision only by getting the inward eye first opened. The diseased mind must be healed that they may be able to look at what is before them, and see it as it is. On this principle Jesus proceeded with the two brethren. He accommodated Himself to their humor, and led them on from despair to hope, and then the outward senses recovered their perceptive power, and told who the stranger was.[5]

A.B. BRUCE IN THE TRAINING OF THE TWELVE

I have learned experimentally, that the best thing for me to do is to have my day marked off in sections, and to come to God for a constant renewal of life as I go on. David says, "Seven times a day do I praise Thee because of Thy righteous judgments"

(Psalm 119:164). You may find it necessary to mark your day into longer or shorter sections, but there must be a constant coming to Him in the midst of the activities of life. When I was in South India, I visited Miss Amy Carmichael at Dohnavur. One of the customs of what is perhaps the most beautiful mission station in the whole world, is to pause at the striking of the hour. In the tower of prayer that rises, flower-covered, above the chapel, there are chimes which can be heard throughout the compound. The whole outward activity of the mission ceases when the chimes begin the hour. The older girls, in their beautiful saris, walking along the flowered pathways, will stop and bow in meditation. The children in the playing fields will cease their games for a brief moment. The big brothers will get down from their bicycles as they go on some errand, and will stand a moment in silence while the chimes play. It is all like a moving picture that turns, for a moment, into a stereopticon slide, and then it resumes its motion. Unhappy the Christian life that does not have its chimes in it somewhere during the day, to stop the earthly activities while we listen to the heavenly peal, think upon the Savior a moment, talk directly to Him, listen to His voice in some verse that He will recall to mind, and then step into the work and the activity of the moment. God has taught me to look ahead like one who walks along the road, asking God to keep and sustain until the next tree, the next milestone, the next bend in the road, at which point I draw the breath that comes from another atmosphere than this, and step out towards the next point.[6]

DONALD GREY BARNHOUSE IN KESWICK'S AUTHENTIC VOICE

ENJOY HIS PRESENCE

Have you chosen to walk the path of the Emmaus Road today? Are you living in the atmosphere of the Presence of Jesus Christ? In the midst of your day, will you search Him out, listen to His Word, and then talk with Him about everything?

I come to the garden alone

while the dew is still on the roses;

And the voice I hear, falling on my ear,

The Son of God discloses.

Refrain

And He walks with me,

And He talks with me,

And He tells me I am His own;

And the joy we share

As we tarry there,

None other has ever known.

He speaks, and the sound of His voice

Is so sweet the birds hush their singing,

And the melody that He gave to me

Within my heart is ringing.

I'd stay in the garden with Him

Though the night around me be falling,

But He bids me go; through the voice of woe,

His voice to me is calling.

And He walks with me,

And He talks with me,

And He tells me I am His own;

And the joy we share

As we tarry there,

None other has ever known.[7]

IN THE GARDEN BY C. AUSTIN MILES

REST IN HIS LOVE

"…And surely I am with you always, to the very end of the age" (Matthew 28:20 NIV).

WHEN YOUR HEART BEGINS TO BURN

Were not our hearts burning within us while he talked with
us on the road and opened the Scriptures to us?

LUKE 24:32 NIV

PREPARE YOUR HEART

Once you have chosen the road to Emmaus, your life is never the same. Why? Because Jesus walks with you. With Jesus, there is always reasoning, conversation, and sharing of truth. He has something to say to you. And He says it like no other can. There is a secret to hearing Him speak. You must open the Bible. And you must be indwelt and filled with His Spirit who is given to you the moment you invite Jesus into your life. When you open your Bible, the Lord Jesus will meet you all across the pages of Scripture.

As you begin your time with the Lord today, think about and pray through the words of this prayer from *The Valley Of Vision: A Collection of Puritan Prayers And Devotions.*

My Father,
 In a world of created changeable things,
Christ and his Word alone remain unshaken.
O to forsake all creatures,
To rest as a stone on him the foundation,
To abide in him, be borne up by him!
For all my mercies come through Christ,
Who has designed, purchased, promised, effected them.
How sweet it is to be near him, the Lamb,
Filled with holy affections!
When I sin against thee I cross thy will, love, life,
And have no comforter, no creature, to go to.
My sin is not so much this or that particular evil,
But my continual separation, disunion, distance from thee,
And having a loose spirit towards thee.
But thou hast given me a present, Jesus thy Son,

As mediator between thyself and my soul,
A middle-man who in a pit
Holds both him below and him above,
For only he can span the chasm breached by sin,
And satisfy divine justice.
May I always lay hold upon this mediator,
As a realized object of faith,
And alone worthy by his love to bridge the gulf.
Let me know that he is dear to me by his Word;
I am one with him by the Word on his part,
And by faith on mine;
If I oppose the Word I oppose my Lord when he is most near;
If I receive the Word I receive my Lord wherein he is nigh.
O thou who hast the hearts of all men in thine hand,
Form my heart according to the Word,
According to the image of thy Son,
So shall Christ the Word, and his Word, be my strength and comfort.[8]

THE VALLEY OF VISION: A COLLECTION OF PURITAN PRAYERS AND DEVOTIONS

READ AND STUDY GOD'S WORD

1. Studying God's Word activates God's power in your life through the Holy Spirit. Truths about Jesus leap off of every page. Read Luke 24:14-35 again paying special attention to verses 25-27. What did Jesus explain as He conversed with His disciples?

2. Read Luke 24:32 and write this verse out, word-for-word.

3. Keeping in mind what you have learned, what is it that will make your heart burn for Christ?

4. The Message translates verse 32 this way: Didn't we feel on fire as he conversed with us on the road, as he opened up the Scriptures for us? What do you think it means to feel on fire for Jesus Christ?

5. Look at the following verses and record what you learn about the words of Christ.

Matthew 7:24-27

Mark 13:31

John 8:31-32

John 15:7

Optional Verses: Luke 7:2-9, John 14:23-26, Philippians 2:14-16, Colossians 3:16

ADORE GOD IN PRAYER

Have you ever prayed using words from the Bible? A.T. Pierson points out that "the Holy Scriptures will suggest the very words which become the dialect of prayer. We know not what we should pray for as we ought (Romans 8:26)—neither what nor how to pray. But here is the Spirit's own inspired utterance, and, if the praying be molded on the model of His teaching, how can we go astray? Here is our God-given liturgy and litany—a divine prayer book. We have here God's promises, precepts, warnings, and counsels, not to speak of all the Spirit-inspired literal prayers therein contained; and, as we reflect upon these, our prayers take their cast in this matrix. We turn precept and promise, warning and counsel into supplication, with the assurance that we cannot be asking anything that is not according to His will, for are we not turning His own word into prayer?"[9] Will you take these words to heart today as a lesson in prayer? The Word of the Lord is so life-changing it can make your heart burn. And it is powerful to make you pray appropriately in every circumstance of life. Turn now to Psalm 25 and pray through these words to your Lord.

YIELD YOURSELF TO GOD

The two disciples on the road to Emmaus had a most profitable journey. Their companion and teacher was the best of tutors; the interpreter one of a thousand, in whom are hid all the treasures of wisdom and knowledge. The Lord Jesus condescended to become a preacher of the gospel, and He was not ashamed to exercise His calling before an audience of two persons, neither does He now refuse to become the teacher of even one. Let us court the company of so excellent an Instructor…This unrivalled tutor used as His class-book the best of books. Although able to reveal fresh truth, He preferred to expound the old. He knew by His omniscience what was the most instructive way of teaching, and by turning at once to Moses and the prophets, He showed us that the surest road to wisdom is not speculation, reasoning, or reading human books, but meditation upon the Word of God. The readiest way to be spiritually rich in heavenly knowledge is to dig in this mine of diamonds, to gather pearls from this heavenly sea. When Jesus Himself sought to enrich others, He wrought in the quarry of Holy Scripture. The favored pair were led to consider the best of subjects, for Jesus spoke of Jesus, and expounded the things concerning Himself. Here the diamond cut the diamond, and what could be more admirable? The Master of the House unlocked His own doors, conducted the guests to His table, and placed His own delicacies upon it. He who hid the treasure in the field Himself guided the searchers to it. Our Lord would naturally speak of the sweetest of topics, and he could find none sweeter than his own person and work: with an eye to these we should always search the Word. O for grace to study the Bible with Jesus as both our teacher and our lesson![10]

CHARLES HADDON SPURGEON IN MORNING AND EVENING

Conversing together on the discourse of Jesus after His departure, they said one to another, "Did not our heart burn within us while He talked with us by the way, and while He opened to us the Scriptures?" The light they had received might be small, but it was new light, and it had all the heart-kindling, thought-stirring power of new truth. That conversation on the road formed a crisis in their spiritual history. It was the dawn of the gospel day; it was the little spark which kindles a great fire; it deposited in their minds a thought which was to form the germ or center of a new system of belief; it took away the veil which had been upon their faces in the reading of the Old Testament, and was thus the first step in a process which was to issue in their beholding with open face, as in a glass, the glory of the Lord, and in their being changed into the same image, from glory to glory, by the Lord the Spirit…Let us note the circumstances in which this new light arose for the disciples. Their heart were set a-burning when they had become very dry and withered: hopeless, sick, and life-weary, through sorrow and disappointment. It is always so: the fuel must be dry that the spark may take hold…So it has been in many an instance since then. The fire of hope has been kindled in the heart, never to be extinguished, just at the moment when men were settling down into despair; faith has been revived when a man seemed to himself to be an infidel; the light of truth has arisen to minds which had ceased to look for the dawn; the comfort of salvation has returned to souls which had begun to think that God's mercy was gone forever.[11]

A.B. BRUCE IN THE TRAINING OF THE TWELVE

How did the disciples get their burning hearts? It was through the way in which Christ opened the Scriptures to them. He made it all look different and new, and they saw what they had never seen before. They could not help feeling how wonderful and how heavenly the teaching was.[12]

ANDREW MURRAY IN THE SECRET OF SPIRITUAL STRENGTH

Here are three ways of putting treasure into our storehouse:

1. Whenever the Spirit of God makes a word live to you, take time to let that word sink deep into your heart. This way is open to us all.

2. Whenever the Bible is read aloud listen with the inward ear. Then, whether you can immediately recall it or not, it is stored in that wonderful storehouse of memory, and in time of need it will be there for use. This, too, is a way open to us all.

3. This way is, perhaps, only open to the fairly young. If we do not use it when we can, we lose more than can be told. It is the way we call learning by heart (memorization). I suggest that you choose chapters like Isaiah 53, John 14, 15, 16, 17, or Psalms like 27, 91 and others, or paragraphs like Romans 8:31-39, and learn them steadily, verse by verse. Keep a dated record, and you will be astonished to find how much you have put in your storehouse by the end of the year.[13]

AMY CARMICHAEL IN THOU GIVEST, THEY GATHER

ENJOY HIS PRESENCE

Do you see the secret to having a heart on fire? It is to draw near to Christ in His Word. As you take time in His Word, He will speak to you through the Holy Spirit, and your heart will ignite with love for Him. Your passion for the Lord will grow and soon you will not be able to keep it to yourself. It will overflow just as it did in the lives of the disciples when they said: ... we cannot help speaking about what we have seen and heard (Acts 4:20). Take some time now to think about the priorities in your life. Is Jesus Christ your first priority? Do you take time in His Word so that He can explain all He wants you to know about Him? How are you going to be extravagant with His Word and live in His Word today? Write a prayer in your journal in the back of this book in response to what He has shown you today.

REST IN HIS LOVE

"I have much more to say to you, more than you can now bear. But when he, the Spirit of truth, comes, he will guide you into all truth. He will not speak on his own; he will speak only what he hears, and he will tell you what is to come. He will bring glory to me by taking from what is mine and making it known to you" (John 16:12-14 NIV).

RECOGNIZING JESUS

Then their eyes were opened and they recognized Him.

Luke 24:31 niv

Prepare Your Heart

The words of this stranger on the road were so engaging and his companionship so comforting that the two disciples on their way to Emmaus invited the man to stay with them. Something happened during His stay that was to change their life forever. He opened their eyes and they recognized who He was. It was Jesus! Before they could even say anything, He vanished. The realization began to sink in. They were some of the privileged ones visited by Him following His resurrection from the dead.

Who is this Jesus who died and then rose from the dead appearing to more than five hundred people following His resurrection? As they walked together on the road to Emmaus, Jesus, beginning with Moses and all the prophets, explained to them the things concerning Himself in all the Scriptures (Luke 24:17). What is so significant about this? What He explained to them was His own fulfillment through His life, death and resurrection of over 300 prophecies written in the Old Testament over a 1500-year period of time. There was an expectation that had grown among the Jewish people as a result of these prophecies. It was an expectation of Messiah, a man anointed by God who would rule and free them from Roman rule. What the people did not realize was that while the promised One was King, He also was a suffering Servant, one who would save His people from their sins by dying in their place. That is why there was such a dashing of hopes when He died on the cross.

How exciting it must have been to these two who were walking on the road to hear Jesus explain the meaning of every promise from Genesis to Malachi concerning Himself. What a theology lesson this was. Wouldn't you love to have been on the road with them that day? The exciting news is that you can experience what these two disciples experienced. How? By traveling the road to Emmaus, discussing and reasoning the truths about Jesus, and then asking Him to stay with you. There is one thing you notice, and that is the time factor involved. They did not just want to hear facts. They wanted the companionship of a Person who explained those facts in relation to Jesus. And that is what you must pursue. Time with Jesus in His Word. You will realize the presence of Jesus more and more in your own life as you live with His Word in His Presence. He will open your eyes and you will see as you have never seen before.

Brennan Manning describes the first time he realized the presence of Christ. It happened as a result of meditating on the truth that Jesus died on the cross. He says: "I felt a hand grip my heart. I could barely breathe. It was abrupt and startling. The awareness of being loved was no longer gentle, tender and comfortable. The love of Christ, the crucified Son of God, for me, took on the wildness, passion, and fury of a sudden spring storm. Like a bursting dam, spasms of convulsive crying erupted from the depths of my being. He died on the Cross for me! I had known that before, but in the way that Cardinal Newman describes as notional knowledge—abstract, far away, largely irrelevant to the gut issues of life, just another trinket in the dusty pawnshop of dogmatic beliefs. But in one blinding moment of salvific truth, it was real knowledge calling for personal engagement of my mind and heart. Christianity was no longer simply a moral code but a love affair, the thrill, the excitement, the incredible, passionate joy of being loved and falling in love with Jesus Christ."[14]

As you begin your time with the Lord, think about the words of this hymn and ask the Lord to open your eyes.

> Open my eyes, that I may see
>
> glimpses of truth thou hast for me;
>
> place in my hands the wonderful key
>
> that shall unclasp and set me free.
>
> Silently now I wait for thee,
>
> ready, my God, thy will to see.
>
> Open my eyes, illumine me, Spirit divine!

CLARA H. SCOTT 1841-1897

Do you long for Jesus to stay with you, teach you from the Bible, and open your eyes that you might know Him? Ask the Lord to open your eyes today that you might see Him.

READ AND STUDY GOD'S WORD

1. Read Luke 24:28-35 again. Describe the experience of these disciples once they arrived in Emmaus.

2. In Luke 24:31 you see that the two disciples recognized Jesus. That word *recognize* is *epiginosko* in the Greek and means to become fully acquainted with someone.[15] Wuest continues to explain that it is "knowledge gained by experience, thus personal knowledge. The compound verb with the prefix *epi* means personal knowledge gained by experience and which is clear."[16] It also carries the idea that one now can recognize a thing to be what it really is, to understand.[17] The root of this verb is *ginosko* and means to know and understand by experience.[18] How were they able now to become fully acquainted with Jesus? The text says that their eyes were opened. In the Greek the word for "opened" is *dianoigo* (Strong's number 1272) and means to cause to see what was not seen before and to make able and willing to understand and receive.[19] What do you think they now understood about Jesus?

3. Because these disciples of Jesus were willing to invite Jesus to stay with them and because they took time with Him, He opened their eyes and they were able to become deeply acquainted with Him. This in-depth knowledge included an understanding of His fulfillment of Old Testament prophecies. He was the Messiah that all Jewish people had hoped for. This is a powerful truth. This knowledge gained by personal experience with Jesus is what will change your life forever. Look at the following verses and record what you learn about knowing Christ.

John 14:6-9

John 17:3

1 Corinthians 1:30

1 Corinthians 13:12

2 Corinthians 3:13-18

Optional Verses: John 2:3-6, 2 Corinthians 4:6-7

4. Paul says in Philippians 3:8, "Yes, indeed, I certainly do count everything as loss compared with the priceless privilege of knowing Christ Jesus my Lord." Why do you think knowing Him such a priceless privilege?

ADORE GOD IN PRAYER

O Lord Jesus Christ, give me such communion with you that my soul may continually thirst for that time when I shall behold you in your glory. In the meanwhile, may I behold your glory in the mirror of your Word and be changed into your image.[20]

F.B. MEYER IN DAILY PRAYERS

YIELD YOURSELF TO GOD

The disciples on the road to Emmaus had a revelation of the living, risen Christ. The Scripture says, "They knew him." He revealed Himself, and then He vanished from their sight. Was that vision of Christ worth much? It was gone in a moment, yet it was worth heaven, eternity, everything …Thank God, Christ can reveal Himself to each one of us by the power of the Holy Spirit. Yet, how He does so is a secret thing between Christ and each individual believer. Take this assurance, "Their eyes were opened, and they knew Him," and believe that it was written for you.[21]

ANDREW MURRAY IN THE SECRET OF SPIRITUAL STRENGTH

All of a sudden everything became clear to the two men and they realized why they had been moved by the manner in which the Stranger had expounded the Scriptures to them on the way. Although Jesus had departed so soon after they had recognized Him, all doubt was now banished from their hearts. They know now that He is risen and that He lives as the Messiah, the promised Redeemer. And this certainty immediately brings such a light and joy into their hearts, that they have an irresistible urge to give others also a share in their joy. So without delay they went back to Jerusalem the same evening…If the men of Emmaus had not invited Jesus into their home, He would have passed on, and how poor would their lives have been then! But because He had spoken to them thus on the way, their hearts burned with love for Him and they invited Him in and thus received the richest blessings, even the Lord Himeslf as the Living King of their lives. How often does He address us also on life's way. And He still desires to enter where He is invited.[22]

NORVAL GELDENHUYS in COMMENTARY ON THE GOSPEL OF LUKE

He makes our heart burn within us as He opens to us the Scriptures. His Word is not mere intellectual light, but spiritual life and celestial fire. It is the eyes of our heart that need to be enlightened more than the faculties of our understanding. It is little use to read the Bible simply as a duty or a study. We want to read it with burning hearts and glowing love as the love letter of His affection and the mirror of His face.[23]

A.B. SIMPSON in THE CHRIST IN THE BIBLE COMMENTARY VOLUME FOUR

We all know how the presence of someone we deeply love lifts our spirits and suffuses us with a radiant sense of peace and well-being. So the one who loves God supremely is lifted into rapture by His conscious Presence. Then were the disciples glad, when they saw the Lord. If only we would stop lamenting and look up. God is here. Christ is risen. The Spirit has been poured out on high. All this we know as theological truth. It remains for us to turn it into joyous spiritual experience. And how is this accomplished? There is no new technique; if it is new it is false. The old, old method still works. Conscious fellowship with Christ is by faith, love and obedience. And the humblest believer need not be without these.[24]

A.W. TOZER in THAT INCREDIBLE CHRISTIAN

ENJOY HIS PRESENCE

Do you count knowing Christ a priceless privilege? How well do you know Him today? As you close your time with Him today, write a prayer in your journal indicating your desire to know Him more. Thank Him for how He has opened your eyes today.

REST IN HIS LOVE

"Blessed are the eyes which see the things you see, for I say to you, that many prophets and kings wished to see the things which you see, and did not see them, and to hear the things which you hear, and did not hear them" (Jesus in Luke 10:23-24).

HEARTS SET AFLAME FOR CHRIST

They got up and returned at once to Jerusalem…Then the
two told what had happened on the way…

LUKE 24:33, 35 NIV

PREPARE YOUR HEART

What happens when a heart is ignited and set on fire? The fire spreads. And it happens quickly. Notice that once the disciples' hearts caught fire, they immediately went back to Jerusalem to tell everyone. That is what always happens. It only takes a spark to get a fire going. And that fire from hearts set aflame for Christ is still burning even today.

Corrie Ten Boom had a heart on fire for Jesus Christ. Once released from Ravensbruck concentration camp, one might have thought that Corrie should spend the rest of her life recovering from the trauma. She prayed: "Lord, I have received my life back from You. Thank You. Will You tell me how to use it? Give me understanding, and a discernment because I will need to see everything through Your eyes. My work must be to save souls for eternity, to tell about You. As Paul has said in 2 Corinthians 5:20, …*to be Your personal representative…*"[25] Now that's a heart on fire for Jesus Christ! A heart on fire is willing to go anywhere, do anything, and is sold out for His sake. Hearts on fire are exclusively attached to Him for His purposes. Corrie went on to become "a tramp for the Lord," as she called herself, and influenced thousands of lives for Jesus Christ. Billy Graham said that her life was "one of the most amazing lives of the century."[26] One friend recalled that when people met Corrie they were always struck by the radiance of her twinkling blue eyes.[27] Why did they twinkle? Because there was a passionate fiery love that burned in her heart for Jesus Christ.

Today, as you spend time with the Lord, the question for you is: how is your heart? Is your heart on fire for Christ? Ask the Lord to give you a heart that burns with love for Him.

READ AND STUDY GOD'S WORD

1. What a day it must have been when the disciples realized Jesus had risen from the dead. All their greatest hopes were answered in that revelation. Read Luke 24:31-53 and notice all that happened in the presence of the disciples. What did they see and learn about Jesus?

2. Read Acts 1:1-11 and describe what these last moments with Jesus were like. Summarize what Jesus said to His disciples.

3. This recognition of Jesus by His disciples was life-changing for them. Jesus empowered His disciples to be His witnesses, as seen in Acts 2:1-12. Once empowered from on high by the Holy Spirit, they took the commission of Jesus seriously to be His witnesses. Where once they were fearful, fleeing for their very lives, now they were bold and courageous in telling others the truth about Jesus. A great example of this is the boldness of Peter as he shared the gospel of Jesus with a huge crowd of people (Acts 2:22-41). Read Acts 2:41. What happened as a result of Peter's message?

4. When your heart is set aflame for Jesus Christ, you cannot help but answer His call in your life. Read 2 Corinthians 2:14-17 and record what you learn about how He will influence others in and through you. (Optional Verses: Matthew 5:14-16, 2 Corinthians 5:17-21)

ADORE GOD IN PRAYER

Are there loved ones in your life who need to know the love of Jesus? Will you pray for them today? Your prayers are part of your call from Christ. Turn to your prayer pages and record their names and talk to the Lord about each person today.

YIELD YOURSELF TO GOD

When the two disciples had reached Emmaus, and were refreshing themselves at the evening meal, the mysterious stranger who had so enchanted them upon the road, took bread and broke it, made Himself known to them, and then vanished out of their sight. They had constrained Him to abide with them, because the day was far spent; but now, although it was much later, their love was a lamp to their feet, yea, wings also; they forgot the darkness, their weariness was all gone, and forthwith they journeyed back the threescore furlongs to tell the gladsome news of a risen Lord, who had appeared to them by the way. They reached the Christians in Jerusalem, and were received by a burst of joyful news before they could tell their own tale. These early Christians were all on fire to speak of Christ's resurrection, and to proclaim what they knew of the Lord; they made common property of their experiences. Let their example impress us deeply. We too must bear our witness concerning Jesus. John's account of the sepulcher needed to be supplemented by Peter; and Mary could speak of something further still; combined, we have a full testimony from which nothing can be spared. We have each of us peculiar gifts and special manifestations; but the one object God has in view is the perfecting of the whole body of Christ. We must, therefore, bring our spiritual possessions and lay them at the apostles' feet, and make distribution unto all of what God has given to us. Keep back no part of the precious truth, but speak what you know, and testify what you have seen. Let not the toil or darkness, or possible unbelief of your friends, weigh one moment in the scale. Up, and be marching to the place of duty, and there tell what great things God has shown to your soul.[28]

CHARLES HADDON SPURGEON IN MORNING AND EVENING

He vanished out of their sight. This was deeply significant. Had He lingered longer, the whole meaning of His new relation to them would have been mistaken. Henceforth it was to be by faith and not by sight. There was a moment of vision and the memory of sight, but now they must rise up and walk by simple faith and go forth by the dead reckoning of a life of trust. It is unwholesome to be always looking for spiritual feeling and emotional joy. The normal atmosphere and attitude of the Christian is trust and the fellowship of prayer. We live by faith, not by sight (2 Corinthians 5:7)…A distinguished preacher tells how every morning as he sits down in his library, he places a chair for the Master to sit by his side, and all through the hours of study they talk together, pray together, plan together the work of the day, and when he goes forth to life's more public duties, he is conscious, not of any ecstatic vision or any supernatural revelation, but of an atmosphere illumined and fragrant with the breath of heaven and a heart all aglow from the Presence and fellowship of the Lord.[29]

A.B. SIMPSON IN THE CHRIST IN THE BIBLE COMMENTARY VOLUME FOUR

ENJOY HIS PRESENCE

Tis so sweet to walk with Jesus

Step by step and day by day,

Stepping in His very footprints,

Walking with Him all the way.

Soon with all who walk with Jesus

We shall walk with Him in white,

While He turns our grief to gladness

And our darkness into light.

Jesus keep me closer, closer,

Step by step and day by day,

Stepping in Thy very footprints,

Walking with Thee all the way.[30]

A.B. SIMPSON IN THE CHRIST IN THE BIBLE COMMENTARY

REST IN HIS LOVE

"And Jesus came up and spoke to them, saying, 'All authority has been given to Me in heaven and on earth. Go therefore and make disciples of all the nations, baptizing them in the name of the Father and the Son and the Holy Spirit, teaching them to observe all that I commanded you; and lo, I am with you always, even to the end of the age'" (Matthew 28:18-20).

DEVOTIONAL READING
BY ANNIE JOHNSON FLINT

DEAR FRIEND,

The next two days are your opportunity to review what you have learned this week. You may wish to write your thoughts and insights in your Journal. As you think about all you have learned about the hearts that burn on fire for Christ, write:

Your most significant insight:

Your favorite quote:

Your favorite verse:

As you think back about what you have learned this week, where are you in this journey? Is your heart on fire for Christ?

Think about all you have learned this week, then close by meditating and praying through these words by Annie Johnson Flint:

His lamp am I
To shine where He shall say.
And lamps are not for sunny rooms,
Not for the light of day;
But for dark places of the earth,
Where shame and wrong and crime have birth;
Or for the murky twilight gray,
Where wandering sheep have gone astray;
Or where the light of faith grows dim
And souls are groping after Him;
And sometimes, a flame,
Clear shining through the night,
So bright we do not see the lamp,
But only see the light.
So may I shine—His light the flame—
That men may glorify His name.[31]

ANNIE JOHNSON FLINT

Viewer Guide
❧ WEEK ONE ❧

Lord, Set My Heart On Fire

You have just completed the first week of study in *A Heart On Fire*. Today we are going to share together two main truths from Luke 24 and the journey of those two men on the road to Emmaus. Understanding these truths will encourage you in your intimate relationship with the Lord. So grab your Bible and let's get into the Word of God.

"Were not our hearts burning within us while he talked with us on the road and opened the Scriptures to us" (Luke 24:32)?

Two Truths To Help You Grow In Your Relationship With The Lord

1. The Lord wants to give you a _____.

What is a heart on fire? It is a heart that has a passionate excitement and love for Jesus that is so great that it is _____ and _____ to others.

2. Your heart will begin to burn on fire for Jesus Christ when you open up your Bible and _____ to Jesus.

Your heart will be on fire and burn just as much as you are in the _____. Colossians 3:16

Why I Love the Word of God

1. In the Word I see _____. John 5:39-40, 1 Corinthians 13:12

2. In the Word I find _____in the storms of life. Romans 15:4, Psalm 119:50, Jeremiah 15:16

3. God uses the Word to _____my life.
Hebrews 4:12, 2 Timothy 3:16

4. The Word is a sure _____.
Matthew 7:24-27

5. The Bible is the _____of God.
Isaiah 40:8, Ephesians 6:17, Hebrews 4:12

6. The Word of God is _____.
Psalm 119:60, John 8:32, John 17:17

What is necessary to give the Word to others?

1. We must _____the Word. 2 Timothy 1:14

2. We must _____the Word. 2 Timothy 2:15

3. We must _____on the Word. Joshua 1:8

4. We must _____on the Word. James 1:22-25

5. We must be _____outspoken with the word. _____
the Word in season and out of season. 1 Peter 3:15

❧   *Video messages are available on DVDs or as Downloadable M4V Video. Audio messages are available on Audio CDs or as Downloadable MP3 Audio. Visit the Quiet Time Ministries Online Store at www.quiettime.org.*

THE PRICELESS PRIVILEGE

Philippians 3:8

I certainly do count everything as loss compared with the priceless privilege
of knowing Christ Jesus my Lord.

PHILIPPIANS 3:8 WMS

KNOW HIM

I certainly do count everything as loss compared with the
priceless privilege of knowing Christ Jesus my Lord.
PHILIPPIANS 3:8 WMS

PREPARE YOUR HEART

John F. Walvoord says: "The riches of divine revelation embodied in Jesus Christ are as measureless as the ocean and His perfections as numberless as the stars. To attempt to state in complete theological form all that should be said about Jesus Christ leaves the writer with a sense of futility. He has dipped from the ocean of infinite glory and perfections of his Lord and Saviour."[1] In the weeks to come we will dip into measureless ocean and drink deeply of many facets of the brilliance of Jesus Christ. However much we drink there is always more of Him. Even John said after knowing Him for three years: "There are many other things which Jesus did, which if they were written in detail, I suppose that even the world itself would not contain the books that would be written" (John 21:25). With that in mind, what are you to do with all that you are going to learn about Jesus, the One and Only, as John called Him (John 1:18)? That is what you will think about this week.

G. Campbell Morgan was the son of a Baptist minister. His home life had such an atmosphere of devotion to Christ that he was drawn to the Lord. When he was ten years old, D.L. Moody came to England for the first time. Moody's ministry and the dedication of his parents made such an impression on him, that Morgan preached his first sermon at the age of thirteen. Soon he was preaching regularly in the area where he lived. He was a devoted student of the Bible and that made him a prominent Bible teacher in his time. He worked with Moody and Sankey in their evangelistic tour of Great Britain in 1883. His reputation soon spread beyond England to the United States. After the death of Moody in 1899, Morgan became the director of the Northfield Bible Conference. Morgan became the teacher who strengthened and deepened the faith of the thousands of converts from Moody's ministry. During his lifetime, he published over 60 books and booklets. His favorite Bible expositions were on the character of Christ. In fact, his most popular work is *The Crises Of Christ*. He wrote this book at the age of forty and said that in it he set forth Christ in His relation to God and His purpose, and to man in his need.[2] Thirty-three years later he remarked that he saw Christ in greater clarity and more amazing glory. He also said that he felt totally unworthy to present the majesty and mystery of the Person and Mission of Christ. Those are words spoken by one who came to intimately know Christ in his everyday experience. At the age of 10 he began the pursuit and even in his seventies he continued to engage in the goal of knowing Christ.

Are you engaged in the pursuit of knowing Christ? As you begin your time with the Lord today, pray and ask the Lord to reveal Himself to you as you draw near to Him.

READ AND STUDY GOD'S WORD

1. Paul made a profound statement about his life pursuit in Philippians 3:8. Read this verse and write it out, word-for-word.

2. It is helpful to look at a significant verse in a number of different translations. Meditate on the following translations of Philippians 3:8. Underline your favorite translated phrases and write any of your insights or observations related to each translation of the verse. Be sure to personalize your insights whenever possible i.e. it is a priceless privilege for *me* to know Christ.

I certainly do count everything as loss compared with the priceless privilege of knowing Christ Jesus my Lord. For His sake I have lost everything, and value it all as mere refuse, in order to gain Christ…Philippians 3:8 WMS

Yes, everything else is worthless when compared with the priceless gain of knowing Christ Jesus my Lord. I have discarded everything else, counting it all as garbage, so that I may have Christ…Philippians 3:8 NLT

Yes, furthermore I count everything as loss compared to the possession of the priceless privilege—the overwhelming preciousness, the surpassing worth and supreme advantage—of knowing Christ Jesus my Lord, and of progressively becoming more deeply and intimately acquainted with Him, of perceiving and recognizing and understanding Him more fully and clearly. For His sake I have lost everything and consider it all to be rubbish (refuse, dregs), in order that I may win (gain) Christ, the Anointed One. Philippians 3:8 AMP[3]

Yes, indeed, therefore, at least, even I am still setting all things down to be a loss for the sake of that which excels all others, my knowledge of Christ Jesus my Lord which I have gained through experience, for whose sake I have been caused to forfeit all things, and I am still counting them dung, in order that Christ I might gain…Philippians 3:8 Wuest's Expanded Translation[4]

Yes, all the things I once thought were so important are gone from my life. Compared to the high privilege of knowing Christ Jesus as my Master, firsthand, everything I once thought I had going for me is insignificant…Philippians 3:8 MSG

More than that, I count all things to be loss in view of the surpassing value of knowing Christ Jesus my Lord, for whom I have suffered the loss of all things, and count them but rubbish so that I may gain Christ…Philippians 3:8 NASB

What is more, I consider everything a loss compared to the surpassing greatness of knowing Christ Jesus my Lord, for whose sake I have lost all things. I consider them but rubbish, that I may gain Christ…Philippians 3:8 NIV

3. What is your favorite *translation* of this verse and why?

4. What is your favorite *phrase* in all of these translations and why?

5. What do you learn from this declaration by Paul? What is he really saying here?

Adore God in Prayer

Pray the words of this prayer by Peter Marshall: "I do need Thee, Lord. I need Thee now. I know that I can do without many of the things that once I thought were necessities, but without Thee I cannot live, and I dare not die. I needed Thee when sorrow came, when shadows were thrown across the threshold of my life, and Thou didst not fail me then. I needed Thee when sickness laid a clammy hand upon my family, and I cried to Thee, and Thou didst hear. I needed Thee when perplexity brought me to a parting of the ways, and I knew not how to turn. Thou didst not fail me then, but in many ways, bit and little, didst indicate the better way. And though the sun is shining around me today, I know that I need Thee even in the sunshine, and shall still need Thee tomorrow. I give Thee my gratitude for that constant sense of need that keeps me close to Thy side. Help me to keep my hand in Thine and my ears open to the wisdom of Thy voice. Speak to me, that I may hear Thee giving me courage for hard times and strength for difficult places; giving me determination for challenging tasks. I ask of Thee no easy way, but just Thy grace that is sufficient for every need, so that no matter how hard the way, how challenging the hour, how dark the sky, I may be enabled to overcome. In Thy strength, who hast overcome the world, I make this prayer. Amen."[5]

Yield Yourself to God

> The expression, "the knowledge of Christ Jesus my Lord," does not refer to the knowledge which the Lord Jesus possesses, but the knowledge of the Lord Jesus which Paul gained through the experience of intimate companionship and communion with Him. Paul came to know His heart, His will, as one comes to know another through intimate fellowship and close association with that person.[6]
>
> KENNETH WUEST IN WORD STUDIES OF THE GREEK NEW TESTAMENT

Christ has come, the Light of the world. Long ages may yet elapse before His beams have reduced the world to order and beauty, and clothed a purified humanity with light as with a garment. But He has come: the Revealer of the snares and chasms that lurk in darkness, the Rebuker of every evil thing that prowls by night, the Stiller of the storm-winds of passion; the Quickener of all that is wholesome, the Adorner of all that is beautiful, the Reconciler of contradictions, the Harmonizer of discords, the Healer of diseases, the Saviour from sin. He has come: the Torch of truth, the Anchor of hope, the Pillar of faith, the Rock for strength, the Refuge for security, the Fountain for refreshment, the Vine for gladness, the Rose for beauty, the Lamb for tenderness, the Friend for counsel, the Brother for love. Jesus Christ has trod the world. The trace of the Divine footsteps will never be obliterated. And the Divine footsteps were the footsteps of a Man. The example of Christ is such as men can follow. On! Until mankind wears His image. On! Towards yon summit on which stands, not an angel, not a disembodied spirit, not an abstract of ideal and unattainable virtues, but THE MAN JESUS CHRIST.[7]

PETER BAYNE IN THE TESTIMONY OF CHRIST IN CHRISTIANITY

ENJOY HIS PRESENCE

As you learn new truths about Christ, always remember the goal is to know Him, to be intimately acquainted with Him in a personal relationship. Close by meditating on these words by Bernard of Clairvaux, and use them to talk with your Lord:

> Jesus, the very thought of thee
>
> with sweetness fills the breast;
>
> but sweeter far thy face to see,
>
> and in thy presence rest.
>
> O hope of every contrite heart,
>
> O joy of all the meek,
>
> to those who fall, how kind thou art!
>
> How good to those who seek!

But what to those who find? Ah, this

nor tongue nor pen can show;

the love of Jesus, what it is,

none but his loved ones know.

Jesus, our only joy be thou,

as thou our prize wilt be;

Jesus, be thou our glory now,

and through eternity.

REST IN HIS LOVE

"Yes, furthermore I count everything as loss compared to the possession of the priceless privilege—the overwhelming preciousness, the surpassing worth and supreme advantage—of knowing Christ Jesus my Lord, and of progressively becoming more deeply and intimately acquainted with Him, of perceiving and recognizing and understanding Him more fully and clearly" (Philippians 3:8 AMP[8]).

RECEIVE AND BELIEVE HIM

...as many as received Him, to them He gave the right to become
children of God, even to those who believe in His name.

JOHN 1:12

PREPARE YOUR HEART

Gipsy Smith, a young evangelist, was a contemporary of G. Campbell Morgan. Smith became a Christian as a result of his father's example, hearing Ira Sankey sing, and a visit to the home of John Bunyan. He stood at the foot of Bunyan's statue and vowed to live for God. He got his Bible, an English dictionary, and a Bible dictionary and carried those resources everywhere he went. People laughed at him because he couldn't even read. He told them he didn't care, that one day he would be a preacher. He went on to become a powerful evangelist in his time. His base was Cambridge but he made numerous trips to America. He would conduct crusades and thousands would make decisions for Christ. One highlight of his life was a trip to South Africa where he conducted tent meetings. Over 300,000 people attended with 18,000 decisions for Christ. His main thrust always was to bring people to a point of decision. In fact, in the flyleaf of a book of his messages, he said that "they were delivered to crowded audiences with a burning desire to bring those who heard them to an immediate decision for Christ."[9] This was not something he dreamed up on his own, but a passion emblazoned in his soul by Christ.

That is the heart of Jesus. The message of Jesus is filled with invitations and challenges. To know Him is to go to places where you have never been and become more than you thought you were. When Jesus entered a village some would welcome Him into their homes and into their lives. Others ignored him. And there were certain people who were outraged by His presence. As He taught, some rejected Him. Others listened to what He said and embraced Him, putting their trust in Him. They followed Him wherever He went.

As Christ opens up His Word and makes Himself known to you, He will ask you for decisions and commitments. Part of your journey with Him is to understand how to receive Him and how to believe in Him. What does that mean? That is the subject of your time with Him today.

As you begin your time alone with the Lord, think about the words of this hymn:

'Tis so sweet to trust in Jesus,

and to take him at his word;

just to rest upon his promise,

and to know, "Thus saith the Lord."

Refrain:

Jesus, Jesus, how I trust him!

How I've proved him o'er and o'er!

Jesus, Jesus, precious Jesus!

O for grace to trust him more!

O how sweet to trust in Jesus,

just to trust his cleansing blood;

and in simple faith to plunge me

neath the healing, cleansing flood! *Refrain*

Yes, 'tis sweet to trust in Jesus,

just from sin and self to cease;

just from Jesus simply taking

life and rest, and joy and peace. *Refrain*

I'm so glad I learned to trust thee,

precious Jesus, Savior, friend;

and I know that thou art with me,

wilt be with me to the end. *Refrain*

LOUISA M.R. STEAD, c. 1850-1917

READ AND STUDY GOD'S WORD

1. John tells us something very important about Jesus' ministry. Read John 1:11-13. Describe what happened.

2. In John 1:11-12 the Greek words used for received are *paralambano* and *lambano*. These words mean "to embrace and acknowledge a teacher's instructions" and "to receive a person as a friend or guest into one's house or society."[10] The Greek word for believe is *pisteuo* and means "to put one's trust in and to be firmly persuaded about something."[11] This belief creates a complete dependence on the one who is trusted. How do these definitions help you understand the meaning of John 1:11-13? Write in your own words what it means for you to receive and believe in Jesus.

3. Throughout His life on earth, Jesus called for decisions as He taught. Look at the following verses and write out the decisions He desired from those who listened.

Matthew 4:18-20

Matthew 5:23-24

Matthew 6:6

Matthew 6:25

Matthew 7:24

Optional Verses: Mark 6:34-44, Mark 8:27-29, Mark 10:17-27, Luke 5:1-11, John 6:26-29, John 11:20-27, 39-40

4. Summarize in 1-2 sentences what you have learned in your study of God's Word today.

ADORE GOD IN PRAYER

What decisions is the Lord asking for in your life today? Write a prayer in your journal as your response to Him.

YIELD YOURSELF TO GOD

Love saw more in Matthew than anybody; and sees more in you, my brother, than anybody else; and if no one wants you, He does, and if no one loves you, He does. If no one cares, He cares; and if you think there is not a friend in the world, you have more friends than you think, and they are closer to you than you dream. God is here, and He says, Come to Me, follow Me, and I will save you; I will give you a chance for this world and the next. Only follow Me. Matthew never did a wiser or nobler thing than when he took Christ home. Everybody there had a chance of blessing that day. Think of what it would mean for your home if you, my brother, took Christ home with you. Your wife and children would have a chance they have never had before. If both of you—husband and wife—bow at His dear feet together, what joy there will be in heaven and on earth! It would mean your home for Jesus. You will give Christ a chance with every child in your home in taking Him there. Matthew took Jesus home with him; and He will go home with you if you will ask Him, and He will go with you this night. God help you! I can believe there are scores and hundreds who mean to follow Jesus. Who will leave all to follow Jesus? Who will sacrifice everything for Jesus' sake? Who will take their stand for Jesus, and who will go home and say to their friends, "I have come to tell you what great things the Lord hath done for me?" Jesus calls to you. Will you follow?[12]

GIPSY SMITH IN AS JESUS PASSED BY

To many Christians Christ is little more than an idea, or at best an idea; He is not a fact. Millions of professed believers talk as if He were real and act as if He were not. And always our actual position is to be discovered by the way we act, not by the way we talk. We can prove our faith by our committal to it, and in no other way… Real faith knows only one way and gladly allows itself to be stripped of any second way or makeshift substitutes. For true faith, it is either God or total collapse. And not since Adam first stood up on the earth has God failed a single man or woman who trusted Him…What we need very badly these days is the company of Christians who are prepared to trust God as completely now as they know they must do at the last day. [13]

A.W. Tozer in The Root Of The Righteous

Do you know how to receive? You say, Sir, I suppose you mean, I need to pray. No sir, I do not mean that. You have been praying long enough. I want you to leave off praying for Christ and taking Christ. I will explain…Will you take? Jesus does love you. Jesus is always near you…He is with you and me always…Jesus, Jesus, Jesus! Not it, not an experience, not emotion, not faith, but Jesus. You have been worrying about your faith. Give it up! Do not think about your faith; think about Jesus, and you will have faith without knowing it. You have been worrying about your feeling. It does not matter, it goes up and down with the barometer. Have done with it, and live in the presence of Jesus. [14]

F.B. Meyer in The Christ Life For Your Life

Enjoy His Presence

In light of all that you have learned from the devotional reading and your time in God's Word, what is the Lord asking you to do when He asks you to receive and believe? How are you responding to Him? In what areas do you need to receive Him and believe Him today? Always remember that when you open your life to the Lord Jesus Christ, you will shine brightly for Him. Close by writing a prayer of response to the Lord in your journal.

Rest in His Love

"Do not be afraid any longer, only believe" (Jesus in Mark 5:36).

ASK AND SEEK HIM

If you abide in Me, and My words abide in you, ask whatever you wish, and it will be done for you.

JOHN 15:7

PREPARE YOUR HEART

George Muller learned something early on in his ministry that served him well for the rest of his life. His friend, Mr. Henry Craik, served the Lord in ministry in Bristol. Mueller felt strongly that there was wide sphere of ministry there for his friend. Not long after that, Craik invited Mueller to join him in ministry in Bristol. Mueller began to pray about God's call in his life, and whether a field of ministry more suited to his gifts might be opening to him. One week later he left for Bristol. On the journey he had no freedom to speak or to give out tracts. He saw that he had substituted the work of the Lord and action for communion and meditation. He had neglected his quiet hour with the Lord that fed his spiritual life. A.T. Pierson describes it this way: "We are prone to think that converse with Christian brethren, and the general round of Christian activity, especially when we are much busied with preaching the Word and visits to inquiring or needy souls, make up for the loss of aloneness with God in the secret place. We hurry to a public service with but a few minutes of private prayer, allowing precious time to be absorbed in social pleasures, restrained from withdrawing from others by a false delicacy, when to excuse ourselves for needful communion with God and his word would have been perhaps the best witness possible to those whose company was holding us unduly! How often we rush from one public engagement to another without any proper interval for renewing our strength in waiting on the Lord, as though God cared more for the quantity than the quality of our service."

In your discovery of the priceless privilege of knowing Christ, it is necessary to understand the priority of spending time alone with Him. There are countless activities and people and pursuits that can crowd out this precious space with Him. It is a resolve you must have at the outset. And that resolve must be renewed day by day. Otherwise, when you least expect it, you can lose your quiet time.

Ask God to speak to you as you draw near to Him in His Word today.

READ AND STUDY GOD'S WORD

1. Jesus taught often about the necessity of prayer and the inner closet of time with Him. Look at the following passages of Scripture and record what you learn about prayer and quiet time.

Matthew 6:5-6

Matthew 7:7-11

Luke 18:1

John 15:7

2. How important was prayer to the disciples after Jesus rose from the dead and ascended to heaven? Look at the following verses and record what you learn about prayer in the early church.

Acts 1:14

Acts 1:24-25

Acts 2:42

Acts 6:4

Acts 12:5

Optional Verses: Acts 4:23-24, Acts 14:23, Acts 20:36-38

3. What is your favorite insight about prayer?

ADORE GOD IN PRAYER

Lord, we will seek You constantly so that you may increase our worth to Your work. But what joy we know we shall find, because you found us. Hallelujah![15]

CORRIE TEN BOOM IN EACH NEW DAY

YIELD YOURSELF TO GOD

Don't think of prayer as an impersonal requirement. Realize that it is a Person, the Lord Jesus Christ, with all authority and with all love, who expects us to pray. These excerpts from His words show that He Himself expects us to pray:

- Matthew 6:5 And when you pray…

- Matthew 6:6 But when you pray…

- Matthew 6:7 And when you pray…

- Matthew 6:9 This, then, is how you should pray…

- Luke 11:9 So I say to you: Ask…; seek…; knock…

- Luke 18:1 Then Jesus told his disciples…they should always pray.

Suppose Jesus appeared to you personally, much as He did to the Apostle John on the Isle of Patmos in Revelation 1, and said that He expected you to pray. Wouldn't you become more faithful in prayer, knowing specifically that Jesus expected that of you? Well, the words of Jesus quoted above are as much His will for you as if He spoke your name and said them to you face to face.[16]

DONALD WHITNEY IN SPIRITUAL DISCIPLINES FOR THE CHRISTIAN LIFE

Here then we have a threefold witness to the secret of true prosperity and unmingled blessing: devout meditation and reflection upon the Scriptures, which are once a book of law, a river of life, and a mirror of self—fitted to convey the will of God, the life of God, and the transforming power of God. That believer makes a fatal mistake who for any cause neglects the prayerful study of the word of God. To read God's holy book, by it search one's self, and turn it into prayer so into holy living, is the one great secret of growth in grace and godliness. The worker for God must first be a worker with God: he must have power with God and must prevail with Him in prayer, if he is to have power with men and prevail with men in preaching or in any form of witnessing and serving. At all costs let us make sure of that highest preparation for our work—the preparation of our own souls; and for this we must take time to be alone with His word and His Spirit, that we may truly meet God, and understand His will and the revelation of Himself. If we seek the secrets of the life George Muller lived and the work he did, this is the very key to the whole mystery, and with that key any believer can unlock the doors to a prosperous growth in grace and power in service. God's word is HIS WORD—the expression of His thought, the revealing of His mind and heart. The supreme end of life is to know God and make Him known; and how is this possible if we neglect the very means He has chosen for conveying to us that knowledge! Even Christ, the Living Word, is to be found enshrined in the written word. Our knowledge of Christ is dependent upon our acquaintance with the Holy Scripture, which are the reflection of His character and glory—the firmament across the expanse of which He moves as the Sun of righteousness.[17]

A.T. PIERSON IN GEORGE MUELLER OF BRISTOL

How can we, who are not monks and do not live in the desert, practice the prayer of the heart? How does the prayer of the heart affect our daily ministry? The answer to these questions lies in the formulation of a definite discipline:

- The prayer of the heart is nurtured by short, simple prayers.

- The prayer of the heart is unceasing.

- The prayer of the heart is all inclusive.

…This way of simple prayer, when we are faithful to it and practice it at regular times, slowly leads us to an experience of rest and opens us to God's active presence. Moreover, we can take this prayer with us into a very busy day…

…To love and work for the glory of God cannot remain an idea about which we think once in awhile. It must become an interior, unceasing doxology…

…A final characteristic of the prayer of the heart is that it includes all our concerns. When we enter with our mind into our heart and there stand in the presence of God, then all our mental preoccupations become prayer…[18]

HENRI NOUWEN IN THE WAY OF THE HEART

ENJOY HIS PRESENCE

Think now about the priority of prayer and seeking the Lord in your own life. Is quiet time the most important part of your day? Do you rush to make it through? What will it take today to begin to implement this great secret that George Mueller discovered?

REST IN HIS LOVE

"In the early morning, while it was still dark, Jesus got up, left the house, and went away to a secluded place, and was praying there" (Mark 1:35).

LOVE HIM

If anyone really loves me, he will observe my teaching, And My Father will love him, and both of us will come into face-to-face fellowship with him; yes, we will make our special dwelling place with him.

JOHN 14:23 WMS

PREPARE YOUR HEART

John Flavel lived in the 1600's, studied at Oxford, and had such an intense love for the Lord Jesus Christ that those who knew him often remarked about his winsome character. He was a minister and was known for his reading, meditation and prayer. Imagine being known as a person of deep devotion and godly character like John Flavel. His actions and priorities were a direct result of the intensity of his love for Christ.

Today, as you begin your time with the Lord, what is it that characterizes your life? One thing that the Lord wants from you above all else is your love. In fact, when Jesus was asked what was the greatest commandment of all, He said: "You shall love the Lord your God with all your heart, and with all your soul, and with all your mind, and with all your strength" (Mark 12:30). As you continue looking at the responses that are necessary as you discover the priceless privilege of knowing Christ, one thing reigns supreme: love for Christ. How strong does your heart beat for the Lord? Is the fire in your heart for Him burning with a high intensity? Ask the Lord to give you a heart of love for Him today.

> I cannot bring Thee praise like golden noon-light
> Shining on earth's green floor.
> My song is more like silver of the moonlight,
> But I adore.
> I cannot bring Thee, O Beloved, ever
> Pure song of woodland bird;
> And yet I know the song of Thy least lover
> In love is heard.
> O blessed be the Love that nothing spurneth:
> We sing—Love doth unfold

Our little song in love. Our silver turneth
To fine-spun gold.[19]

AMY CARMICHAEL IN MOUNTAIN BREEZES

READ AND STUDY GOD'S WORD

1. How important is your love to the Lord Jesus? Read John 14:21-24 and notice every occurrence of love in this chapter. What do you learn about the Lord's love and our love for Him?

2. His desire for our love is seen more clearly in a conversation He had with Peter after his resurrection from the dead. Read John 21:15-19 and record what you learn about the priority of love for Jesus.

3. Read the following verses and write what you learn about loving the Lord, personalizing your insights (i.e. in 1 Corinthians 2:9 "what God has prepared for *me* who loves Him").

   1 Corinthians 2:9

   Ephesians 6:24

   James 1:12

   James 2:5

   1 Peter 1:8

ADORE GOD IN PRAYER

Jesus, Thy boundless love to me

No thought can reach, no tongue declare;

O knit my thankful heart to Thee,

And reign without a rival there:

Thine wholly, Thine alone I am:

Be Thou alone my constant flame.

O grant that nothing to my soul

May dwell, but Thy pure love alone;

O may Thy love possess me whole,

My joy, my treasure, and my crown:

Strange fires far from my soul remove:

May every act, word, thought, be love.

In suffering, be Thy love my peace;

In weakness, be Thy love my power;

And, when the storms of life shall cease,

Jesus, in that important hour,

In death, as life, be Thou my guide,

And save me, who for me hast died.[20]

PAUL GERHARDT, 1607-1676 TR. JOHN WESLEY, 1703-1791

YIELD YOURSELF TO GOD

Think about the following words by John Flavel and underline any that stand out to you:

1. Is Jesus Christ altogether lovely? Then I beseech you set your souls upon this lovely Jesus. I am sure such an object as has been here represented, would compel love from the coldest breast and hardest heart. Away with those empty nothings, away with this vain deceitful world, which deserves not the thousandth part of the love you give it. Let all stand aside and give way to Christ. O if only you knew

his worth and excellency, what he is in himself, what he has done for you, and deserved from you, you would need no arguments of mine to persuade you to love him!

2. Esteem nothing lovely except as it is enjoyed in Christ, or used for the sake of Christ. Love nothing for itself, love nothing separate from Jesus Christ. In two things we all sin in love of created things. We sin in the excess of our affections, loving them above the proper value of mere created things. We also sin in the inordinacy of our affections, that is to say we give our love for created things a priority it should never have.

3. Let us all be humbled for the corruption of our hearts that are so eager in their affections for vanities and trifles and so hard to be persuaded to the love of Christ, who is altogether lovely. O how many pour out streams of love and delight upon the vain and empty created thing; while no arguments can draw forth one drop of love from their stubborn and unbelieving hearts to Jesus Christ! I have read of one Joannes Mollius, who was observed to go often alone, and weep bitterly; and being pressed by a friend to know the cause of his troubles, said "O! it grieves me that I cannot bring this heart of mine to love Jesus Christ more fervently."

4. Represent Christ to the world as he is, by your behaviour towards him. Is he altogether lovely? Let all the world see and know that he is so, by your delights in him and communion with him; zeal for him, and readiness to part with any other lovely thing upon his account. Proclaim his excellencies to the world, as the spouse did in these verses. Persuade them how much your beloved is better than any other beloved. Show his glorious excellencies as you speak of him; hold him forth to others, as he is in himself: altogether lovely. See that you "walk worthy of him unto all well pleasing," Col. 1:10. "Show forth the praises of Christ," 1 Pet. 2:19. Let not that "worthy name be blasphemed through you," James 2:7. He is glorious in himself, and he is sure to put glory upon you; take heed that you do not put shame and dishonours upon him; he has committed his honour to you, do not betray that trust.

5. Never be ashamed to be counted as a Christian: he is altogether lovely; he can never be a shame to you; it will be your great sin to be ashamed of him. Some men

glory in their shame; do not let yourself be ashamed of your glory. If you will be ashamed of Christ now, he will be ashamed of you when he shall appear in his own glory, and the glory of all his holy angels. Be ashamed of nothing but sin; and among other sins, be ashamed especially for this sin, that you have no more love for him who is altogether lovely.

6. Be willing to leave everything that is lovely upon earth, in order that you may be with the altogether lovely Lord Jesus Christ in heaven. Lift up your voices with the bride, Rev. 20:20 "Come Lord Jesus, come quickly." It is true, you must pass through the pangs of death into his intimacy and enjoyment; but surely it is worth suffering much more than that to be with this lovely Jesus. "The Lord direct your hearts into the love of God, and the patient waiting for Jesus Christ," 2 Thess. 3:5.

7. Let the loveliness of Christ draw all men to him. Is loveliness in the creature so attractive? And can the transcendent loveliness of Christ draw none? O the blindness of man! If you see no beauty in Christ that causes you to desire him, it is because the god of this world has blinded your minds.

8. Strive to be Christ-like, if ever you would be lovely in the eyes of God and man. Certainly, my brethren, it is only the Spirit of Christ within you, and the beauty of Christ upon you, which can make you lovely persons. The more you resemble him in holiness, the more will you show of true excellence and loveliness; and the more frequent and spiritual your communication and communion with Christ is, the more of the beauty and loveliness of Christ will be stamped upon your spirits, changing you into the same image, from glory to glory. Amen.[21]

BY JOHN FLAVEL IN CHRIST ALTOGETHER LOVELY

Christ rightly known is most surely Christ beloved. No sooner do we discern His excellencies, behold His glories, and partake of His bounties, than our heart is at once moved with love towards Him. Let Him but speak pardon to our guilty souls, we shall not long delay to speak words of love to His most adorable person. It is utterly impossible for a man to know himself to be complete in Christ, and to be destitute of love towards Christ Jesus. A believer may be in Christ, and yet, from a holy jealousy, he may doubt his own affection to his Lord; but love is most assuredly in his bosom, for that breast which has never heaved with love to Jesus is yet a stranger to the blood of sprinkling. He that loveth not, hath not seen Christ, neither known Him. As seed expands in the moisture and the heat, and sends forth its green blade, so when the soul becomes affected with the mercy of the Saviour, it puts forth its shoots of love to Him and desire after Him…One of the earliest and most important signs of love to Jesus is the deed of solemn dedication of ourselves, with all we have and are, most unreservedly to the Lord's service…Every true believer, of course, ought to devote himself to the service of the Redeemer; yea, he must and will, for he is constrained by love. He will do it not once only, but daily.[22]

CHARLES SPURGEON IN THE SAINT AND HIS SAVIOUR

ENJOY HIS PRESENCE

Do you love the Lord Jesus Christ? Will you tell Him of your love for Him? Write a prayer that expresses this love.

LOVE'S RESPONSE
"The disciple whom Jesus loved,"
Why! that's me!
Loved completely, perfectly.
How can it be?
He calls me His chosen, beloved,
Kept for eternity.
How can I respond, my Lord,
Except by loving Thee?[23]

CONNI HUDSON

REST IN HIS LOVE

"Blessed is a man who perseveres under trial; for once he has been approved, he will receive the crown of life which the Lord has promised to those who love Him" (James 1:12).

FOLLOW HIM

If anyone wishes to come after Me, he must deny himself,
and take up his cross and follow Me.
MATTHEW 16:24

PREPARE YOUR HEART

One of the decisions that every believer in Christ will be asked by Him is to follow. He said, over and over, to those He came in contact with: "Follow Me." Down through the centuries, this invitation is repeated. Follow Me. This is more than just an invitation or a request. It is a clarion call to a singular commitment to Jesus. It is the call to discipleship. In Matthew 4:19, He said, "Follow Me, and I will make you fishers of men." Influencing the world is a high calling. When you follow Him, you will follow His lead, His example of mercy, kindness, and grace, and you will love and serve Him. The answer to this discipleship call touches every area of your life. It means that you always live a cut above the norm. You represent not just yourself, but Him. You will be known to those around you as His disciple. You will be seen as one who has been with Him. Every activity, every relationship, every opportunity is seen in the light of that decision to follow Him. There is no turning back. You are going to discover so many powerful truths about Jesus in the days ahead. Always in the background, this call from Him will sound clearly: "Follow Me." How can you refuse your Lord when He speaks? Say, "Yes Lord. Where you lead, I will go."

Ask the Lord to speak to you today as you draw near to Him in your quiet time.

READ AND STUDY GOD'S WORD

1. Those early days in the ministry of Christ must have been exciting. His teaching must have thrilled those with hearts hungry for God. Read the following passages of Scripture. Record everything you learn about discipleship. Personalize your observations as you write them out.

Matthew 4:19-25

Matthew 9:7-13

Matthew 16:24

Luke 14:25-27

Optional Verses: Matthew 10

2. What was it like to be a disciple of Jesus Christ following His resurrection and ascension into heaven? Read Acts 4:1-14, 32-35 and record your most significant insights about discipleship.

3. Describe what you think it means to be a disciple of Jesus Christ. What does it mean to follow Him, deny yourself, and take up your cross?

ADORE GOD IN PRAYER

As you respond to all that the Lord has shown you in His Word today, take some time now to talk with Him. Turn to your prayer pages and review those needs that are written there. Bring each request to Him. Write out any answers to prayer.

> Lord Jesus, I thank you that a new day affords another opportunity for consecration and devotion. You have turned a fresh page in my life's story. It comes from you without blemish or soil; help me to keep it so. Forgive the past blotted with my failures and sins, and help me to walk in the light.[24]
>
> F.B. MEYER IN DAILY PRAYERS

YIELD YOURSELF TO GOD

Our Lord implies that the only men and women He will use in His building enterprises are those who love Him personally, passionately and devotedly beyond any of the closest ties on earth. The conditions are stern, but they are glorious.[25]

OSWALD CHAMBERS IN MY UTMOST FOR HIS HIGHEST

Discipleship means personal, passionate devotion to a Person, Our Lord Jesus Christ. There is a difference between devotion to a Person and devotion to principles or to a cause. Our Lord never proclaimed a cause; He proclaimed personal devotion to Himself. To be a disciple is to be a devoted love-slave of the Lord Jesus. Many of us who call ourselves Christians are not devoted to Jesus Christ. No man on earth has this passionate love to the Lord Jesus unless the Holy Ghost has imparted it to him. We may admire Him, we may respect Him and reverence Him, but we cannot love Him. The only Lover of the Lord Jesus is the Holy Ghost, and He sheds abroad the very love of God in our hearts. Whenever the Holy Ghost sees a chance of glorifying Jesus, He will take your heart, your nerves, your whole personality, and simply make you blaze and glow with devotion to Jesus Christ.[26]

OSWALD CHAMBERS IN MY UTMOST FOR HIS HIGHEST

ENJOY HIS PRESENCE

Will you respond to the Lord's call, *follow Me,* today? It is a daring, passionate decision that requires both humility and courage. Once you make this decision there is an invisible mark in your life that means there is a claim on you—it is the claim of Christ. It means that you follow Him wherever He leads. Is there anything in your life that is keeping you from such an important decision? This decision will alter the course of your life and take you on that adventure of having a heart on fire for Christ and engaging in the priceless privilege of knowing Him. Close your time with the Lord by thinking about, singing, and praying through the words of this hymn. Then write a prayer of commitment to the Lord Jesus Christ in your journal.

> All to Jesus I surrender;
>
> all to him I freely give;
>
> I will ever love and trust him,
>
> in his presence daily live.

Refrain: I surrender all, I surrender all,

all to thee, my blessed Savior, I surrender all.

All to Jesus I surrender;

humbly at his feet I bow,

worldly pleasures all forsaken;

take me, Jesus, take me now. *Refrain*

All to Jesus I surrender;

make me, Savior, wholly thine;

fill me with thy love and power;

truly know that thou art mine. *Refrain*

All to Jesus I surrender;

Lord, I give myself to thee;

fill me with thy love and power;

let thy blessing fall on me. *Refrain*

All to Jesus I surrender;

now I feel the sacred flame.

O the joy of full salvation!

Glory, glory, to his name! *Refrain*

J.W. Van Deventer

Rest in His Love

"And He said to them, 'Follow Me, and I will make you fishers of men.' Immediately they left their nets and followed Him" (Matthew 4:19-20).

DEVOTIONAL READING
BY CHARLES HADDON SPURGEON

Dear Friend,

The next two days are your opportunity to spend time reviewing what you have learned this week. You may wish to write your thoughts and insights in your journal in the back of this study book. As you think about all that you have learned about the priceless privilege of knowing Christ, record your most important discoveries in the space provided:

Your most significant insight:

Your favorite quote:

Your favorite verse:

Meditate on these words by Charles Haddon Spurgeon in *Morning and Evening*:

> …press forward and seek to know much of the Son of God who is the brightness of His Father's glory, and yet in unspeakable condescension of grace became man for our sakes; know Him in the singular complexity of His nature: eternal God, and yet suffering, finite man; follow Him as He walks on the waters with the tread of deity, and as He sits upon the well in the weariness of humanity. Be not satisfied unless you know much of Jesus Christ as your Friend, your Brother, your Husband, your all…[27]

CHARLES HADDON SPURGEON IN MORNING AND EVENING

Viewer Guide
≈ WEEK TWO ≈

The Real Life Of Privilege

In Week Two of *A Heart On Fire*, you have had the opportunity to study more in-depth what it means to have an intimate relationship with Christ. In our time together in this message, we want to look why knowing Christ is such an incredible privilege.

"Yes, indeed I certainly do count everything as loss compared with the priceless privilege of knowing Christ Jesus my Lord" (Philippians 3:8 WMS).

The Promise of Privilege

It's priceless. When something is priceless, there's nothing that compares and there's not enough money in the world to buy it.

The Place of Privilege

Knowing _____is the place of privilege. It means you experience His Person, who He is, intimately, moment by moment in your daily life.

1. You experience the power of His _____.

2. You experience the fellowship of His _____.

3. You experience _____with Him in death and in life. You have a future hope that no one can take from you.

The Priority of this Privilege

The _____of knowing Christ takes first priority because everything else pales in comparison to knowing Him.

The Experience of this Privilege

1. You will know how He _____.

2. You will know and understand His _____more and more.

3. You will experience times of _____.

4. You will know what He _____.

5. You will know how He _____.

≈≈ *Video messages are available on DVDs or as Downloadable M4V Video. Audio messages are available on Audio CDs or as Downloadable MP3 Audio. Visit the Quiet Time Ministries Online Store at www.quiettime.org.*

THE DIVINE ROMANCE

John 3:16

For God so loved the world that he gave his one and only Son, that whoever believes in him shall not perish but have eternal life.

JOHN 3:16 NIV

CHOSEN AS HIS BELOVED

So, as those who have been chosen of God, holy and beloved…

COLOSSIANS 3:12

PREPARE YOUR HEART

*od so loved the world…*These words are the beginning of probably one of the most well-known and loved verses in the Bible: John 3:16. They tell the truth that is more than just a story and definitely more than a fairy tale. Because God so loved the world, He also loves you. There is much depth in this statement. God is a romancer of those He loves. He constantly woos them to Himself. Not only is He a romancer of people, but He is also a romancer of the individual. That means His eye is on you. He desires you more than anything else in this world. His plan for you is borne out of His love for you. This week, your goal is to understand that all of life is really about a romance. It is the great romance between you and your Lord. This romance involves all of those components that make a great story: tension, pain, drama, a daring rescue, and a happy ending. The wonderful thing about this story is that it is true. And it involves you and your Lord.

There is no place where the heart of God is seen with more clarity than in the Old Testament. And this is especially true when you read the words of the prophets. What you hear in their prophecies is what God wants to say to His people. It is the cry that comes from the heart of a God who is constantly reaching out to a people who many times ignore Him or do not realize He is with them.

As you begin your quiet time today, read these words from the prophet Isaiah in Isaiah 41:8-10 and see if you can *catch the romance* that is found deep in the heart of your Lord: "But you, O Israel, my servant, Jacob, whom I have chosen, you descendants of Abraham my friend, I took you from the ends of the earth, from its farthest corners I called you. I said, 'You are my servant'; I have chosen you and have not rejected you. So do not fear, for I am with you; do not be dismayed, for I am your God. I will strengthen you and help you; I will uphold you with my righteous right hand." Keep in mind that God's way of choosing and his character never change. He chose Israel and He has chosen you according to Colossians 3:12. Ask God to speak to you today as you draw near to Him in quiet time.

READ AND STUDY GOD'S WORD

1. God chooses people for a love relationship with Him. It is amazing, but it is true. He chose the people of Israel to be His people. Look at the following verses and record what you learn about God's choice of His people.

Deuteronomy 4:32-40

Deuteronomy 7:7-9

2. God chose Israel to be His people and He promised to be their God. They responded to His love with rebellion, idolatry and disobedience. The consequence of their sin was exile to a foreign land. And now you will move forward in the history of Israel to a time when God brought His people back to the land they loved: Jerusalem. Today you will look briefly at the prophecy of Zechariah. His prophecy is considered to be one of the most important prophecies in the Old Testament, second only to Isaiah. Zechariah's words occurred just prior to 400 years of silence from God. The next time the people would hear God speak was in Jesus, the Incarnate and Living Word. His prophecy sums up all that the previous prophets had said and is the most Messianic of all the prophecies. It is a prophecy about being chosen; specifically, God's choice of His people in spite of their own sad inner state. Fifty thousand wartorn, weary exiles had returned to their homeland. They were filled with a desire to rebuild the temple that had been destroyed. The temple had been central to the life of the people. The people began to rebuild but soon abandoned the project and built houses instead. It was a barren life without their God. They were weak, tired, discouraged with no hope for their lives. They had no sense of being special and felt forgotten, rejected, and abandoned by God. And so God once again reaches out to His people through His prophet, Zechariah.

Read the following verses and record those phrases that show you something about the heart of God and the depth of His love for His people.

Zechariah 1:14-17

Zechariah 2:7-8

Zechariah 2:12-13

Optional Verses: Zechariah 2:3-5, Zechariah 2:10-11, Zechariah 3:1-5

3. And now, we move forward in time to see that God's choice is seen in the New Testament as well. Those who are in a relationship with Him through Jesus Christ are also chosen by Him. Look at the following verses and record what you learn. Be sure to look for the great results of being chosen and also the responsibilities of the chosen.

1 Corinthians 1:26-31

Ephesians 1:3-6

Colossians 3:12

1 Peter 2:9-10

Optional Verses: 1 Corinthians 6:19-20, 2 Thessalonians 2:13-14, Revelation 17:14

4. Optional: Behind God's choice stands His great love for you. Read the following verses and record what you learn about His love. John 3:16-17, Romans 5:6-8, 1 John 3:1, 1 John 4:8-10

ADORE GOD IN PRAYER

May these words be the prayer of your heart today:

Thee will I love, my Strength, my Tower,
Thee will I love, my Joy, my Crown,
Thee will I love with all my power,
In all Thy words, and Thee alone;
Thee will I love, till the pure fire
Fill my whole soul with chaste desire.

Ah, why did I so late Thee know,
Thee, lovelier than the sons of men!
Ah, why did I no sooner go
To Thee, the only ease in pain!
Ashamed, I sigh, and inly mourn,
That I so late to Thee did turn.

Give to mine eyes refreshing tears,
Give to my heart chaste, hallowed fires,
Give to my soul, with filial fires,
The love that all heaven's host inspires;
That all my powers, with all their might,
In Thy sole glory may unite.

Thee will I love, my Joy, my Crown,
Thee will I love, my Lord, my God;
Thee will I love, beneath Thy frown,
Or smile, Thy sceptre, or Thy rod;
What though my flesh and heart decay,
Thee shall I love in endless day.[1]

JOHANN SCHEFFLER, 1624-1677, TR. JOHN WESLEY, 1703-1791

YIELD YOURSELF TO GOD

Do you know, beyond all doubt, that you are God's own child and you are loved by Him without measure? It is true. Your soul is loved, with a love so tender, by the One who is the highest of all. His is a love so wonderful, far beyond anything we created beings can fully fathom. No one in this life, can know how passionately the Creator longs for us. Enter into this love, then, by His empowering grace. Be diligent as you go to prayer. Still the nagging, worrying voices that tell you to doubt your Lover's complete trustworthiness—and fix your thoughts on His good, lofty, and limitless compassion—so that you remain in His love. Trust Him. Learn what it means to hide your soul in Him in this way, in utter trust. After that, your prayers will be filled with true reverence—that is, a joyful respect not mixed with resentment, demands, or bargaining. For then our natural will is to have God himself—nothing less. And God's good will is simply to have us. To wrap us in himself, and in eternal life. Never stop willing or loving, until you are united with Him in happy completeness….This is the sturdy foundation on which everything else in your spiritual life depends, now and forever.[2]

JULIAN OF NORWICH IN I PROMISE YOU A CROWN
ARRANGED AND PARAPHRASED BY DAVID HAZARD

ENJOY HIS PRESENCE

In the Old Testament when the people of God realized that God had chosen them, it motivated them to give their hearts to God and live for Him. Their inner devotion was renewed and they wanted to serve Him by doing the work He had called them to do. In short, it lit their hearts on fire for God and fueled their passion for Him. What is your response today as you think about being chosen by God?

REST IN HIS LOVE

"…you are a chosen race, a royal priesthood, a holy nation, a people for God's own possession, so that you may proclaim the excellencies of Him who has called you out of darkness into His marvelous light" (1 Peter 2:9).

THE GREAT DILEMMA

*I looked and there was no one to help, and I was astonished and there
was no one to uphold; so My own arm brought salvation to Me...*

ISAIAH 63:5

PREPARE YOUR HEART

In the beginning God created the heavens and the earth. He created human beings. And He
pronounced that all He had created was good. And then something happened to change the
idyllic paradise that He created and the perfect relationship He had with human beings. The ones
He created made a choice that was independent of God. Sin entered the world. As a result, sin
created a great, uncrossable chasm between God and man. The penalty of sin is death. J.I. Packer
writes: "Sin, which is in essence an irrational energy rebellion against God—a lawless habit of
self-willed arrogance, moral and spiritual, expressing itself in egoism of all sorts—is something
that God hates in all its forms (Isaiah 61:8, Jeremiah 44:4, Proverbs 6:16-19) and that defiles us
in his sight. Therefore Scripture views it not only as guilt needing to be forgiven, but also as filth
needing to be cleansed."[3]

Because of sin, there is a human dilemma. Man was created with a high purpose: to know
and love God. Man's sin separated all of mankind from God and placed us in a position of need
and helplessness. Herein is the dilemma: man is separated from God and in need of a Redeemer.

Because God is holy, just and righteous, He cannot look upon sin without exercising the justice required to exercise the penalty of death. His wrath is seen because He is righteous and holy.
That is divine justice. And yet, He loves men and women with an everlasting love. That is divine
love. It is an unconditional love for the undeserving. It is a love that desires security and assurance
bestowed on its objects. It is unchangeable and eternal. Thus, there is the divine side of the great
dilemma. He is just, requiring death for sin and yet He loves, requiring action on behalf of those
who are the objects of His love. His love will take action on behalf of the undeserving. His love
will move the undeserving to a favorable position.

There have been celebrated romances throughout history: Prince Edward and Mrs. Simpson,
Anne Morrow and Charles Lindbergh, Spencer Tracy and Katherine Hepburn, Antony and
Cleopatra, Elizabeth Barrett Browning and Robert Browning. Their love has been proclaimed

as great love. But their love pales in comparison to the love your Lord has for you. Imagine One who loves you more than life itself. His is a love that will do what it takes to set you free from that which enslaves you.

Today, as you spend time with your Lord, ask Him to quiet your heart that you might be able to absorb the depth of His love for you. Ask Him to show you how "wide and long and high and deep is the love of Christ, and to know this love that surpasses knowledge..." (Ephesians 3:18-19 NIV). If you have extra time, meditate on the words of Psalm 44:1-8 and think about what God does for His people who are in need.

READ AND STUDY GOD'S WORD

1. In Isaiah 6:1-7 you see the God's call of His prophet, Isaiah. This is one of the clearest pictures we have of the holiness of God and the response of a sinful man. Read this passage and record your insights about the holiness of God.

2. Look at the following verses in Isaiah and record your insights about the need of God's people and what He does as a result.

Isaiah 41:17-20

Isaiah 63:5, 7-9

3. In the prophecy of Jeremiah the human and divine dilemmas are clearly seen. In these verses you see that man's wound is incurable, and there is no one to plead your cause (Jeremiah 30:12). It is described as a virtually impossible situation. It might be seen as the great dilemma. But you also see God's love. Read Jeremiah 30:12-17, 22, and Jeremiah 31:3, and record what you see about God's love and how He expresses His love for His people. (Optional Verses: Jeremiah 31:1-4, 11-14)

4. In Paul's letter to the Romans, he sets forth the helplessness of man and the need for salvation from God. Read the following verses and record your insights.

Romans 3:9-12

Romans 3:23

Romans 6:23

5. Summarize in 1-2 sentences your most significant insight in your study of God's Word today.

ADORE GOD IN PRAYER

Perhaps today you are realizing the human dilemma in your own life. Will you draw near to the Lord and bring every sin, every weakness, every need of your life to Him? Do you see that He wants to meet your need with Himself? Rejoice today that He loves you that much.

YIELD YOURSELF TO GOD

God is holy in His being: He is righteous in His character. Righteousness appears in His dealings with others. The term righteousness is a relative one; it assumes the existence of others. It is a word of relationship: whether in attitude or in government, God will ever be righteous. But holiness is not a word of relationship, but of nature, of being. God is holy: if there were no creatures He would yet be holy, the Holy One, whose name is Holy. It is in this holiness of God that we must look for the necessity of propitiation (satisfaction). That there must be propitiation does not indicate, primarily, that God is offended and must be appeased; but that God is holy and cannot by sinful creatures be approached. Only holy beings (like the seraphim, the cherubim of glory, and the elect angels) can possibly abide in His presence. Sin cannot come near Him. It is not that He hates sinners (He gave His Son to ransom them!) but it is that He is holy and cannot look upon sin. And if there be sin, there must be wrath against it: not merely the vindication of God's offended government, but the infinite abhorrence of His holy nature! He dwelleth in light unapproachable. It is death to draw near; not because God is vindictive,-- He is love: but because He is holy, and we are sinful, unclean, and unholy.[4]

WILLIAM NEWELL IN ROMANS, VERSE BY VERSE

So, dear soul, cursed with the sin which thou hast taken into thy heart, God hates the sin, but He loves thee! He knew all about it before He chose thee. He will never be surprised. He will never be disappointed. He will never love you less. … Your weakness will command His strongest love. He sits down beside you. The fever is on your head and body. He knows it will take a long vigil, long care, long patience. He has counted the cost, He is prepared for a long sickness. He has taken you in hand, your passions, your impurity, your garrulous gossip, your sulkiness, your jealousy, your vainglory, your love of money, your love of sin; God knows it all. But He has come, and will never leave you for a moment. If you will let Him, He will make short work. If you resist Him, you will make the work longer. But He will never leave you, He will never give you up, and however often you fall, go back to Him again.[5]

F.B. MEYER IN THE CHRIST LIFE FOR YOUR LIFE

ENJOY HIS PRESENCE

Do you see the love, the devotion, and the faithfulness of your Lord today? Close your time with Him by thanking Him for loving you in spite of your tendency to stray. Ask Him to give you a heart on fire for Him, one that says "yes" to His invitation to the divine romance.

REST IN HIS LOVE

"I have loved you with an everlasting love; Therefore I have drawn you with lovingkindness…" (Jeremiah 31:3).

THE ANOINTED ONE

The Spirit of the Lord God is upon me, because the Lord has anointed me to bring good news to the afflicted; He has sent me to bind up the brokenhearted, to proclaim liberty to captives and freedom to prisoners.

ISAIAH 61:1

PREPARE YOUR HEART

C. S. Lewis was an atheist for many years. He was not one to believe in an emotional religion or entertain something that was not true. At the age of 28, C.S. Lewis became friends with Thomas Dewar Weldon, a teacher of philosophy at Magdalen College where they both had been elected Fellows. During a momentous conversation between the two, Lewis discovered that Weldon was a Christian. He was stunned. As a result, C.S. Lewis began to read Christian writers and philosophers. One spring day in 1929, he boarded a bus at Magdalen College. His head was swimming with words from philosophers and writers as he considered the truths of the existence of God. When the bus reached its destination, C.S. Lewis had come to grips with the fact of the existence of God. But his search did not end there. God wanted him for His own. In that same year, Lewis began to think about his own heart and the meaning of his existence. One evening in September, Lewis had a long talk on Christianity with J.R.R. Tolkien (a devout Roman Catholic) and Hugo Dyson. The next day C.S. Lewis, on a journey to the zoo, continued thinking about Christ, and by the time he reached his destination, he had come to a decision about Christ. C.S. Lewis came to a point where he realized his own responsibility to God and knelt before Him, acknowledging Him as Lord and Savior. He described himself as probably the most reluctant convert in all of England, and he saw God as the Great Pursuer. In a letter to Sheldon Vanauken who was considering Christianity, C.S. Lewis closed his letter by intimating that he doubted if Vanauken could escape God's pursuit of him.

God has a plan that stands sure and cannot be thwarted. This plan is seen in the salvation of those who turn to Him. God's plan is vividly demonstrated in the miraculous answer to the great dilemma: His Divine Love and Justice and man's sin and need for a Redeemer. In His great plan, He determined to rescue His people Himself. Throughout the Old Testament, you will discover the facts of His determination to come and save His own people from their sin. There is the promise of a Messiah, one who would come first, as a Suffering Servant, dying in the place of the people so that the penalty for sin would be paid. Then, He would come as a Conquering King, ushering in the Kingdom of God and a new heaven and a new earth. You see, God will have you for Himself. Just as He has gone to the ends of the earth for one such as C.S. Lewis or Sheldon Vanauken, so He has done the same for you. Today you will look at this One who came from heaven to earth for you, who said Yes and went all the way to the cross.

As you begin your time with the Lord today, turn to Psalm 2 and meditate on these words that speak of the Lord's Anointed who will accomplish God's purpose. Ask God to speak to your heart as you draw near to Him.

READ AND STUDY GOD'S WORD

1. All God's prophets in the Old Testament possessed a strong sense of the call of God. They carried with them a great sense of purpose as they lived for God during their day. According to Walt Kaiser, Jr., prophets did more than foretelling. They also were called to forthtelling where they would "set forth the word of God against the backdrop of the failure of the people to obey the moral law of God."[6] They also predicted future events, often with a focus on the coming Messiah. Take some time now to look at the following prophecies connected to the coming Messiah, the One who would save His people from their sins.[7] Read through these prophecies quickly to get the overall impact of the Messiah. (The verses are listed for your convenience if you would like to look at any of them firsthand in your own Bible.)

Born of the seed of the woman (Genesis 3:15 fulfilled in Galatians 4:4, Matthew 1:20)
Born of a virgin (Isaiah 7:14 fulfilled in Matthew 1:18, 24-25, Luke 1:26-35)
He would be the Son of God (Psalm 2:7 fulfilled in Matthew 3:17)
Of the seed of Abraham (Genesis 22:18 fulfilled in Matthew 1:1, Galatians, 3:16)
Son of Isaac (Genesis 21:12 fulfilled in Luke 3:23-24)
Son of Jacob (Numbers 24:17 fulfilled in Luke 3:23-24)
Tribe of Judah (Genesis 49:10, Micah 5:2 fulfilled in Luke 3:23-24, Hebrews 7:14)
Family line of Jesse (Isaiah 11:1 fulfilled in Luke 3:23, 32)
House of David (Jeremiah 23:5 fulfilled in Luke 3:23, 31)
Born at Bethlehem (Micah 5:2 fulfilled in Matthew 2:1, Luke 2:4-7)
Presented with gifts (Psalm 72:10, 12-15 fulfilled in Matthew 2:1, 11)
Herod kills children (Jeremiah 31:15 fulfilled in Matthew 2:16)
He will be pre-existent (Micah 5:2 fulfilled in Colossians 1:17)
He will be called Lord (Psalm 110:1 fulfilled in Luke 2:11, Luke 20:41-44)
He will be called Immanuel (Isaiah 7:14 fulfilled in Matthew 1:23, Luke 7:16)

He will be a prophet (Deutereonomy 18:18 fulfilled in Matthew 21:11)

He will be a priest (Psalm 110:4 fulfilled in Hebrews 3:1, Hebrews 5:5-6)

He will judge (Isaiah 33:22 fulfilled in John 5:30, 2 Timothy 4:1)

He will be king (Psalm 2:6, Zechariah 9:9 fulfilled in Matthew 27:37, John 18:33-38)

He will have a special anointing of Holy Spirit (Isaiah 11:2 fulfilled in Matthew 3:16-17)

He will be zealous for God (Psalm 69:9 fulfilled in John 2:15-17)

He will be preceded by a messenger (Isaiah 40:3, Malachi 3:1 fulfilled in Matthew 3:1-2)

His ministry will begin in Galilee (Isaiah 9:1 fulfilled in Matthew 4:12-13, 17)

He will have a ministry of miracles (Isaiah 35:5 fulfilled in Matthew 9:35)

He will be a teacher of parables (Psalm 78:2 fulfilled in Matthew 13:34)

He will enter the temple (Malachi 3:1 fulfilled in Matthew 21:12)

He will enter Jerusalem on a donkey (Zechariah 9:9 fulfilled in Luke 19:35-37, Matthew 21:6-11)

He will be a stone of stumbling to the Jews (Psalm 118:22 fulfilled in 1 Peter 2:7)

He will be a light to the Gentiles (Isaiah 60:3, 49:6 fulfilled in Acts 13:47-48)

He will rise from the dead (Psalm 16:10 fulfilled in Luke 24:46, Acts 2:31, Matthew 28:6)

He will ascend to heaven (Psalm 68:18 fulfilled in Acts 1:9)

He will sit at the right hand of God (Psalm 110:1 fulfilled in Hebrews 1:3, Acts 2:34-35)

He will be betrayed by a friend (Psalm 41:9 fulfilled in Matthew 10:4)

He will be sold for 30 pieces of silver (Zechariah 11:12 fulfilled in Matthew 26:15)

Thirty pieces of silver thrown in God's house (Zechariah 11:13 fulfilled in Matthew 27:5)

The money will be used for a potter's field (Zechariah 11:13 fulfilled in Matthew 27:7)

He will be forsaken by his disciples (Zechariah 13:7 fulfilled in Mark 14:50)

He will be accused by false witness (Psalm 35:11 fulfilled in Matthew 26:59-61)

He will be silent before accusers (Isaiah 53:7 fulfilled in Matthew 27:12-19)

He will be wounded and bruised (Isaiah 53:5 fulfilled in Matthew 27:26)

He will be struck and spit upon (Isaiah 50:6, Micah 5:1 fulfilled in Matthew 26:67)

He will be mocked (Psalm 22:7,8 fulfilled in Matthew 27:31)

He will fall under the cross (Psalm 109:24-25 fulfilled in John 19:17)

His hands and feet will be pierced (Psalm 22:16 fulfilled in Luke 23:33)

He will be crucified with thieves (Isaiah 53:12 fulfilled in Matthew 27:38)

He will make intercession for his persecutors (Isaiah 53:12 fulfilled in Luke 23:34)

He will be rejected by his own people (Isaiah 53:3 fulfilled in John 7:4, 48)

He will be hated without a cause (Psalm 69:4 fulfilled in John 15:25)

His friends will stand afar off (Psalm 38:11 fulfilled in Luke 23:49)

People will shake their heads at him (Psalm 109:25 fulfilled in Matthew 27:39)

He will be stared at (Psalm 22:17 fulfilled in Luke 23:35)

His garments will be taken, divided and lots will be cast for them (Psalm 22:18 fulfilled in John 19:23-24)

He will suffer thirst (Psalm 69:21 fulfilled in John 19:28)

Vinegar will be offered to him (Psalm 69:21 fulfilled in Matthew 27:34)

He will cry out about being forsaken (Psalm 22:1 fulfilled in Matthew 27:46)

He will commit himself to God (Psalm 31:5 fulfilled in Luke 23:46)

His bones will not be broken (Psalm 34:20 fulfilled in John 19:34)

His heart will be broken (Psalm 22:14 fulfilled in John 19:34)

His side pierced (Zechariah 12:10 fulfilled in John 19:34)

Darkness will come over the Land (Amos 8:9 fulfilled in Matthew 27:45)

He will be buried in a rich man's tomb (Isaiah 42:9 fulfilled in Matthew 27:57-60)

You have just read 61 of more than 300 prophecies of the coming Messiah. What are the odds that someone could fulfill even eight of these prophecies? Someone has actually figured it out. It's $1 \times 10(17)$—100,000,000,000,000,000.[8] To illustrate it, let's say that you take that many silver dollars and lay them on the face of Texas. They will cover all of the state two feet deep. Now mark one of these silver dollars and stir the whole mass thoroughly, all over the state. Blindfold a man and tell him that he can travel as far as he wishes, but he must pick up one silver dollar and say that this is the right one. What chance would he have of getting the right one? Just the same chance that the prophets would have had of writing these eight prophecies and having them all come true in any one man, from their day to the present time.

What makes this especially astounding is that Jesus did not fulfill just 8 or even 61 of the prophecies of the coming Messiah. Jesus fulfilled all of the Messianic prophecies in the Old Testament; over 300 of them! What impresses you the most as you read through all these different prophecies?

2. Look at the following passages and record your most significant observations about the One who is the promised Messiah.

Isaiah 9:2-7

Isaiah 61:1-3

Zechariah 2:10-11

Optional Verses: Psalm 22, Isaiah 40:1-11, Isaiah 42:1-4, Isaiah 60:1-6

3. Optional: What an amazing thing it must have been when Jesus set foot on this earth. It was as though a light was turned on that could never be turned off again. Look at the following verses and record what you learn about Jesus and the fulfillment of prophecy. If you are short on time, you might choose 2-3 verses. Matthew 3:1-3 (fulfilling Isaiah 40:1-11), Matthew 11:1-6, Matthew 16:13-20, Luke 1:25-33, Luke 4:14-21, John 1:14-18, Hebrews 1:1-3, 1 Peter 2:21-25

4. How can your heart begin to burn, on fire for Jesus Christ? It will burn as you begin to realize who He is and all that He does, especially on your behalf. Discover the priceless privilege of knowing Him today by turning to Philippians 2:5-11. Write out everything you learn about the Lord Jesus Christ. Think about what it took for Him to accomplish the plan of God on your behalf.

ADORE GOD IN PRAYER

Pray through the words of this prayer written by one of the Puritans many years ago.

O Father of Jesus,
Help me to approach thee with deepest reverence,
Not with presumption,
Not with servile fear, but with holy boldness.

Thou art beyond the grasp of my understanding,
But not beyond that of my love.
Thou knowest that I love thee supremely,
For thou art supremely adorable, good, perfect.
My heart melts at the love of Jesus,
My brother, bone of my bone, flesh of my flesh,
Married to me, dead for me, risen for me;
He is mine and I am his,
Given to me as well as for me;
I am never so much mine as when I am his,
Or so much lost to myself until lost in him;
Then I find my true manhood (or womanhood).
But my love is frost and cold, ice and snow;
Let his love warm me,
Lighten my burden,
Be my heaven;
May it be more revealed to me in all its influences
That my love to him may be more fervent
And glowing;
Let the mighty tide of his everlasting love
Cover the rocks of my sin and care;
Then let my spirit float above those things
Which else had wrecked my life.
Make me fruitful by living to that love,
My character becoming more beautiful every day.
If traces of Christ's love-artistry be upon me,
May he work on with his divine brush
Until the complete image be obtained
And I be made a perfect copy of him,
My Master.
O Lord Jesus, come to me,
O Divine Spirit, rest upon me,
O Holy Father, look on me in mercy
For the sake of the well-beloved.[9]

THE VALLEY OF VISION: A COLLECTION OF PURITAN PRAYERS AND DEVOTIONS

YIELD YOURSELF TO GOD

In Jesus of Nazareth, God gave to the world again a Man, perfect in His humanity, and therefore perfect in His revelation of the facts concerning Himself. In Jesus there was a fulfillment of all that was highest and best in the ideas of God, which had come to men by the revelations of the past. The continuous work of God from the moment when man fell from his high dignity, by the act of his rebellion, and so obscured his vision of God, was that of self-revelation. Through processes that were long and tedious, judged from the standpoint of human lives, God with infinite patience spoke in simple sentences, shone forth in gleams of light, and so kept enshrined within the heart of man, facts concerning Himself, which man was unable to discover for himself. So degraded was human intelligence, that speaking after the manner of men only, it may be said that it took whole centuries for God to enshrine in the consciousness of the race, some of the simple and most fundamental facts concerning Himself. Man's ruin was so terrible, and so profound, as witness the darkened intelligence, the deadened emotion, and the degraded will, that there was but one alternative open to the Eternal God. Either He must sweep out and destroy utterly the race, or else in infinite patience, and through long processes, lead it back to Himself. He chose the pathway of reconciliation in His infinite grace, at what cost the story of Christ alone perfectly reveals.[10]

G. CAMPBELL MORGAN IN THE CRISES OF CHRIST

At last, then, at long last the Divine Yes has sounded through him. Jesus is the Yes to all of God's promises: that there is a God, a Father lying behind this universe caring for all creation; that this Father is manifested in the face of Jesus Christ, for ours is a Christlike God; that humankind can be different and life can be utterly changed; that our emptiness can become fullness as every recess of our inner and outer lives is invaded and empowered by the Holy Spirit. To all these promises Jesus Christ is the Divine Yes, and we belong to Him. If you belong to Jesus, you belong to the Kingdom that cannot be shaken through death or old age. Christianity means to say Yes to his Yes. Surrender to his will and you will be saying Yes to his Yes. The whole universe is behind it. You will walk the earth a conqueror, afraid of nothing.[11]

E. STANLEY JONES IN THE DIVINE YES

ENJOY HIS PRESENCE

When you stop to think about it, there is nothing greater than the fact of God's love in Jesus Christ. He gave up everything to gain the eternal best for you. Now, think about this. If He has gone to such great lengths to accomplish salvation, will He not go to any length to have you for His very own? No matter how far down you think you are, or how lost, no matter how dark your circumstance, you are never out of His reach. Will you fall before Him today and surrender yourself in every way to Him? If you will, then you are taking the first steps in that priceless privilege of knowing Him, experiencing Him firsthand. It is not just mere acquaintance, but a relationship of deep intimacy. Close your time by writing a prayer to Him.

REST IN HIS LOVE

"He personally carried away our sins in his own body on the cross so we can be dead to sin and live for what is right. You have been healed by his wounds! Once you were wandering like lost sheep. But now you have turned to your Shepherd, the Guardian of your souls" (1 Peter 2:24-25 NLT).

THE PROOF OF GOD'S AMAZING LOVE

By His knowledge the Righteous One, My Servant, will
justify the many, as He will bear their iniquities.

ISAIAH 53:11

PREPARE YOUR HEART

Rodney Smith, as a young boy, would accompany his father to gypsy camps where his father would play the fiddle and he, working with his father, would play the crowd, collecting money in his little hat. The family lived the transient life of gypsies. His father would frequent beer houses, and sometimes little Rodney would go with him. His father, out of great guilt, had prayed that God would change his life but couldn't seem to find the transformation he was seeking. One day Rodney's father was sitting with his two brothers. They had not been together for some time and so they began talking. Soon Rodney's father said what was truly on his heart. He said that he had a great burden that needed to be removed. He had a hunger that needed satisfying or he felt he would die. Amazingly, his brothers said that they had felt the exact same things in recent weeks. Though these men had been apart from each other, God had been dealing with them in the same way and at the same time. They traveled together to Cambridge, fully intending to find a church where they expected to find answers. They stopped at a local beer house at one end of the town. They shared with the lady who ran this house how they felt. She began to cry and brought out a book that she thought would mean something to them. It was Pilgrim's Progress by John Bunyan. Since they could not read, she began reading it to them. When they got to the part about the burden falling off of Pilgrim when he looked at the cross, they got very excited. They knew that was exactly what they wanted. On Sunday they went to church three times. By going to church, Rodney's father was convicted of his sin. But he had not yet received Christ. Some time later he attended a meeting. At that meeting he heard the hymn:

There is a fountain filled with blood, Drawn from Emmanuel's veins,

And sinners, plunged beneath that flood, Lose all their guilty stains.

I do believe, I will believe, That Jesus died for me.

As a result of those words, Rodney's father gave his life to Jesus Christ. His brother also surrendered his life to Christ. Rodney, his young son, who was watching all of this, was dumbfounded, ran out of the room, and went home. As a result of the father's conversion and subsequent sharing of the experience, at least 13 others, including many family members came to Christ that day. The home of gypsies now became a Christian home. Rodney held back from making any kind of commitment. One day he said to himself: "Rodney, are you going to wander around as a gypsy boy and a gypsy man without hope, or will you be a Christian and have some definite object to live for?" A determined calm came over him. He said out loud: "By the grace of God, I will be a Christian and I will meet my mother in heaven!" He made his decision. He knew he would live for Christ. The entire course of that family was transformed. Rodney Smith became known as Gipsy Smith, the well known evangelist who led hundreds to Christ during the time of Fanny Crosby and G. Campbell Morgan.

One thing is certain. The fact that Jesus Christ broke through human history, came to earth, and died for our sins has changed the course of everything. His appearing fulfilled the prophecies of His coming and opened the way for your salvation and future of eternal life in heaven.

This is one of the greatest truths in the romance of God with you. Your eternal destiny was at stake. And you were lost and without hope in the world. He did what it took to secure everything for you. All it takes is one look at God in the face of Jesus Christ and you know of His solid love for you. He never gives an empty promise. He fulfilled every promise He made in the Old Testament that He was going to come to earth to die for our sins.

In preparation for your time alone with the Lord today, ask God to quiet your heart. Meditate on the words of that hymn that meant so much to Gipsy Smith's father:

There is a fountain filled with blood, Drawn from Emmanuel's veins,

And sinners, plunged beneath that flood, Lose all their guilty stains.

I do believe, I will believe, That Jesus died for me.

READ AND STUDY GOD'S WORD

1. In the divine romance between a holy God and His people, a great rescue by a Righteous One was necessary. It was a rescue by one who is called the Christ; Messiah. What would the Messiah be like, what would He do, and why would He do it? Read Isaiah 53 and write out everything you learn about the promised Messiah, referred to as the suffering servant.

The Servant Of The Lord in Isaiah 53

The Servant Of The Lord in Isaiah 53 (Cont'd)

2. Psalm 32:1 says "Blessed is he whose transgressions are forgiven, whose sins are covered." Read John 19:16-30. What do you think Jesus meant when He cried out, "It is finished"?

3. Think about what Jesus' death on the cross accomplished for us according to Romans 5:7-11. Underline your favorite parts of this passage of Scripture. "In human experience it is a rare thing for one man to give his life for another, even if the latter be a good man, though there have been a few who have had the courage to do it. Yet the proof of God's amazing love is this: that it was while we were sinners that Christ died for us. Moreover, if he did that for us while we were sinners, now that we are men justified by the shedding of his blood, what reason have we to fear the wrath of God? If, while we were his enemies, Christ reconciled us to God by dying for us, surely now that we are reconciled we may be perfectly certain of our salvation through his living in us. Nor, I am sure, is this a matter of bare salvation—we may hold our heads high in the light of God's love because of the reconciliation which Christ has made" (Romans 5:7-11 PHILLIPS).

4. What is your response to the supreme act of divine love, Jesus' death on the cross for you? Paul articulated his response in Romans 8:31-39. Read the following verses in the Phillips Translation and underline your favorite phrases within this passage. Think about what these words mean to you today. "In face of all this, what is there left to say? If God is for us, who can be against us? He who did not grudge his own Son but gave him up for us all—can we not trust such a God to give us, with him, everything else that we can need? Who would dare to accuse us, whom God has chosen? The judge himself has declared us free from sin. Who is in a position to condemn? Only Christ, and Christ died for us, Christ rose for us, Christ reigns in power for us, Christ prays for us! Who can separate us from the love of Christ? Can trouble, pain or persecution? Can lack of clothes and food, danger to life and limb, the threat of force of arms? Indeed some of us know the truth of that ancient text: For thy sake we are killed all the day long; We were accounted as sheep for the slaughter. No, in all these things we win an overwhelming victory through him who has proved his love for us. I have become absolutely convinced that neither death nor life, neither messenger of Heaven nor monarch of earth, neither what happens today nor what may happen tomorrow, neither a power from on high nor a power from below, nor anything else in God's whole world has any power to separate us from the love of God in Christ Jesus our Lord" (Romans 8:31-39 PHILLIPS).

ADORE GOD IN PRAYER

Jesus Christ is your Savior and died for your sins. Is there something in your life that you are holding back from Him? A sin to confess? Or an area of your life that needs to be brought to Him at the cross? Take some time now to draw near to Him and ask Him to search your heart today. You can know that according to 1 John 1:9 that if we confess our sins, He is faithful and righteous to forgive us our sins and to cleanse us from all unrighteousness.

> Oh, living loving Savior, we present unto Thee our bodies, our souls, our all. We hold not one thing back; but as the woman cast in all her living, we give ourselves as living sacrifices on Thee, the living altar. Our lips, our love, our all. Take them as Thine forever, and may we each go out consecrated irrevocably. Take my life, and let it be consecrated, Lord, to Thee. Yes, Lord, let us give Thee all, and love Thee much, for we have been much forgiven.[12]
>
> REV. CHARLES A. FOX IN KESWICK'S AUTHENTIC VOICE

YIELD YOURSELF TO GOD

Blessed be the God and Father of our Lord Jesus Christ, who has blessed us with all spiritual blessings in the heavenly places in Christ (Ephesians 1:3). Such is the work which is now fully accomplished in and for the lowliest sinner who has believed on the Lord Jesus Christ. It is all superhuman and God alone could do it. If man could have any part in that work it would at that point of contact be imperfect, and therefore be blasted and ruined forever…That He might thus be free to satisfy His boundless love for us, He met all the issues of sin for a lost and ruined world, and so perfectly has He wrought that man need now but believe and thus receive the bounty of His grace.[13]

LEWIS SPERRY CHAFER IN SALVATION

Many men are touched into momentary regrets, many men are moved and melted to tears, but the deep places of their souls and the strong currents of their daily lives are not changed…We are children, we are God's Jacobs, whom He has redeemed for Himself with the precious blood of His Son, and whom He has called unto His Kingdom by the almightiness of His Holy Spirit. God is near to us; God is kind to us; the God to whom we come is, as we are finding out, a limitless God. But do we all remember this: that He is also a holy God…We come to Christ because Christ is the Lover of our souls; but do let us recognize and be very sure that we are coming to the Christ of Gethsemane and the Christ of Calvary, to whom those questionable things and those contaminating things which we have been tolerating, for which we have been making excuse, meant the bloody sweat and the accursed tree and the hiding of God's face. Coming back to such a Father, back to such a Saviour, we must abhor every sin…God is in serious earnest, and you and I have to be in serious earnest too. Many, O Lord my God, are my infirmities; many they are, and great: but Your medicine is mightier. Search me, and know my heart; try me, and know my thoughts; and see if there be any way of wickedness in me, and lead me in the everlasting way. Come, and let us return to the Lord; for He has torn, and He will heal us: He has smitten, and He will bind us up.[14]

"A SUMMONS TO NEWNESS OF LIFE" BY REV. ALEXANDER SMELLIE, M.A., D.D.

When once you have accepted Jesus Christ as your Savior from sin, when once you have made Him your Lord and your king, then you must, if you are to be loyal, true, honorable, then you must dedicate every moment of your life to His service.

You must let it be seen everywhere that you are now not your own, but that you belong to Him, that the profession you made the other night or years ago when you said As for me and all I am concerned with and have any authority over, I will serve the Lord – that profession must be lived out. Every day and every hour of every day, not only in the Church but in the home, in the workshop, in the business, in the office, in the political arena, in public and in private, I am Christ's man, I am Christ's woman, and I must act, I must live, I must walk, I must so conduct myself, so transact my business, so think and so speak that the Divine stamp will be on me and will be felt and seen everywhere. I must live with this ever before me: I am risen with Christ, and by my life, my neighbors, my friends, my servants, my master, my acquaintances and relatives must see that my heart is set on things above.[15]

GIPSY SMITH IN "HID WITH CHRIST" IN AS JESUS PASSED BY AND OTHER ADDRESSES

ENJOY HIS PRESENCE

As you close your time with the Lord today, meditate on the words of this classic hymn, *And Can It Be That I Should Gain*, written by Charles Wesley.

And can it be that I should gain

an interest in the Savior's blood!

Died he for me? who caused his pain!

For me? who him to death pursued?

Amazing love! How can it be

that thou, my God, shouldst die for me?

'Tis mystery all: th' Immortal dies!

Who can explore his strange design?

In vain the firstborn seraph tries

to sound the depths of love divine.

'Tis mercy all! Let earth adore;

let angel minds inquire no more.

He left his Father's throne above
(so free, so infinite his grace!),
emptied himself of all but love,
and bled for Adam's helpless race.
'Tis mercy all, immense and free,
for O my God, it found out me!

Long my imprisoned spirit lay,
fast bound in sin and nature's night;
thine eye diffused a quickening ray;
I woke, the dungeon flamed with light;
my chains fell off, my heart was free,
I rose, went forth, and followed thee.

No condemnation now I dread;
Jesus, and all in him, is mine;
alive in him, my living Head,
and clothed in righteousness divine,
bold I approach th' eternal throne,
and claim the crown, through Christ my own.

REST IN HIS LOVE

"For while we were helpless, at the right time Christ died for the ungodly" (Romans 5:6).

TOGETHER FOREVER

The LORD their God will save them on that day as the flock of his people. They will sparkle in his land like jewels in a crown. How attractive and beautiful they will be!
ZECHARIAH 9:16-17 NIV

PREPARE YOUR HEART

While in prison for his faith in Christ, John Bunyan wrote one of the great Christian classics of all time: *Pilgrim's Progress*. It is the story of Christian who travels from the City of Destruction through the Wicket Gate to the Celestial City. As you prepare for your time with the Lord today, meditate on John Bunyan's description of the Celestial City. This description is based on the truths found in Revelation 19-22. It is the ultimate fulfillment of all the promises of God. It is the realization of all that God has desired for those He romances and wins as His own. Ask God to quiet your heart and give you eyes to see as you contemplate the most holy ground of heaven and eternity.

> Now, upon the bank of the river, on the other side, they saw the two shining men again, who there waited for them; wherefore, being come out of the river, they saluted them, saying, We are ministering spirits, sent forth to minister for those that shall be heirs of salvation. Thus they went along towards the gate.
>
> Now, now look how the holy pilgrims ride,
> Clouds are their chariots, angels are their guide:
> Who would not here for him all hazards run,
> That thus provides for his when this world's done.
>
> Now you must note that the city stood upon a mighty hill, but the Pilgrims went up that hill with ease, because they had these two men to lead them up by the arms; also, they had left their mortal garments behind them in the river, for though they went in with them, they came out without them. They, therefore, went up here with much agility and speed, though the foundation upon which the city was framed was higher than the clouds. They therefore went up through the regions

of the air, sweetly talking as they went, being comforted, because they safely got over the river, and had such glorious companions to attend them. The talk they had with the Shining Ones was about the glory of the place; who told them that the beauty and glory of it was inexpressible. "There," said they, "is the Mount Zion, the heavenly Jerusalem, the innumerable company of angels, and the spirits of just men made perfect." "You are going now," said they, "to the paradise of God, wherein you shall see the tree of life, and eat of the never-fading fruits thereof; and when you come there, you shall have white robes given you, and your walk and talk shall be every day with the King, even all the days of eternity. There you shall not see again such things as you saw when you were in the lower region upon the earth, to wit, sorrow, sickness, affliction, and death, for the former things are passed away. You are now going to Abraham, to Isaac, and Jacob, and to the prophets—men that God hath taken away from the evil to come, and that are now resting upon their beds, each one walking in his righteousness." The men then asked, "What must we do in the holy place?" To whom it was answered, "You must there receive the comforts of all your toil, and have joy for all your sorrow; you must reap what you have sown, even the fruit of all your prayers, and tears, and sufferings for the King by the way. In that place you must wear crowns of gold, and enjoy the perpetual sight and vision of the Holy One, for there you shall see him as he is. There also you shall serve him continually with praise, with shouting, and thanksgiving, whom you desired to serve in the world, though with much difficulty, because of the infirmity of your flesh. There your eyes shall be delighted with seeing, and your ears with hearing the pleasant voice of the Mighty One. There you shall enjoy your friends again that are gone thither before you; and there you shall with joy receive, even every one that follows into the holy place after you. There also shall you be clothed with glory and majesty, and put into an equipage fit to ride out with the King of Glory. When he shall come with sound of trumpet in the clouds, as upon the wings of the wind, you shall come with him; and when he shall sit upon the throne of judgment; you shall sit by him; yea, and when he shall pass sentence upon all the workers of iniquity, let them be angels or men, you also shall have a voice in that judgment, because they were his and your enemies. Also, when he shall again return to the city, you shall go too, with sound of trumpet, and be ever with him."

READ AND STUDY GOD'S WORD

1. God has something in mind for you that extends far beyond the here and now all the way to eternity. Jesus knew it and you must know it too. Look at the following verses and record what you learn about the future He has planned for you. Be sure to personalize your observations.

Isaiah 54:4-8

Isaiah 62:1-5

Daniel 7:13-14

Zechariah 9:16-17

2. Because Jesus knew what was to come, He was filled with hope. Record what you learn about His hope in these verses.

Luke 23:39-43

Hebrews 12:2

3.. Jesus is your Eternal Partner, the One with whom you will spend eternity. Look at the following verses and record what you learn about your relationship with Him.

Ephesians 5:22-30

Revelation 21:9-11

Optional Verses: 1 Corinthians 6:15-17, Revelation 19:7-9, Revelation 22:1-5

ADORE GOD IN PRAYER

Someday the things of this world will fade away and you will fully enjoy the fruit of your relationship with your Lord. In the meantime, there are those things that weigh on your heart, things that daily need to be taken to the throne of your Lord. Will you now, take each need, each person, each difficult circumstance to the Lord and leave it all there with Him? You may use your prayer pages in the back of this book to write out your requests. Then, thank the Lord for the promises of eternal life that give you a hope that anchors your soul on the firm foundation of the Lord.

YIELD YOURSELF TO GOD

What the delight of God will be in this new earth with men, and what their capacity for knowing God and progressing in that blessed and only real knowledge, can be measured only by eternity, and the infinity of God Himself; which is to say, it is utterly without limit! Marvelous and yet reasonable fruit of the redemption that is in Christ Jesus who suffered for sins…that He might bring us to God…Oh, how little do we know our God! How small is our widest thought of Him! Do we not see this great Bible He has given us going right forward against all obstacles, over all mountains, through all valleys, yea, to Gethsemane and Calvary—to come to this sweet, eternal consummation, that God may be with men, their God? That He may wipe every tear from their eyes, that He may banish into the far forgotten past, mourning, crying, and pain; and say, Behold I make all things new? For God is love…let this thought overwhelm us…Let us, too, know it and believe it; and thus enter by faith this glorious new creation scene; bending low under this weight of glory, though yet we tread this earth. Let us know this love that passeth knowledge, and breathing the fragrant air of the city of God, walk daily through its gates of pearl and walk by faith its golden streets, giving thanks unto the Father, who made us meet to be partakers of the inheritance of the saints in light.[16]

WILLIAM R. NEWELL IN REVELATION

We are like to one who hath in his hand the guide-book of a country to which he is journeying; he finds in it fair pictures of the scenery of the land and the architecture of the cities, and as he reads each page he says to himself, I am going there! This is what I shall soon behold! It would be a wretched thing to have such a book in one's hand and to be entering upon a life-long banishment from home and the home-country. Then should we have to say, "This was my country once, but I shall never see it again. Fair are its skies and lovely are its vales, but mine eye shall ache in vain to gaze upon them. I am exiled forever from my own dear land!" It is not so with us who are believers in Christ: our faces are towards Immanuel's land, the land which floweth with milk and honey, and we have a portion among the blessed; a mansion is being made ready for each one of us, and we have this promise: Go thou thy way till the end be: for thou shalt rest, and stand in thy lot at the end of the days. Rejoice, then, beloved, for if your portion on earth be slender, if your condition here be sorrowful, if your trials multiply, if your strength declines, yet it is but a little while and he that will come shall come, and shall not tarry. Well doth our hymn tell us that an hour with our Lord will make up for it all. We shall forget the pains of a long life in one half-hour of the vision of the Well-beloved…It seems but a few days to you who are aged people since you climbed your mother's knee, and yet in far less time you will behold the face of your soul's Bridegroom. Then all trouble will be ended, and eternal joy will crown your head… The true Christian life, when we live near to God, is the rough draft of the life of full communion above. We have seen the artist make with his pencil, or with his charcoal, a bare outline of his picture. It is nothing more, but still one could guess what the finished picture will be from the sketch before you. One acquainted with the artist could see upon the canvas all the splendor of color peeping through the dark lines of the pencil.[17]

CHARLES HADDON SPURGEON IN SPURGEON'S SERMONS, VOLUME 15

ENJOY HIS PRESENCE

Think about all that you have learned about this divine romance between the Lord and His chosen beloved. How would you describe it to someone else? What does this divine romance mean to you?

REST IN HIS LOVE

"Then he showed me a river of the water of life, clear as crystal, coming from the throne of God and of the Lamb, in the middle of its street…There will no longer be any curse; and the throne of God and of the Lamb will be in it, and His bond-servants will serve Him; they will see His face, and His name will be on their foreheads" (Revelation 22:1, 3-4).

DEVOTIONAL READING
BY CHARLES HADDON SPURGEON

Dear Friend,

The next two days are your opportunity to spend time reviewing what you have learned this week. You may wish to write your thoughts and insights in your journal in the back of this study book. As you think about all that you have learned about the Divine Romance, record your most important discoveries.

Your most significant insight:

Your favorite quote:

Your favorite verse:

Will you not desire to get beyond the hem and beyond the garment, to himself, and to his heart, and there forever take up your abode? Who desires to be forever a babe in grace, with a half-awakened, dreamy, twilight consciousness of the Redeemer? Brethren, be diligent in the school of the cross; therein is enduring wisdom. Study your Saviour much. The science of Christ crucified is the most excellent sciences; and to know him and the power of his resurrection, is to know that which is best worth knowing. Ignorance of Jesus deprives many saints of those divine rapture which carry others out of themselves, therefore let us be among those children of Zion who are taught of the Lord…To believe a thing, is, as it were, to see the cool crystal water sparkling in the cup; but to meditate upon it is to drink thereof. Reading gathers the clusters, contemplation squeezes forth their generous juice. Meditation is of all things the most soul-fattening when combined with prayer…Think, my brethren, of our Lord Jesus: he is God, the Eternal, the Infinite, the ever-blessed; yet he became man for us—man of the substance of his mother, like ourselves. Meditate upon his spotless character; review the sufferings which he endured on Calvary; follow him into the grave, and from the grave to the resurrection, and from the resurrection up the starry way to his triumphant throne. Let your souls dwell upon each of his offices, as prophet, priest, and king; pore over each one of his characters, and every scriptural title; pause and consider every phase of him, and when you have done this, begin again, and yet again…The most of you are too busy, you have too much to do in the world, but what is it all about? Scraping together dust, loading yourselves with thick clay. Oh, that you were busy after the true riches, and could step aside awhile to enrich yourselves in solitude, and make your hearts vigorous by feeding upon the person and work of your ever-blessed Lord! You miss a heaven below by a too eager pursuit of earth. You cannot know these joyful raptures if meditation be pushed into a corner…I believe those are the happiest saints who are most overwhelmed with a sense of the greatness, goodness, and preciousness of Christ. I believe these to be the most useful saints, also and to be in the Christian church as a tower of strength.[18]

CHARLES HADDON SPURGEON IN SPURGEON'S SERMONS, VOLUME 9

Viewer Guide
~ WEEK THREE ~

The Proof Of God's Amazing Love

In Week Three of *A Heart on Fire*, we have had the opportunity to take an in-depth look at God's love for His people. I want to take some time in this message to talk about the divine romance and explore with you the proof of God's amazing love. So grab your Bible, and let's get into the Word of God together.

"Yet the proof of God's amazing love is this: that it was while we were sinners that Christ died for us" (Romans 5:8 PHILLIPS)

The Theme of Romans—The Revelation of God's Righteousness, Romans 1:16-17
The Outline of Romans:
The Need For God's Righteousness Romans 1-3
The Way To God's Righteousness Romans 4-5
The Power and Provision of God's Righteousness Romans 6-8
The Scope Of God's Righteousness Romans 9-11
The Practical Applications of God's Righteousness Romans 12-16

The Great Dilemma — Romans 5:5-8

1. The nature of divine justice, _____, and righteousness.

2. The nature of divine _____.

The Act of Divine Love — Romans 5:5-10

Summed up in a Person — _____.

When We Survey the Wondrous Cross of Jesus Christ

1. Jesus accomplished _____for us. Romans 3:21-24

2. Jesus accomplished _____ for us. Romans 3:25

3. Jesus accomplished _____ for us. Romans 4:7, Ephesians 1:7

4. Jesus accomplished _____ for us. Romans 5:18

5. Jesus accomplished _____ for us. Romans 5:10

6. Jesus accomplished our _____ as sons and daughters. Romans 8:15

7. Jesus accomplished _____ for us. Romans 6:22

8. Jesus accomplished _____ for us. Romans 8:30

The Result of Divine Love

We may be in a _____ with God.

The Result of Divine Love

1. No more reason to _____ the wrath of God.

2. We may hold our heads high in the light of God's _____.

＊ *Video messages are available on DVDs or as Downloadable M4V Video. Audio messages are available on Audio CDs or as Downloadable MP3 Audio. Visit the Quiet Time Ministries Online Store at www.quiettime.org.*

WHEN GOD BECAME MAN

John 1:14

And the Word became flesh, and dwelt among us, and we saw His glory,
glory as of the only begotten from the Father, full of
grace and truth.

JOHN 1:14

WE WANT TO SEE JESUS

There were some Greeks among those who were coming up to worship at the feast, and then went to Philip who was from Bethsaida in Galilee, and kept making this request of him, "Sir, we want to see Jesus."
JOHN 12:20-21 WMS

PREPARE YOUR HEART

A light dawned in this world that changed all of life forever. The Second Person of the Triune God became man. He had the appearance of man, with flesh and blood, and human emotions. He could feel pain. He could identify with the weakness of man. He had personality. He got tired. He cried. He conversed. He smiled. He laughed. Finally, for a brief period in all of time, the world could see what God is like.

Paul writes in Philippians 2:6-11 that "Christ Jesus, who, being in very nature God, did not consider equality with God something to be grasped, but made himself nothing, taking the very nature of a servant, being made in human likeness, and being found in appearance as a man, he humbled himself and became obedient to the point of death, even death on a cross! Therefore God exalted him to the highest place and gave him the name that is above every name, that at the name of Jesus every knee should bow, in heaven and on earth and under the earth, and every tongue confess that Jesus Christ is Lord, to the glory of God the Father." Jesus Christ is the Second Person of the Trinity; fully God and fully man.

Now these are life-altering words. Why? Because if they are really true, then it is absolutely imperative that you know what this One who walked this earth had to say and what He was like. In fact, you need to know everything about His life on earth. You need to know what He did. You need to know if He said anything that has implications for you today where you live. Because if what He said involves you, and He is God, then it is absolutely relevant in your life. Why? Because it never changes, corresponds with reality, and is more true than anything else in your life. If there is something outside the realm of time that corresponds with reality, it is the measure for all that is true. God is the measure of what is true. He determines what is true. He has no beginning and no end. He is eternal. He is unchangeable. He cannot lie.

If you wish to know whether a line is straight, you hold a ruler next to it. If you wish to draw a straight line, you use a ruler. The ruler, the measure of all that is true and real is God Himself. If God became man and walked on planet earth, then you must know what He said and did.

The man who claimed to be God lived more than two thousand years ago. His name was Jesus. When He lived on earth in human form, with flesh and blood, He accomplished more in three short years of ministry than anyone else who has ever lived. In your quiet times this week, your goal will be one thing: to see Jesus. Who is He? What has He done? Who did He claim to be? What you learn will not be truth determined by you. It will be truth discovered by you in God's Word. When Jesus was talking with the Jews, He said, "You search the Scriptures because you believe they give you eternal life. But the Scriptures point to me! (John 5:39 NLT)" In God's Word, you will discover Jesus. And you will find that He is the truth.

Truth is not determined by anyone who wants to determine it, as the world believes. It is discovered by all who wish to seek it out. Therefore not all beliefs are valid. Only what is true is valid and real. The strength and sincerity of one's belief does not make it true. Only what corresponds with reality is true. Therefore what you believe is important, not how strong and great your ability to believe.

Truth exists whether you choose to believe it or not. Something that is true does not become true for you once you discover it. For example, if there is a 100 foot cliff that is about a mile down a road and two people are traveling on that road, it's existence is not true for the one who knows about it and untrue for the one who does not. The 100 foot cliff is there and both will experience the consequences if they do not heed the warning signs and turn around. Spiritual truth from God including the way of salvation through Jesus is true whether one chooses to believe it or not.

These are weighty things to say, but you must think about this. Wrap your mind around it. In the world today there are many belief systems. In fact the world has redefined tolerance to say that all beliefs are equally valid and to say they are not is considered "intolerant." The world today says that you need to determine truth for yourself. What's right for you is right for you. What someone else believes is also right, even if it contradicts what someone else believes. "All beliefs are okay" says the postmodernist. Believing in truth and in Jesus as the exclusive way to God is considered radical in this day and age. But what if it is true? Then who cares how the world thinks? You must build your life on what is true. Truth will win out in the end. It has to. Why? Because it is true. Plain and simple. So your goal is not to determine truth, but to discover it. You will find it in the places where God has revealed Himself. He has revealed Himself in a general way in all of creation (the heavens and earth), and in a special way in Jesus and in His Word. Do you want to know God? Then, look at Jesus. Where can you look at Him? In the Word of God. You will see Jesus on every page of your Bible.

As you begin your quiet time, think about these words by Amy Carmichael. May they be your prayer today.

> I could not see
> For the glory of that light.
> Let the shining of that glory
> Illumine our sight.
> Things temporal
> Are transparent in that air.
> But the things that are eternal
> Are manifest there.
> Jesus our Lord,
> By the virtue of Thy grace,
> In the shining of Thy glory
> Let us see Thy face.[1]

AMY CARMICHAEL IN TOWARD JERUSALEM

READ AND STUDY GOD'S WORD

1. John records an incident that is seemingly insignificant. Some Greek people came to Philip, one of the disciples of Jesus, possibly because of his Greek name. There were many Greeks (non-Jews) who were hungry for God. In fact, some would convert to Judaism. Once they converted to Judaism, they were expected to be circumcised as an identification with the Jewish people. If they refused circumcision, they were then called Godfearers. While it is not known whether this group that came to Philip was part of the Godfearers, they definitely had an interest in Jesus. In addition, it is important to note that in the letters of Paul we see that Jesus made salvation available not for the Jews only, but also for the Gentiles (Greeks and others).

With this in mind, read about this event in the life of Jesus in John 12:20-33. Then answer the following questions:

What did the Greeks want?

What did Jesus talk about upon hearing their request? And what would happen when Jesus was lifted up (verse 32)?

2. Oh, to see the face of Jesus. Just one look at Him will change your life forever. You can see Him even now. How? He reveals Himself to you in God's Word by the Holy Spirit who is in you. As soon as you invited Jesus into your life, put your faith in Him as your Savior and Lord, and trusted Him for forgiveness of sins and eternal life, you were indwelt by the Holy Spirit. Part of that new spiritual birth was the gift of spiritual eyes to see spiritual things. Look at the following verses and write out what you learn about spiritual sight, the Holy Spirit, and the ability to see Jesus.

John 14:7-11

John 16:12-15

2 Corinthians 4:6

2 Corinthians 4:18

Hebrews 12:1-3

Optional Verses: John 14:25-26, 1 Corinthians 2:10-16, 1 Corinthians 13:11-12, 2 Corinthians 3:15-18, Ephesians 1:13-14, Ephesians 1:18-19

3. In light of what you have studied today, what have you learned about how to see Jesus? What does it mean to see Jesus and how is it that you can see Jesus?

ADORE GOD IN PRAYER

Why do you need to see Jesus today? If you could meet with Him alone and talk, what would you talk to Him about? Turn to your journal and write a prayer to Him sharing those things that are on your heart.

YIELD YOURSELF TO GOD

…the Spirit makes known the personal presence in and with the Christian and the church of the risen, reigning Savior, the Jesus of history, who is the Christ of faith… It is as if the Spirit stands behind us, throwing light over our shoulder, on Jesus, who stands facing us. The Spirit's message to us is never, Look at me, listen to me; come to me; get to know me, but always, Look at him, and see his glory; listen to him, and hear his word; go to him, and have life; get to know him, and taste his gift of joy and peace.[2]

J.I. PACKER IN KEEP IN STEP WITH THE SPIRIT

The more you know about Christ, the less will you be satisfied with superficial views of Him; and the more deeply you study His transactions in the eternal covenant, His engagements on your behalf as the eternal Surety, and the fullness of His grace which shines in all His offices, the more truly you will see the King in His beauty. Be much in such outlooks. Long more and more to see Jesus. Meditation and contemplation are often like windows of agate, and gates of carbuncle, through which we behold the Redeemer. Meditation puts the telescope to the eye, and enables us to see Jesus after a better sort than we could have seen Him if we had lived in the days of His flesh.[3]

CHARLES HADDON SPURGEON IN MORNING AND EVENING

ENJOY HIS PRESENCE

Close your time with the Lord by meditating on the words of this well-known beloved hymn, *Turn Your Eyes Upon Jesus* written by Helen H. Lemmel:

O soul, are you weary and troubled?

No light in the darkness you see?

There's a light for a look at the Savior,

And life more abundant and free!

Turn your eyes upon Jesus,

Look full in His wonderful face,

And the things of earth will grow strangely dim,

In the light of His glory and grace.

REST IN HIS LOVE

"But we all, with unveiled face, beholding as in a mirror the glory of the Lord, are being transformed into the same image from glory to glory, just as from the Lord, the Spirit" (2 Corinthians 3:18).

HE WAS IN THE BEGINNING

In the beginning was the Word, and the Word was with God, and the Word was God. He was in the beginning with God. All things came into being through Him, and apart from Him, nothing came into being that has come into being.

JOHN 1:1-3

PREPARE YOUR HEART

As you continue on in your journey to discover the priceless privilege of knowing Christ and have a heart on fire for Him, you are now going to enter holy territory. You are going to catch a glimpse of the depth and pinnacle of the character of Christ. It is that holy ground of the Trinity where you will gaze on His eternal nature as the Son of God. The Trinity is a mystery. The very thought of the Triune God is incomprehensible. To think about Jesus as God will cause you to bow low before Him in worship. You may even wonder, "How can it be?" And yet, Jesus is God. That He claimed to be God is certain. He knew Himself to be God. And those around Him knew His claim to be God. His disciples proclaimed this fact following His death and resurrection. His enemies crucified Him not for what He did, but for who He claimed to be. When the high priest tore his robe at the bold, conclusive words of Jesus, he was accusing Jesus of blasphemy. He understood without question that Jesus said He was God. The mystery is this: there is a Triune God, i.e. Father, Son, and Holy Spirit. Three Persons who are One. They are distinct in personality, yet One.

Your goal today is to begin to try to wrap your mind around the revelation in God's Word that Jesus is God. You will not be able to comprehend it, but God can give you a glimpse of this truth so that you will have a new view of Jesus and see Him in a way you may have never seen Him before.

John begins his gospel: "In the beginning was the Word, and the Word was with God, and the Word was God. He was in the beginning with God. All things came into being through Him, and apart from Him nothing came into being that has come into being." These are probably some of the most powerful words in all of Scripture. John continues by writing that the Word became flesh and dwelt among us. The Word is Jesus. Think about what John is saying here. He is saying that Jesus is Eternal and that Jesus is God. He is saying that Jesus is the expression and explanation of God in language that humans can understand. And he goes on to say that Jesus was involved in

Creation. Oh how exciting the thought of Jesus as Creator! Think about what it must have been like for the Father, the Son, and the Holy Spirit, God three-in-One, working together in unison to paint the universe, fling stars into the sky, mold the earth, and form man into a living, breathing human being. When you learn that all things came into being through Him, you discover that you came into being because of God. You are His thought, His idea, and His design. You are unique in personality and have purpose because He created you.

Today, as you draw near to the Lord, write a prayer asking Him to open the eyes of your heart, that you might see Him in a new and deeper way this week.

READ AND STUDY GOD'S WORD

1. Turn to John 1:1-18. Record everything you learn about Jesus in these verses.

2. Since John says that all things came into being through Him, this means that Jesus was involved in creation. Read Genesis 1 and record all the things that were created by Him. Think about what it must have been like for the Triune God to design all of these things and bring them into existence.

3. Read Colossians 1:15-20 and record what you learn about Jesus.

4. Optional: Probably the one person who was given the most explicit detail about all that was involved in creation was Job. Job experienced some of the deepest suffering in life and he also was given a vivid glimpse into the character and work of God. After a long silence, God finally spoke to Job. Read Job 38:1 – 40:5 and 42:1-6. Keep in mind once again that creation came about by the Triune God. As you read, think about what amazes you the most about God's creation. What was Job's response once he was given this glimpse into the character and ways of God?

Adore God in Prayer

Take some time now to worship your Lord. You may use the passages of Scripture you just spent time in to worship Him for who He is and all that He has created. Thank Him for how He made you and ask Him to accomplish all that He has planned for you.

Yield Yourself to God

"Having existed in sovereign self-sufficiency and love for all eternity past, the triune God sovereignly and eternally determined to create and project into being that which was not himself and yet which was utterly dependent on him for its continuing existence. We must emphasize that God's production of the universe was not dependent in any way on an inherent necessity or intrinsic need in the divine being. Indeed, the triune God would have remained sovereignly self-sufficient and self-fulfilled for all eternity had he not created the universe. That he did create it was simply an outworking of his sovereign, loving will.[4]

RON RHODES IN CHRIST BEFORE THE MANGER

…as far as man is concerned, there was a beginning and there was a Creation. That phrase, "In the beginning," does not mark a birth date for God Almighty. It means the point in time as we think of it when God ceased to be alone and began to make time and space and creatures and beings. …In His existence before Creation, God was already busy; busy with eternal mercies, His mind stirring with merciful thoughts and redemptive plans for a mankind not yet created.[5]

A.W. Tozer in Christ, The Eternal Son

John's Gospel tells us "In the beginning was the Word, and the Word was with God, and the Word was God. He was with God in the beginning. Through him all things were made; without him nothing was made that has been made" (John 1:1-3). How John must have exulted as he walked by Jesus' side, knowing that next to him stood the Creator of the universe in all its vastness! Surely he must have marveled at how the stars above him were the handiwork of his friend, companion, and Savior, Jesus Christ. No wonder John had such a worshipful attitude toward Jesus (John 1:14; 2:11; 20:30-31).[6]

Ron Rhodes in Christ Before The Manger

Enjoy His Presence

What does it mean to you that this same Jesus whom you have come to know and love is Creator of all things? How does that change how you walk with Him each day? Record your insights in the space provided.

Rest in His Love

"Yet for us there is but one God, the Father, from whom are all things and we exist for Him; and one Lord, Jesus Christ, by whom are all things, and we exist through Him" (1 Corinthians 8:6).

HE DWELT AMONG US

And the Word became flesh, and dwelt among us, and we saw His glory, glory
as of the only begotten from the Father, full of grace and truth.

JOHN 1:14

PREPARE YOUR HEART

Can you imagine sitting in the crowd that day when Jesus fed five thousand people with only a few loaves of bread and some fish? What if you had been on the mountain with Him when He began teaching about the kingdom of God that became what is known as the Sermon on the Mount in Matthew 5–7? Imagine sitting under a tree when He and His disciples walked by. Suppose He had walked over to you and struck up a conversation with you about you and your life? The look in His eyes would show you that He loves you more than anyone ever has loved you. And His words to you would demonstrate that He sees more than your outward appearance. He sees all the way to your heart. He knows your thoughts. He knows your past. And He knows your future. His manner and His way with you would prove His kindness and compassion. You must know that because the Word became flesh, and dwelt among us, you may know what God is like. And that means you may know not only what He was like two thousand years ago, but what He is like now, in relationship with you.

When Jesus walked this earth, He had many enemies. There were many who were not remotely interested in seeing what all the excitement was about. There were some who stood on the edge and observed the action. But then there were those who knew He was something special. They knew that He was a fulfilled promise from God. And so, they took every opportunity to do what it would take to be where He was. Today, will you linger long with Him? Will you withdraw from the distractions of this world, slow down, and take some time to sit at His feet and hear what He has to say to you?

As you prepare for your time with the Lord, think about these words by Amy Carmichael:

Have I been so long with thee
And yet hast thou not known Me?

Blessed Master, I have known Thee
On the roads of Galilee.

Have I been so long time with thee
On the roads of Galilee:
Yet, my child, has thou not known Me
When I walked upon the sea?

Blessed Master, I have known Thee
On the roads and on the sea.

Wherefore then hast thou not known Me
Broken in Gethsemane?
I would have thee follow, know Me
Thorn-crowned, nailed upon the Tree.
Canst thou follow, wilt thou know Me
All the way to Calvary?[7]

READ AND STUDY GOD'S WORD

1. John, one of the twelve disciples, gives some very important facts about Jesus. Read John 1:14-18 and record what you discover in these verses about the Lord.

2. One of the truths seen in the gospel of John is that when Jesus lived on earth and dwelt among us, we saw His glory. This means that they saw God's presence and power in Jesus. Basically, what happened was that those who walked with Jesus saw God in action. It was an awesome and amazing experience for all. We live in a technological age with many capabilities. But these things are nothing compared with what Jesus did and can accomplish. Read the following events and write your insights about what Jesus did and what those who were with Him experienced. As you read each of these passages, imagine that you are there.

Luke 9:28-36

John 6:1-15

John 11:11-45

Optional Verses: John 2:1-11, John 4:7-30

3. Jesus revealed Himself to others in many ways. One of the names He gave to others about Himself was Son of Man. He used this name at least eighty times. By that name He designates Himself as the Representative Man and the last Adam (1 Corinthians 15:45).[8] In this name you see His mission to represent all of mankind in paying the penalty of sin by death on the cross. Look at the following verses. What do you learn about the Son of Man?

Matthew 20:18-19

Luke 19:10

Romans 5:17

Optional Verses: Matthew 12:40, 1 Corinthians 15:45-49

4. As you think about all you have learned today, how would you describe what you see about God in Jesus? Consider His gracious plan and purpose making possible your salvation and eternal life. What have you learned about God because of who Jesus is and what He does and how He acts?

ADORE GOD IN PRAYER

People came from everywhere to hear the words of Jesus. They brought Him their impossible situations as well. Today you may be facing an impossible situation. Whatever it is, you can take it to the Lord Jesus. Will you talk to Him today about your impossible circumstance? You may wish to use your prayer pages in the back of this book to write out your requests. Be sure to write the date and any verses that you can claim as a promise associated with your request.

YIELD YOURSELF TO GOD

Now, here is a thought I had one day: it could have been very easy for God to have loved us and never told us. God could have been merciful toward us and never revealed it. We know that among humans it is possible for us to feel deeply and still tell no one. It is possible to have fine intentions and never make them known to anyone. The Scriptures say that no man hath seen God at any time; the only begotten Son, which is in the bosom of the Father, he hath declared Him. The eternal Son came to tell us what the silence never told us. He came to tell us what not even Moses could tell us. He came to tell us and to show us that God loves us and that He constantly cares for us. He came to tell us that God has a gracious plan, and that He is carrying out that plan. Before it is all finished and consummated, there will be a multitude that no man can number, redeemed, out of every tongue and tribe and nation. That is what He has told us about the Father God. He has set Him forth. He has revealed Him—His being, His love, His mercy, His grace, His redemptive intention, His saving intention. He has declared it all. He has given us grace upon grace. Now we have only to turn and believe and accept and take and follow. All is ours if we will receive because the Word was made flesh and dwelt among us.[9]

A.W. TOZER IN CHRIST, THE ETERNAL SON

ENJOY HIS PRESENCE

At a point in time God the Son became man. The Triune God determined that the Second Person of the Trinity would take on human flesh and blood and live with those He created. It was all for only one reason. So that one day He could cry out "It is finished," and satisfy the righteous requirement of God on your behalf. Only Jesus could do it because He is fully God and fully man. It was all by choice in answer to God the Father's heart of love toward you and His desire to love you and be in an eternal relationship with you. Will you take some time now to think about what it means that Jesus, the Second Person of the Triune God became man? Think about how He is fully God and fully man and came out of heaven to earth to do what it took to accomplish your salvation.

> In the Paradise of glory
> is the Man Divine;
> There my heart, O God, is tasting
> Fellowship with Thine.
> Called to share Thy joy unmeasured,
> Now is heaven begun;
> I rejoice with Thee, O Father,
> In Thy glorious Son.
>
> Where the heart of God is resting,
> I have found my rest;
> Christ who found me in the desert,
> Laid me on His breast.
> There in deep unhindered fullness
> Doth my joy flow free—
> On through everlasting ages,
> Lord, beholding Thee.
>
> Round me is creation groaning,
> Death, and sin, and care;
> But there is a rest remaining,
> And my Lord is there.
> There I find a blessed stillness
> In His courts of love;
> All below but strife and darkness,
> Cloudless peace above.
>
> 'Tis a solitary pathway
> To that fair retreat—
> Where in deep and sweet communion

Sit I at His feet.
In that glorious isolation,
Loneliness how blest,
From the windy storm and tempest
Have I found my rest.

Learning from Thy lips for ever
All the Father's heart,
Thou hast, in that joy eternal,
Chosen me my part.
There, where Jesus, Jesus only,
Fills each heart and tongue,
Where Himself is all the radiance
And Himself the song.

Here, who follows Him the nearest,
Needs must walk alone;
There like many seas the chorus,
Praise surrounds the throne.
Here a dark and silent pathway;
In those courts so fair
Countless hosts, yet each beholding
Jesus only, there.[10]

"THE MAN DIVINE" BY T.P.

Do you know the deep and sweet communion found in the courts of the Lord? Ask Him to give you that deep and sweet communion with Him today.

REST IN HIS LOVE

"The people realized that God was at work among them in what Jesus had just done. They said, 'This is the Prophet for sure, God's Prophet right here in Galilee'" (John 6:14 MSG).

THE GREAT ATTRACTION

You see, you cannot help it all; the whole world has gone off after Him!
JOHN 12:19 WMS

PREPARE YOUR HEART

Thomas Haemerken was a priest who lived in Germany from 1379-1471. He is known to many as Thomas à Kempis and authored one of the best-loved books of all time: *Of The Imitation of Christ*. He often delivered sermons about the words and works of Jesus Christ. He constantly read, wrote, and prayed and especially loved sitting in silence and solitude, contemplating the greatness of his Lord. Sometimes when the conversation turned to God or the cares of the soul, he would excuse himself. "My brethren," he would say, "I must go. Someone is waiting to converse with me in my cell."[11] There was no one more important or interesting to Thomas à Kempis than Jesus Christ. He would rather talk with Jesus than anyone else.

Over two thousand years ago, Jesus ministered in and around the area of Galilee for three years. And by the end of three years, He was the most popular man on the planet. The religious leaders of the day, with all their training and earthly power, just could not believe His influence. They said, "The whole world has gone off after Him" (John 12:19).

Why did the world go after Him? What was it about Jesus that was so engaging, so inviting, that you would leave your daily life, alter your entire course, just to run to be with Him? Those around Him wanted to see Him, hear Him speak, and marvel at His next miracle. He constantly surprised and amazed those who followed Him. There was something about Him that was like a magnet, a great attraction.

Do you run after Him today in that same way? Are you attracted to Him? Do you know His beauty, His love, His steadfastness, His direct approach, the fact that He knows everything about you, His ability to get to the heart of a matter with you, and His joy? Write a prayer to God, asking Him to quiet your heart as you think about the great attraction of Jesus today.

READ AND STUDY GOD'S WORD

1. To look at Jesus is like looking at the facets of a diamond. As you hold the diamond up to the light, you see its beauty more and more. Look at Jesus now as He revealed Himself to others during His life on earth. Record what you see about Jesus as you look at the following verses:

Matthew 11:28-30

Matthew 15:30-31

Mark 1:40-42

Luke 8:40-48

John 4:40-42

John 16:33

Optional Verses: Matthew 1:23, Mark 1:23-25, Luke 2:40-49, John 1:29-30, John 3:1-2

2. And now, it is most important that you catch another glimpse into the heart of Jesus. There is one place that shows us His heart and His thoughts more deeply than almost anywhere else in Scripture. Turn to John 17. Jesus prayed this prayer to the Father just prior to His arrest, crucifixion, burial and resurrection. As you read through this prayer, what are your most significant insights about the Person and Character of Jesus Christ?

3. Optional: There were many instances in the life of Christ where someone took extra measures to be near Jesus. Read the following event about Zaccheus in Luke 19:1-10 and note what he did to get close to Jesus.

4. What is it that is so attractive about Jesus Christ? Why do you think the crowds wanted to be near Him? If you were there, where would you have been in relation to Jesus?

ADORE GOD IN PRAYER

Let me turn to you, O Lord, from the sweetest of earthly joys, to find that you are best of all, the fairest among ten thousand, and altogether lovely.[12]

F.B. MEYER IN DAILY PRAYERS

YIELD YOURSELF TO GOD

The numerous physical healings performed by Jesus to alleviate human suffering are only a hint of the anguish in the heart of God's Son for wounded humanity. His compassion surges from the bowels of His being, and operates on a level that escapes human imitation. Jesus resonated with the depths of human sorrow. He became lost with the lost, hungry with the hungry, and thirsty with the thirsty. On the Cross He journeyed to the far reaches of loneliness, so that He could be lonely with those who are lonely and rob loneliness of its killing power by sharing it Himself. He did then and He does now. Jesus vibrates to the hope and fear, the celebrations and desolations of each of us. He is the incarnation of the compassion of the Father…When we speak of Jesus Christ as Emmanuel, God with us, we are saying that the greatest lover in history knows what hurts us. Jesus reveals a God who is not indifferent to human agony, a God who fully embraces the human condition, and plunges into the thick of our human struggle. There is nothing that Jesus does not understand about the heartache that hangs over the valley of history. In His own being He feels every separation and loss, every heart split open with grief, every cry of mourning down the corridors of time.[13]

BRENNAN MANNING IN THE LION AND THE LAMB

When Jesus is present, all is good and nothing seems difficult; but when Jesus is absent, all is hard. When Jesus speaks not inwardly to us, all other comfort is worth nothing; but if Jesus speaks but one word we feel great comfort. Did not Mary rise immediately from the place where she wept, when Martha said to her: "The Master is come, and calleth for thee" (John 11:28)? Happy hour, when Jesus calls from tears to spiritual joy…It is great skill to know how to hold converse with Jesus… Among all therefore that be dear unto us, let Jesus alone be specially beloved. Love all for Jesus, but Jesus for Himself. Jesus Christ alone is singularly to be beloved. He alone is found good and faithful above all friends.[14]

THOMAS À KEMPIS IN OF THE IMITATION OF CHRIST

ENJOY HIS PRESENCE

Thomas à Kempis was radical in his relationship with the Lord Jesus Christ. He had a longing that burned within to leave the company of others to go talk to that Someone who was waiting to converse with him. Are you becoming so intimate with the Lord Jesus, especially as you learn who He is, that your heart burns with that same passion? You see, a heart on fire is a heart that burns with desire for Him—His company, His joy, His wisdom, His guidance, His teaching, and His comfort. You will discover that the fire within grows as you know Him more. Will you draw near and touch the hem of His garment today by faith just as that person did so many years ago when He dwelt among us?

> Pass me not, O gentle Savior, hear my humble cry;
> while on others thou art calling, do not pass me by.

> *Refrain*
> Savior, Savior, hear my humble cry;
> while on others thou art calling, do not pass me by.

Let me at thy throne of mercy find a sweet relief,
kneeling there in deep contrition; help my unbelief. *Refrain*

Trusting only in thy merit, would I seek thy face;
heal my wounded, broken spirit, save me by thy grace. *Refrain*

Thou the spring of all my comfort, more than life to me,
whom have I on earth beside thee? Whom in heaven but thee? *Refrain*

FANNY CROSBY

REST IN HIS LOVE

"Therefore, since we have so great a cloud of witnesses surrounding us, let us also lay aside every encumbrance and the sin which so easily entangles us, and let us run with endurance the race that is set before us, fixing our eyes on Jesus" (Hebrews 12:1-2).

IS HE WHO HE CLAIMED TO BE?

John testified about Him and cried out, saying, "This was He of whom I said, He who comes after me has a higher rank than I, for He existed before me."

JOHN 1:15

PREPARE YOUR HEART

Who is this One who dwelt among us? There are many names throughout the Bible that reveal the character of the Lord Jesus Christ. Mark begins his gospel by writing: "The beginning of the gospel of Jesus Christ, the Son of God…" In this name we see the divine nature of Christ and His eternal Sonship. He is one with the Father and the Holy Spirit as part of the Triune God. This name cannot be applied to any earthly creature. All of Scripture makes the claim that Jesus is God.

Even as Jesus made this claim then, so He makes it now. Jesus is the same yesterday and today and forever (Hebrews 13:8). At one point in His earthly ministry, Jesus asked His disciples a question involving His identity. "Who do people say that the Son of Man is?" They responded, "Some say John the Baptist; and others, Elijah; but still others, Jeremiah, or one of the prophets." Jesus then asked: "But who do you say that I am?" Simon Peter answered, "You are the Christ, the Son of the living God." And Jesus responded, "Blessed are you, Simon Barjona, because flesh and blood did not reveal this to you, but My Father who is in heaven" (Matthew 16:13-17).

Just as He looked directly at those disciples and asked them to make a decision, so He is looking into the eyes of your heart and soul and asking you, "But who do you say that I am?" Once you have begun to examine His character and hear His words, you must make a decision. Who do you say that He is? This is really the heart of the matter for you. Your decision will determine your direction in life. And once you decide for Christ, you will be filled with a purpose you have never before known. You will sense a security, a bedrock of assurance, that will carry you through even the deepest troubles.

As you begin your time with the Lord, think about these words written by Fanny Crosby, writer of more than eight-thousand hymns, who was blind, yet saw spiritually in a way few have.

Blessed assurance, Jesus is mine!

O what a foretaste of glory divine!

Heir of salvation, purchase of God,

born of his Spirit, washed in his blood.

Refrain

This is my story, this is my song,

praising my Savior all the day long;

this is my story, this is my song,

praising my Savior all the day long.

Perfect submission, perfect delight,

visions of rapture now burst on my sight;

angels descending bring from above

echoes of mercy, whispers of love. *Refrain*

Perfect submission, all is at rest;

I in my Savior am happy and blest,

watching and waiting, looking above,

filled with his goodness, lost in his love. *Refrain*

READ AND STUDY GOD'S WORD

1. Jesus was born of a virgin. His was no ordinary birth. Although He was laid in a manger, shepherds and kings alike came from the far reaches of the earth to worship Him. When He was brought to the temple, godly men blessed Him. John the Baptist recognized Him as the Lamb of God who takes away the sins of the world. He forgave sins against God and this was considered blasphemy to the religious leaders of the day. Two events in particular stand out as His clear claims to deity and as an evidence of the fact that He is the Son of God. Read these two passages of Scripture and record what you see about Jesus and the people with whom He came in contact.

Matthew 27:50-28:15

Mark 14:53-64

2. Paul the Apostle experienced the priceless privilege of knowing Christ. The Lord entrusted to him the stewardship of taking the gospel to the Gentiles and writing numerous letters that have become much of what we know as our New Testament. In these letters Paul often wrote about the character of Christ. There is one place in Scripture where his apologetic for the deity of Christ is especially powerful. Turn to Colossians 1:13-20 and record everything you learn about Jesus Christ.

3. Who do you say Jesus is?

ADORE GOD IN PRAYER

My God, my Saviour, sweet to be
Dependent every hour on Thee!
Amid life's bitterness,—how sweet
Thy loving-kindnesses to meet!

Sweet to hold converse with Thee, Lord!
And hear Thee answer by Thy word;
Thy love in all my life to trace,

And live that life—the child of grace.
To feel the very light and glow
Of heaven's own gladness here below,
And drink those sparkling streams, whose rills
Rise 'mid the everlasting hills!

None, walking as Thy word hath taught,
Have ever sought, and found Thee not,
Or brought to Thee a single care
Thou didst not either take or share.

My God, my Saviour, grant that I
May with Thee live, and in Thee die!
'Tis all my spirit asks, but less
Thou know'st would not be happiness.[15]

JOHN S.B. MONSELL IN PARISH MUSINGS

YIELD YOURSELF TO GOD

Christ claimed to be other than the men by whom He was surrounded. He claimed prior existence, in that He said He was, before He came. He claimed infinite existence, in that while He was yet present in the limitations of time and space, He spoke of being in the bosom of the Father, and in heaven itself. He claimed indestructible existence, in that while He spoke of laying down His life, He declared that He would take it again, and that no man could destroy it. He also claimed a natural existence—that is, an existence definable by the terms applicable to man as the crown of creation. He claimed to live as a man; in subjection to God; limited in knowledge and in power; finding all-sufficient resource in God for the accomplishment of the will of God. He claimed, moreover, that He was in the world for the express purpose of saving men, and restoring a lost order; and He explicitly declared that this purpose could not be fulfilled save by His death and resurrection; and that in the accomplishment of death and resurrection He was working in the will of God and in cooperation with Him.[16]

G. CAMPBELL MORGAN IN THE TEACHING OF CHRIST

…turn your eyes upon Jesus and commit yourself fully and completely to Him because He is God and Christ, Redeemer and Lord, the same yesterday, today and forever. In these matters of spiritual blessing and victory, we are not dealing with doctrines—we are dealing with the Lord of all doctrine! We are dealing with a Person who is the Resurrection and the Life and the Source from whom flows all doctrine and truth…nothing about our Lord Jesus Christ has changed down to this very hour. His love has not changed. It hasn't cooled off, and it needs no increase because He has already loved us with infinite love and there is no way that infinitude can be increased. His compassionate understanding of us has not changed. His interest in us and His purposes for us have not changed. He is Jesus Christ, our Lord. He is the very same Jesus. Even though He has been raised from the dead and seated at the right hand of the Majesty in the heavens, and made Head over all things to the Church, His love for us remains unchanged. Even though He has been given all authority and power in heaven and in earth, He is the very same Jesus in every detail. He is the same yesterday, today and forever!…The very same Jesus—a Brother who bears your image at the right hand of the Father, and who knows all your troubles and your weaknesses and sins, and loves you in spite of everything! The very same Jesus—a Saviour and Advocate who stands before the Father taking full responsibility for you and being easier to get along with than the nicest preacher you ever knew and being easier to approach than the humblest friend you ever had. The very same Jesus—He is the sun that shines upon us, He is the star of our night. He is the giver of our life and the rock of our hope. He is our safety and our future. He is our righteousness, our sanctification, our inheritance. You find that He is all of this in the instant that you move your heart towards Him in faith. This is the journey to Jesus that must be made in the depths of the heart and being. This is a journey where feet do not count…"[17]

A.W. Tozer in I Talk Back To The Devil

Enjoy His Presence

Do you realize today the immense claims of Jesus and the fact that He is who He claimed to be? Knowledge of Jesus changes the black and white of your world to rich and vibrant color. It takes you from the superficial and temporal to the deep and eternal nature of the true and real world of the kingdom of Christ. All that He was then is all that He is now. You have a Lord who is ever-present, who can do anything, and who is intensely concerned, compassionate and interested in you! Will you take these truths today, let your mind dwell on them, and then allow them to soak into your heart where you commune intimately with your Lord? Then, watch out. Your heart is going to burn with a passion that perhaps you have not known before. And the world will be turned upside down as He does mighty things in and through you where you live. Close your time by writing a prayer expressing your love and feelings for the Lord Jesus.

REST IN HIS LOVE

"…whenever a person turns to the Lord, the veil is taken away" (2 Corinthians 3:16).

DEVOTIONAL READING
BY JOSH MCDOWELL AND BILL WILSON

DEAR FRIEND,

As you think back about what you have learned this week about Jesus as fully God and fully man, who do you say He is?

What were your most meaningful discoveries this week as you spent time with the Lord?

Your most significant insight:

Your favorite quote:

Your favorite verse:

To know Jesus from history is to know Him from afar. It is only to know about Him rather than to actually know Him. Yet the historical record of His life reveals that He intensely desired that all mankind might know Him personally. On the eve of His crucifixion, when He knew death was imminent and the most important thoughts filled His mind, we find Him praying before His disciples: "Father, the hour has come; glorify Your Son, that the Son may glorify You, even as You gave Him authority over all mankind, that to all whom You have given Him, He may give eternal life. And this is eternal life, that they may know You, the only true God, and Jesus Christ whom You have sent" (John 17:1-3). Either Jesus was supremely egotistical or He was revealing the whole purpose of His life within human history: that anyone from all mankind might come to know Him. Not just know about Him, but actually know Him in a personal way. One of the most powerful evidences that Jesus lived, died, and rose from the dead is the changed lives of His disciples, from those of the first century down to those in the present time. Hundreds of millions of people throughout history have been able to say that they have come to know Him and that He has changed their lives. During the nineteenth century, critical scholars put a dividing line between the Jesus of history and the Christ of faith. Our experience, along with that of Christians throughout history, is that no such barrier exists. Because of the resurrection, the historical Jesus continues to live in history.[18]

JOSH MCDOWELL AND BILL WILSON IN HE WALKED AMONG US

Viewer Guide
❧ WEEK FOUR ❧

Do You Recognize His Face?

In Week Four of *A Heart On Fire*, you had the opportunity to study the Person and claims of Jesus. When we look at Jesus, we can know what God is like, for He is God. Today, I want to look more deeply into face of Jesus with you so that you can know Him more intimately and love Him with all your heart. So, grab your Bibles, and let's share together.

"If you do not believe that I am the one I claim to be, you will indeed die in your sins" (John 8:24 NIV).

The Revelation of Yahweh (I AM) to Moses

By revealing to Moses that He is the I AM, God was saying:
I am _____ my people need for every situation of life.

What We Learn About Yahweh

1. He will _____ in oppressive situations for His people.

2. He is _____, accessible, dynamically near to all who call on Him for forgiveness, deliverance, guidance

3. Yahweh _____ Himself to a particular people whom He chooses, not based on any of their own merit but purely out of a compassionate gracious love found within Himself.

4. Yahweh's intention toward you is not simply an association, or fellowship, but intimate _____ with you. He joins His life with yours. He gives Himself to you.

5. The result of union with Yahweh is deliverance, power, and the_____ for every need, comfort for every care, His presence for every perplexity.

---

6. Yahweh is God's memorial _____.

7. Yahweh keeps His _____.

8. Yahweh is _____.

9. Yahweh is _____.

10. Yahweh commits Himself to a _____. He wants you.

11. Yahweh makes the promise of _____.

12. Yahweh _____ and sees the state of His people.

13. Yahweh _____ His people.

14. Yahweh will _____ His people.

15. Yahweh wants His people to _____ Him.

16. Yahweh acts with _____ towards His people.

The Claim of Jesus — John 8:14-24

I AM in the Greek — *ego eimi*

John 6:35 I am the bread of life
John 8:12 I am the light of the world
John 10:7-9 I am the door
John 10:11, 14 I am the good shepherd
John 11:25 I am the resurrection and the life
John 14:6 I am the way, the truth, and the life
John 15:1,5 I am the true vine

What This Means For You

Yahweh is _____ — He wants to be your God and He wants you for His own.

What Yahweh looks like:

1. He is more than a _____. He is God.

2. He is more than a _____. He is your defender, protector, and provider.

3. He more than an _____. He is the answer to every question. He is the first word and the last word. The alpha and omega.

4. He provides you with more than a _____. Your life with Him is a union. You are united with Him.

How You Can Respond

1. As Yahweh, the I AM, the *ego eimi*, Jesus is for you. If He is for you who can be against you?
Your response? You can _____Him.

2. As Yahweh, the I AM, the *ego eimi*, Jesus is everything you need.
Your response? You can _____ to Him.

3. As Yahweh, the I AM, the *ego eimi*, Jesus is life.
Your response? You can passionately _____Him.

4. As Yahweh, the I AM, the *ego eimi*, Jesus is personally with you.
Your response? You can _____Him.

✤ *Video messages are available on DVDs or as Downloadable M4V Video. Audio messages are available on Audio CDs or as Downloadable MP3 Audio. Visit the Quiet Time Ministries Online Store at www.quiettime.org.*

Week Five

HE IS EVERYTHING
YOU NEED

John 8:58

Jesus said to them, "Truly, truly, I say to you, before Abraham was born, I am."

John 8:58

DAY 1

FOR LIFE AND LIGHT

I am the bread of life…I am the Light of the world.
JOHN 6:35, 8:12

PREPARE YOUR HEART

It is one thing to know who Jesus is and to have invited Him into your life. It is quite another to realize and trust that He is the answer for everything that you face both today and for all the tomorrows of your life. He is more than you know Him to be right now. He is everything you need for every circumstance of life. This truth becomes especially meaningful for you in light of a desperate situation or a deep loss. This does not mean that you won't suffer pain. It doesn't mean you won't experience deep needs. What it does mean is that Jesus is greater than your loss, your pain, or your need. And He is enough to fill the empty places of your life and carry you through to the other side of your difficulty.

Charles Haddon Spurgeon, probably the greatest preacher who has ever lived, understood this truth. Spurgeon preached over 3000 sermons in his day. He was one of the most prolific writers of all time. He was never without words for the need of the hour. And yet he was a man who knew what it was to be in need. He was intimately acquainted with pain. He suffered from deep depression to the point of feeling, at times, as though he had no hope in the world. And yet he knew his Lord better than most.

One day Jesus was speaking to the Jews. When He spoke, He said something so radical that they literally tried to kill Him on the spot. In the course of the conversation, Jesus told them they did not know God. He pressed the point of His own identity by saying, "Your father Abraham rejoiced to see My day, and he saw it and was glad" (John 8:56). He spoke of Abraham as though He actually knew Abraham. The point from Jesus was so apparent that the Jews immediately asked, "You are not yet fifty years old, and have You seen Abraham?" Oh, what a moment for Jesus. He was about to reveal something to them that would so shake their world that they could not possibly forget His words. Jesus replied, "Truly, truly, I say to you, before Abraham was born, I am" (John 8:58). The Bible then says that the Jews "picked up stones to throw at Him, but Jesus hid Himself and went out of the temple." Why did the Jews try to stone Him? Because Jesus was

163

telling them that He existed before Abraham. And He was revealing to them that He is Yahweh, the I AM, the covenant-keeping God who is everything we need for every circumstance of life.

Thankfully, John, the beloved disciple, through the inspiration of the Holy Spirit, included this powerful event in his gospel. Oh what a moment this was filled with drama and emotion. It would be like some person walking into the middle of a group of people and saying, "I am God, the Creator of the Universe." What an astounding claim from Jesus: "I am Yahweh, the I AM." He declared then and now for all the world to know that He is eternal and one with the Father.

What does this mean for you now? No matter what you face today, Jesus is enough. He is everything you need. He will show you the way through. He will lead you. The question is always: "Who and what do you trust in life—Jesus or something else? Every day, one of your greatest decisions is dependence on the One who has the answer for every circumstance, every need, everything you face every moment of your life.

Today, as you draw near to God, ask Him to quiet your heart so that you may hear Him speak.

READ AND STUDY GOD'S WORD

1. Jesus claimed to be Yahweh, I AM, to the Jews throughout the conversation recorded in John 8:31-59. His most direct claim was in His words, "Truly, truly, I say to you, before Abraham was born, I am" (John 8:58). It is important that you understand the background of this name of God: I AM. The Hebrew is Yahweh (YHWH) and is the name that expressed the character of God to His people Israel in the Old Testament. In this name God revealed that He was dependable and faithful and desired complete trust from His people.[1] God called Moses to deliver His people from the oppression of the Egyptians. Read Exodus 3:13-15 and write out what God told Moses about Himself.

2. Read John 8:58-59. Summarize in one sentence the significance of Jesus' words. How does what you have learned help you understand why the Jews wanted to stone Jesus?

3. Jesus revealed seven different aspects of His character as the I AM in the Gospel of John. This week you are going to have the opportunity to look at them and as a result, see how Jesus is the I AM, eternal in nature, one with the Father, and everything you need in life. Today you will look at two specific revelations of His character. Why are they called revelations? A revelation is something that cannot be known unless God tells you. These are powerful truths that you would never know unless the Lord Jesus told you. The good news is that He has said it. And now it is up to you to believe what He says and depend on Him. Read the following verses and record what you learn about Jesus as the I AM and the needs He satisfies:

John 6:35 I AM _____.

What Jesus wants us to understand and needs He satisfies with this aspect of His character:

John 8:12 I AM _____.

What Jesus wants us to understand and needs He satisfies with this aspect of His character:

4. Optional: Look at the following verses and record what you learn about the light. If you are short on time, you might choose 2-3 verses. Psalm 27:1, Exodus 13:21-22, John 1:4-5, John 12:44-46, Ephesians 5:6-14, 1 John 1:5-7

ADORE GOD IN PRAYER

Why do you need the Bread of life and the Light of the world today? In what ways do you need nourishment and need light in the darkness? How do you need to be fed in the depths of your soul? How do you need guidance today? Turn to your prayer pages and list your needs, one by one. Be sure to date each of your requests and to record God's answers when they come. You may have to wait for God's timing, but He will answer you. He promises.

YIELD YOURSELF TO GOD

Jesus is still just the same towards those who seek His fellowship. He wants to be with those who are occupied with the love of His Godhead! Our relationship with Him is summed up in this simple fact—everything you need is found in Jesus Christ, the Son of God. He is God and He is the Son of Man. He is all the guilty sinner needs and He is more than the fondest expectation of the loftiest saint. We can never go beyond Him. We can never learn all that He is able to teach. We can never use all of the spiritual power and victory He is able to provide.[2]

A.W. TOZER IN I TALK BACK TO THE DEVIL

In essence, Jesus said that what bread was to the physical life, He was to the soul. How fitting that Jesus was born in Bethlehem which was known as the House of Bread. Bread has been called the staff of life. It is the basic staple for existence. Other foods are expendable, but not bread. Christ is inexpendable to life and sustenance…The transient pleasures, the phantom charms, the evanescent fame and success are like bubbles. They sparkle, and like children, we reach out to them only to find that when we grasp them their charm vanishes. The intoxicating cups of the world's pleasures will turn to bitterness…We need to take Christ into our inmost being. We need to assimilate the truths and the reality of His presence into our daily lives. He will sustain us. He will replenish our spent strength and our exhausted store of endurance. He will give vitality and vigor to the spiritual life.[3]

BY HENRY GARIEPY IN 100 PORTRAITS OF CHRIST

Another beautiful custom connected with the Feast of Tabernacles is referred to in this discourse, namely, the hanging up of brilliant lamps in the Court of the Women. Pointing, perhaps, to these, Jesus exclaims, "I am the Light of the world. Whoever follows me will never walk in darkness, but will have the light of life" (John 8:12). There may also have been an allusion to another Old Testament type, namely the pillar of fire which led ancient Israel in the wilderness, thus connect Christ with the whole system of Mosaic types, the manna in the wilderness, the rock in Horeb, and the guiding presence of the cloud and Shekinah. The light of life. Christ is the Light of life; not merely a teacher of truth in the abstract, but a practical and personal Guide. The light He gives is the light of life, that is, the light that men can live by, shining on the path of duty, perplexity and trial, illuminating and cheering every step of Christian life.[4]

A.B. SIMPSON IN THE CHRIST IN THE BIBLE COMMENTARY

There is the closest possible connection between light and life. Growth depends on light. No plant will grow, no flower will blossom, no fruit will ripen, if it is deprived of the light of the sun. Health depends on light. Health cannot flourish in darkened hovels where the light cannot come, and the surest way to improve the health of a nation is to tear down the ancient slums and to build homes into which the light can shine. Goodness depends on light. Light is the great destroyer of crime. A darkened street or lane or square may be the scene of vice and immorality and crime. Let it be brilliantly lit, and the evil things automatically disappear, because they cannot stand the light. Light and life are inseparable. Jesus is the one in whom is life, and the life is the light of men (John 1:4).[5]

WILLIAM BARCLAY IN JESUS AS THEY SAW HIM

ENJOY HIS PRESENCE

What kinds of needs does Jesus as the Bread of life and the Light of the world meet today? In what ways do you need nourishment for your soul and light in your life? Will you draw near that He might feed your soul and shine His light in your life? Close by writing a prayer to the Lord thanking Him for who He is and how He has met you today.

REST IN HIS LOVE

"And my God will meet all your needs according to his glorious riches in Christ Jesus" (Philippians 4:19 NIV).

FOR COMFORT AND SECURITY

I am the door of the sheep…I am the good shepherd.
JOHN 10: 7, 11

PREPARE YOUR HEART

One of the outstanding qualities of Charles Haddon Spurgeon the eloquent preacher was his ability to shepherd the people entrusted to him in his congregation. He had a heart for the people. While he could mesmerize a crowd of six thousand, he could also bring great comfort as he sat at the bedside of a dying child. He was extremely concerned for individuals and felt their pain. He wrote hundreds of letters. He would visit sometimes thirty people in one day. After such a day he said, "I was so delighted that I did not know anything about how the time passed."[6]

Lives are changed when someone steps beyond their personal comfort zone, recognizes a need, and meets it with mercy and kindness. Pastors greatly influence lives when they go beyond the necessary care to compassion for the individual. This shepherd heart reflects the heart of the Lord Jesus Christ.

Today you will continue to look at how Jesus revealed Himself to those He loves. In His words He speaks of sheep and the fact that He is the good Shepherd. In these words you will find such comfort and such security. As you begin your time alone with the Lord, turn to Psalm 23 and write your favorite insight about the Lord.

READ AND STUDY GOD'S WORD

1. Today, as you continue the journey of understanding Jesus as the I AM (*ego eimi* in the Greek New Testament and Yahweh - YHWH in the Hebrew Old Testament) you are going to discover one of the most comforting aspects of His nature. Read the following verses and record what you learn about Jesus as the I AM and the needs He satisfies:

John 10:7-10 I AM _____.

What Jesus wants us to understand and needs He satisfies with this aspect of His character:

John 10:11-14 I AM _____.

What Jesus wants us to understand and needs He satisfies with this aspect of His character:

2. Read the following verses and record what you learn about the Shepherd.

Mark 6:33-34

Luke 15:1-7

1 Peter 2:25

1 Peter 5:4

Revelation 7:13-17

3. In what way do you need the Lord Jesus as your Shepherd today?

4. What aspect of Jesus as your Shepherd brings you the greatest comfort today?

ADORE GOD IN PRAYER

Pray through these words by Peter Marshall: "Father, some of Thy children find life hard. It is for them we would ask Thy help now. Many of them are burdened with loads that they need not carry. Many of them clutch black burdens of anxiety and worry, when no child of Thine need be anxious. There are many who carry loads of fear when there is nothing to fear; many who make themselves miserable when they might be filled with Thy peace. We ask Thee O Lord, to teach us all how to live without strain. We have to confess to Thee that most of the things we have worried about have never happened. Teach us the secret of living just one day at a time, knowing that each day brings with it so much joy that we cannot fully explore it, so many blessings that we cannot even count them—much less enter into them all. So help us to be like children, content to live fully each hour as it comes. Then shall we escape the corroding care, the agonizing worry that destroys our peace of mind, renders us unfit for happiness, and dishonors Thee. Then shall we be filled with joy and that peace which no circumstance can take from us. We thank Thee for Thy ceaseless bounty, for that joy and that peace. Amen."[7]

YIELD YOURSELF TO GOD

"I am the Door" (John 10:9 KJV). This title refers to the unique custom of the Eastern sheepfold. At night the shepherd would gather the sheep in a stone or other type of natural or improvised enclosure with a narrow opening. Then he would lie across that opening and literally become the door of the fold…Christ is the Door of salvation: "By Me if any man enter in, he shall be saved" (John 10:9 KJV). Many have tried to climb the wall of redemption by vain philosophy, human effort, religious systems—but apart from Christ there is no salvation…Through Christ, the Door, we enter and become part of the great flock of God. Christ is the Chief Shepherd and Bishop of our souls.[8]

HENRY GARIEPY IN 100 PORTRAITS OF CHRIST

If He is your Shepherd, then He wants to care for you in the very best possible way; for He is a good Shepherd, and cares for His sheep…But you may ask me, if all this is true of the Shepherd, what is the part of the sheep? The part of the sheep is very simple. It is only to trust and to follow. The Shepherd does all the rest. He leads the sheep by the right way. He chooses their paths for them, and sees that those paths are paths where the sheep can walk in safety. When He putteth forth His sheep, He goeth before them. The sheep have none of the planning to do, none of the decisions to make, none of the forethought or wisdom to exercise; they have absolutely nothing to do but to trust themselves entirely to the care of the good Shepherd, and to follow Him whithersoever He leads. It is very simple. There is nothing complicated in trusting, when the One we are called upon to trust is absolutely trustworthy; and nothing complicated in obedience, when we have perfect confidence in the power we are obeying. Let me entreat you, then, to begin to trust and to follow your Shepherd now and here. Abandon yourself to His care and guidance, as a sheep in the care of a shepherd, and trust Him utterly… Thousands of the flock of Christ can testify that when they have put themselves absolutely into His hands, He has quieted the raging tempest, and has turned their deserts into blossoming gardens. I do not mean that there will be no more outward trouble, or care, or suffering; but these very places will become green pastures and still waters inwardly to the soul. The Shepherd knows what pastures are best for His sheep, and they must not question or doubt, but must trustingly follow Him. Perhaps He sees that the best pastures for some of us are to be found in the midst of opposition or of earthly trials. If He leads you there, you may be sure they are green pastures for you, and you will grow to be made strong by feeding in them.[9]

HANNAH WHITALL SMITH IN THE GOD OF ALL COMFORT

There were ninety and nine that safely lay
In the shelter of the fold,
But one was out on the hills away
Far off from the gates of gold;
Away on the mountains wild and bare
Away from the tender Shepherd's care,
Away from the tender Shepherd's care.

Lord, Thou hast here Thy ninety and nine,
Are they not enough for Thee?
But the Shepherd made answer: *This of Mine*
Has wandered away from Me;
And although the road be rough and steep
I go to the desert to find My sheep,
I go to the desert to find My sheep.

But none of the ransomed ever knew
How deep were the waters crossed,
Nor how dark was the night that the Lord passed through
E'er He found His sheep that was lost,
Out in the desert He heard its cry,
Sick, and helpless, and ready to die,
Sick, and helpless, and ready to die.

Lord, whence are those blood-drops all the way
That mark out the mountain track?
They were shed for one who had gone astray
Ere the Shepherd could bring him back.
Lord, whence are Thy hands so rent and torn?
They are pierced tonight by many a thorn,
They are pierced tonight by many a thorn.

But all through the mountains, thunder-riven,
And up from the rocky steep,
There arose a cry to the gate of heaven:
Rejoice! I have found My sheep.
And the angels echoed around the throne,
Rejoice! For the Lord brings back His own!
Rejoice! For the Lord brings back His own![10]

CHARLES SLEMMING IN HE RESTORETH MY SOUL

ENJOY HIS PRESENCE

Where in your life do you need to run to the good Shepherd, the Guardian of your soul (1 Peter 2:25) today? Are there things in your life that have caused you to withdraw because of the pain and even distance yourself from the Lord? If you will run to your Shepherd and find His comfort, these very things can become the very platform of something new that will make not only a difference in your life, but possibly in the lives of hundreds of others. When you run to Him in the most desperate of times, it is then that you truly discover the priceless privilege of knowing Him. Then, your heart will burn in a new way, on fire for Him. And that fire will spread to others who need to know Him too.

Savior, like a shepherd lead us,

much we need thy tender care;

in thy pleasant pastures feed us,

for our use thy folds prepare.

Blessed Jesus, blessed Jesus!

Thou hast bought us, thine we are.

Blessed Jesus, blessed Jesus!

Thou hast bought us, thine we are.

BEVERLY THRUPP (1779-1847)

REST IN HIS LOVE

"For just as the sufferings of Christ flow over into our lives, so also through Christ our comfort overflows" (2 Corinthians 1:5 NIV).

FOR HOPE THAT ANCHORS THE SOUL

I am the resurrection and the life; he who believes in Me will live even if he dies, and everyone who lives and believes in Me will never die. Do you believe this?

JOHN 11:25-26

PREPARE YOUR HEART

John and Betty Stam were two missionaries who literally gave their lives for Jesus Christ. They served the Lord in China in the 1930's. They were captured by the communists and condemned to death. As they were being led through the town where they had served the Lord, the postmaster who knew them asked, "Where are you going?" John Stam replied that he did not know where they (the guards) were going, but then he added, "We are going to heaven." John and Betty had a hope that could not be shaken. It is said that as they were executed, there was a look of joy on the face of John Stam that told of the unseen Presence with them during their final ordeal.[11]

If you know the Lord Jesus Christ, then you have a hope that can never be taken away from you. It is the hope of heaven. This hope will anchor your soul, especially in the midst of pain and difficulties. How is it an anchor? Because you can know that this life is not everything, there is something better, something eternal, where life really is found. This hope is yours for one reason: because of Jesus Christ. He died that you might live forever. He rose from the dead and ascended to heaven to secure your eternal destiny. Do you know this hope today? Draw near to the Lord, and ask Him to quiet your heart that you might realize the hope of heaven.

READ AND STUDY GOD'S WORD

1. Many fear the process and inevitability of death. And perhaps you also experience this fear from time to time. Jesus knows about your fear, and He deals with it in the presence of all so that we might know something that is going to give us a firm hope. While He lived on earth He had a favorite place that He would frequent--the town of Bethany. He would often visit His friends Martha, Mary and Lazarus in Bethany. One day He received a message from Martha and Mary that their brother, Lazarus, was sick. This led to one of the great miracles performed by Jesus and another revelation of His character. Read John 11:18-45. What does Jesus reveal about Himself in John 11:25?

John 11:25 I AM _____.

What Jesus wants us to understand and needs He satisfies with this aspect of His character:

2. Read 1 Corinthians 15:19-21, 51-57 and write out why the resurrection brings us such hope.

3. Jesus says I am the resurrection and the life. In these words you see the hope of eternal life. You see that there is something beyond the here and now, something that lasts forever. Look at the following verses and record what you learn about this future hope.

John 14:1-3

1 Corinthians 2:9

2 Corinthians 5:1-9

Hebrews 6:17-19

Hebrews 11:13-16

1 John 5:11-15

4. What truth have you learned today that gives you the most hope?

ADORE GOD IN PRAYER

Turn to your journal pages and write a prayer to the Lord thanking Him for the hope of heaven. Ask Him to open your heart more and more to these truths so that you will have a firm anchor for your soul in the storms of life.

YIELD YOURSELF TO GOD

Charles Fuller once announced that he would be speaking the following Sunday on heaven. During that week a beautiful letter was received from an old man who was very ill. The following is part of his letter:

> Next Sunday you are to talk about heaven. I am interested in that land, because I have held a clear title to a bit of property there for over 55 years. I did not buy it. It was given to me without money and without price. But the Donor purchased it for me at tremendous sacrifice. I am not holding it for speculation since the title is not transferable. It is not a vacant lot. For more than half a century I have been sending materials out of which the greatest Architect and Builder of the Universe has been building a home for me which will never need to be remodeled nor repaired because it will suit me perfectly, individually, and will never grow old. Termites can never undermine its foundations for they rest on the Rock of Ages. Fire cannot destroy it. Floods cannot wash it away. No locks nor bolts will ever be placed upon its doors, for no vicious person can ever enter that land where my dwelling stands, now almost completed and almost ready for me to enter in and abide in peace eternally, without fear of being rejected. There is a valley of deep shadow between the place where I live in California and that to which I shall journey in a very short time. I cannot reach my home in that City of Gold without passing through this dark valley of shadows. But I am not afraid because the best Friend I ever had went through the same valley long, long ago and drove away all its gloom. He has stuck by me through thick and thin, since we first became acquainted 55 years ago, and I hold to his promise in printed form, never to forsake me or leave me alone. He will be with me as I walk through the valley of shadows, and I shall not lose my way

when He is with me. I hope to hear your sermon on Heaven next Sunday from my home in Los Angeles, CA, but I have no assurance I shall be able to do so. My ticket to Heaven has no date marked for the journey, no return coupon, and no permit for baggage. Yes, I am all ready to go and I may not be here while you are talking next Sunday evening, but I shall meet you there someday.[12]

ENCYCLOPEDIA OF 7700 ILLUSTRATIONS BY PAUL LEE TAN

ENJOY HIS PRESENCE

Here are some conclusions you can make because of the hope of heaven: This present life doesn't last forever. It is brief and momentary compared to eternity. This present life is only the first page of the book, not the last. This present life is not all there is, nor is it the best there is. This life will never completely satisfy—it is not designed to because God has something better. Our hearts are to be set on heaven. Tozer asks the question: "Are you so comfortable in this world that you have little desire to leave it?" Heaven is our home, not this world. The existence of heaven changes our view about death. To be absent from the body is to be present with the Lord. Death is the gateway to heaven.

As you think about all of this, do you have the hope of heaven today? Will you rest your heart and mind on that which anchors your soul—eternal life? Close your time today by thanking the Lord for giving you a hope that cannot be taken from you, one that is certain and unshakeable.

Think of stepping on shore, and finding it heaven.

Think of taking hold of a hand, and finding it God's hand.

Think of breathing new air, and finding it celestial air.

Think of feeling invigorated, and finding it immortality.

Think of passing from storm and tempest, to an unknown calm.

Think of waking up, and finding it home.[13]

QUOTES FROM THE QUIET HOUR

REST IN HIS LOVE

"These things I have written to you who believe in the name of the Son of God, so that you may know that you have eternal life" (1 John 5:13)

FOR YOUR RELATIONSHIP WITH GOD

I am the way, and the truth, and the life; no one comes to the Father but through Me.

JOHN 14:6

PREPARE YOUR HEART

Have you ever told someone you believed in Jesus and experienced this response? "Well, what's right for you is right for you and what's right for me is right for me. That's your truth and I have my truth." Countless people believe that there are many ways to God. Some think it really doesn't matter what you believe as long as you are sincere. This way of thinking is encouraged everywhere including the media.

Today, we are going to examine the words of Jesus that command a decision from everyone. Either what Jesus says is true or not. Jesus has said, "I am the way, and the truth, and the life; no one comes to the Father but through Me" (John 14:6). This is an absolute, exclusive claim. He is saying that He is the only way to God. Therefore, a person cannot believe in Him as the way to God and in something else as another way to God. This truth cannot be said more plainly than this. When you hear someone on the radio or television say that there are many beliefs that are right (though they are contradictory), and that there are many ways to God, then you must decide. Are they correct or is what Jesus said the truth? When you begin to truly understand this claim and revelation of who Jesus is, you will become firm in your convictions, and you will stand strong. You can no longer be shaken from your firm position in Christ. If you want to know the way to God, there is only one place to turn: Jesus. If you want to know the truth, there is only one place to look: Jesus. If you want life, there is only one way to live, one place to run: Jesus. It's Jesus through and through. A singular, solitary belief: Jesus is the only way to God.

Draw near to the Lord now and ask Him to open your eyes that you might behold wonderful things in His Word. Write a prayer to the Lord about any needs or burdens on your heart.

READ AND STUDY GOD'S WORD

1. During a conversation with His disciples, Jesus revealed something very important about Himself—He is the only way to God. It was an exclusive claim. One that commanded their attention and a decision. Just prior to this revelation, Jesus tells His followers that He is going to

prepare a place for them. Thomas said, "Lord, we do not know where You are going, how do we know the way" (John 14:5). Following Jesus' response, He reveals to Philip that He is God, that "He who has seen Me has seen the Father" (see John 14:7-15). Now, read John 14:6 and record what you learn about Jesus as the I AM and the need He satisfies:

John 14:6 I AM _____.

What Jesus wants us to understand and needs He satisfies with this aspect of His character:

2. From Jesus' words, we understand that He is the truth. In a world that is constantly changing that you can know truth. Look at the following verses and record what you learn about the truth. Be sure to personalize your insights as you write them out.

John 1:14-17

John 8:31-32

John 16:13

John 17:17

John 18:37-38

3 John 1:1-4

Optional Verses: John 3:20-21, John 4:23-24, John 8:45-47, 2 Timothy 3:1-7, 2 Peter 1:10-21

4. What is your favorite insight about truth today?

ADORE GOD IN PRAYER

O LORD GOD,
Thou hast commanded me to believe Jesus;
And I would flee to no other refuge,
Wash in no other fountain,
Build on no other foundation,
Receive from no other fullness,
Rest in no other relief.
His water and blood were not severed in their flow at the cross,
May they never be separated in my creed and experiences;
May I be equally convinced of the guilt and pollution of sin,
Feel my need of a prince and saviour,
Implore of him repentance as well as forgiveness,
Love holiness, and be pure in heart,
Have the mind of Jesus, and tread in his steps.
Let me not be at my own disposal,
But rejoice that I am under the care of one
Who is too wise to err,
Too kind to injure,
Too tender to crush.
May I scandalize none by my temper and conduct, but
Recommend and endear Christ to all around,
Bestow good on every one as circumstances permit,
And decline no opportunity of usefulness.
Grant that I may value my substance,
Not as the medium of pride and luxury,
But as the means of my support and stewardship.

Help me to guide my affections with discretion,
To owe no man anything,
To be able to give to him that needeth,
To feel it my duty and pleasure to be merciful and forgiving,
To show to the world the likeness of Jesus.[14]

THE VALLEY OF VISION: A COLLECTION OF PURITAN PRAYERS AND DEVOTIONS

YIELD YOURSELF TO GOD

To recognize that truth is in Jesus and to do nothing about it means that in effect one ranges oneself with the enemies of the Lord. It means also that there is some powerful spiritual force holding back the would-be believer from what is recognized as the right course of action. The man in that position is not free but a slave. Jesus makes it plain that his adversaries are slaves to sin and in the closest possible relationship to the Evil One. True freedom is to be found in the liberty which Christ gives.[15]

LEON MORRIS IN THE GOSPEL ACCORDING TO JOHN

…in Jesus we come face to face with truth and reality. In him we penetrate beyond the guesses and the gropings, beyond the perhaps and the maybes, and arrive at The Truth; we pass beyond the counterfeits and the substitutes, the imitations and the shadows, and arrive at reality. Because Jesus is the truth, he alone can tell us about God and bring us into the things which are real.[16]

WILLIAM BARCLAY IN JESUS AS THEY SAW HIM

ENJOY HIS PRESENCE

Have you looked to Jesus Christ as the way, the truth, and the life? Look to no other, but Him alone. He has made the claim and now you can trust Him in for the rest of your life. You will find that when you stand on what is true, you have a firm foundation that cannot be shaken. God bless you as you continue to walk with Him and hold on to Him in every circumstance of your life

REST IN HIS LOVE

"This is eternal life, that they may know You, the only true God, and Jesus Christ whom You have sent" (John 17:3).

FOR A FRUITFUL AND SATISFYING LIFE

I am the true vine...
JOHN 15:1

PREPARE YOUR HEART

How can a vibrant and vivacious woman choose to leave a life in the theater and become a missionary in China? Through her mother's prayers and a disappointing romance, Isobel Kuhn turned to Christ and surrendered her life to Him. She then attended Moody Bible Institute and sailed to China as a missionary among the Lisu tribe, an oppressed people who indulged in evil practices. They labored for years, winning a few converts to Christ. Then, God gave Isobel the great idea to begin a Bible school during the rainy season. As a result, many within the tribe became Christians and took the gospel to other villages. Isobel and her husband, John, suffered greatly during their time in China. During World War II their young daughter was held prisoner in a concentration camp. Isobel had learned to do one thing in the midst of every trial. She would fall on her knees in prayer and weep before the Lord, asking for his help. He answered her every time. She found the Lord to be her very life. And in Him she was satisfied. The result was much fruit in her ministry among the Lisu people in China.

There is nothing so exciting as seeing lives changed for Jesus Christ. Everyone wants to feel as though their lives count for something. Jesus wants more than that for you. He wants your life to count for eternity. You can invest in things that will last forever. How can that happen? By drawing upon your source in life and allowing Him to work in and through you. Ministry is Jesus Christ in action. If you try to work for the Lord, you will burn out. If you will allow Him to work in and through you, you will burn for Him and others will be drawn to His light.

Meditate on the words of this hymn by Henry Lyte (1793-1847) and ask the Lord to show you what it means to abide in Him today.

> Abide with me; fast falls the eventide;
>
> the darkness deepens; Lord, with me abide.
>
> When other helpers fail and comforts flee,
>
> Help of the helpless, O abide with me.

I need thy presence every passing hour.

What but thy grace can foil the tempter's power?

Who, like thyself, my guide and stay can be?

Through cloud and sunshine, Lord, abide with me.

I fear no foe, with thee at hand to bless;

ills have no weight, and tears not bitterness.

Where is death's sting? Where, grave, thy victory?

I triumph still, if thou abide with me.

Hold thou thy cross before my closing eyes;

shine through the gloom and point me to the skies.

Heaven's morning breaks, and earth's vain shadows flee;

in life, in death, O Lord, abide with me.

READ AND STUDY GOD'S WORD

1. Today, you are going to learn how to have a fruitful and satisfying life. Your Teacher will be the Lord Himself. Because He is the Master Teacher, he uses a visual aid of a vine and branches to help you remember these powerful truths. Read John 15:1-17 and record what you learn about the Lord Jesus Christ, about yourself, and the result of abiding in Christ.

John 15:1, 5 I AM _____.

What Jesus wants us to understand and needs He satisfies with this aspect of His character:

Jesus, the Vine:

You, the branch:

Result of abiding in Christ (John 15: 7-8, 11, 16)

2. Jesus desires that you, as a branch, abide in Him. To abide in Christ means to remain in vital contact with Him. If indeed, He is the source of everything you need for every circumstance of life, then you can see how imperative it is that you abide in Him. Look at the following truths about who Jesus is. The verses are listed for your convenience in looking at any that are especially significant to you. As you read through this list, underline any truths about Christ that stand out to you to today.

Jesus Is…

Your Sufficiency—"My grace is sufficient for you…" 2 Corinthians 12:9
Your Companion—"Lo, I am with you always…" Matthew 28:20
Your Brother—"…Made like His brethren." Hebrews 2:17
Your Liberator—"The Son makes you free." John 8:36
Your Friend—"You are my friends…" John 15:14
Your Helper—"I can do all things through Him." Philippians 4:13
Your Guardian—"The Good Shepherd lays down His life for the sheep." John 10:11
Your Example—"Walk in the same manner as He walked…" 1 John 2:6
Your Fellowship—"Our fellowship is with the Father and with His Son…" 1 John 1:3
Your Peace—"My peace I give to you…do not let your heart be troubled…" John 14:27
Your Forgiver—"He is faithful and righteous to forgive us our sins…" 1 John 1:9
Your Purifier—"I am the one who wipes out your transgressions…" Isaiah 43:25
Your Intercessor—"Christ Jesus is He…who also intercedes for us." Romans 8:34
Your Mediator—"One Mediator also between God and men…Jesus Christ." 1 Timothy 2:5

Your Sanctifier—"…We have been sanctified through…Jesus Christ…" Hebrews 10:10

Your Perfecter—"He has perfected for all time those who are sanctified." Hebrews 10:14

Your Finisher of Faith—"Jesus, the Author and Perfecter of faith." Hebrews 12:2

Your Lord—"He is Lord of lords…" Revelation 17:14

Your King—"He is…King of kings…" Revelation 17:14

Your Life—"He who has the Son has the life…" 1 John 5:12

Your Road—"I am the way…" John 14:6

Your Truth—"I am…the truth…" John 14:6

Your Hope—"Christ Jesus, who is our hope." 1 Timothy 1:1

Your Light—"I am the Light of the world." John 9:5

Your Master—"For the Son of Man is Lord of the Sabbath." Matthew 12:8

Your Hiding Place—"You are my hiding place." Psalm 32:7

Your Protector—"You preserve me from trouble." Psalm 32:7

Your Glory—"But you, O LORD, are…my glory…." Psalm 3:3

Your Wonderful Counselor—"His name will be called Wonderful Counselor." Isaiah 9:6

Your Mighty God—"His name will be called…Mighty God." Isaiah 9:6

Your Eternal Father—"His name will be called Eternal Father." Isaiah 9:6

Your Prince of Peace—"His name will be called Prince of Peace." Isaiah 9:6

Your Shield—"But you, O LORD, are a shield around me…" Psalm 3:3

Your Strength—"The LORD is my strength." Exodus 15:2

Your Resurrection—"I am the Resurrection." John 11:25

Your Song—"The LORD is…my song." Exodus 15:2

Your Victory—"The Lord…He has given me victory." Exodus 15:2

Your Comforter—"He will wipe away every tear from their eyes…" Revelation 21:4

Your Joy—"To God my exceeding joy." Psalm 43:4

Your Pleasure—"In your right hand there are pleasures forever." Psalm 16:11

Your Savior— "Christ Jesus our Saviour." Titus 1:4

Your Baptizer—"He will baptize you with the Holy Spirit." Matthew 3:11

Your Liberty—"Where the Spirit of the Lord is, there is liberty." 2 Corinthians 3:17

Your Abiding Place—"In Him we live and move and exist." Acts 17:28

Your Love—"You shall love the Lord your God with all your heart." Matthew 22:37

Your Lover—"I have loved you with an everlasting love; therefore I have drawn you with lovingkindness." Jeremiah 31:3

Your Lovingkindness— "He who trust in the LORD, lovingkindness shall surround him." Psalm 32:10

Your Bridegroom—"As the bridegroom rejoices over the bride, so your God will rejoice over you." Isaiah 62:5

Your All in All—"Christ is all and in all." Colossians 3:11.

Your Everything—"In Him you have been made complete…" Colossians 2:10

What is your favorite truth regarding who Jesus is? What causes your heart to burn with that contagious love for Him?

4. Jesus desires that you bear much fruit and experience an abundant life (John 10:10). That is the result of abiding in Him. Read Galatians 5:22-25 and write out what you learn about fruit. (Optional Verses: Philippians 1:22-23, Colossians 1:1-12, Hebrews 12:11, Hebrews 13:15-16, James 3:13-18)

ADORE GOD IN PRAYER

O true and living Vine, make me fruitful today in good works to do your will. You have given me a desire for a holy life; accomplish this by the grace of your Spirit dwelling in me and working through me continually.[17]

F.B. MEYER IN DAILY PRAYERS

YIELD YOURSELF TO GOD

Abide in Me means "hold and profess the truth I have spoken to you and give yourselves out merely as my witnesses." The other abiding, on the other hand, signifies the indwelling of the Spirit of Jesus in the hearts of those who believe. Jesus gives His disciples to understand that, while abiding in His doctrine, they must also have His Spirit abiding in them; that they not only hold fast the truth, but be filled with the Spirit of truth.[18]

A.B. BRUCE IN THE TRAINING OF THE TWELVE

By Christ's death and resurrection, apprehended and trusted, we enter into eternal life; and by wholehearted yieldedness to Christ as Lord and Master, we enter into the experience of abounding life...let us believe Christ when He says He came that we might live like that; and let us believe that He has given to us His Holy Spirit for its realization...We need not wait for Him. He is waiting for us. In this place and moment He is offering Himself to us as the source of strength and satisfaction, as well as the place of safety; and if we will but receive Him, fear will be exchanged for trust, doubt for certainty, ineffectiveness for success, defeat for victory, and sadness for joy. We have tried trying and have failed; why not now try trusting? We have wrought in our own strength and have found it to be weakness; why not now take hold of His strength? The faith we once exercised for the possession of divine life, let us now exercise for the experience of abounding life; and as Christ met us then, so He will meet us now.[19]

REV. W. GRAHAM SCROGGIE IN KESWICK'S AUTHENTIC VOICE

The thought of what the vine is to the branch, and Jesus to the believer, will give new force to the words, Abide in me! It will be as if He says, Think, soul, how completely I belong to thee. I have joined myself inseparably to thee; all the fullness and fatness of the Vine are thine in very deed. Now thou once art in me, be assured that all I have is wholly thine. It is my interest and my honour to have thee a fruitful branch; only Abide in me. Thou art weak, but I am strong; thou art poor, but I am rich. Only abide in me; yield thyself wholly to my teaching and rule; simply trust my love, my grace, my promises. Only believe; I am wholly thine; I am the Vine, thou art the branch. Abide in me.   What sayest thou, O my soul? Shall I longer hesitate, or withhold consent? Or shall I not, instead of only thinking how hard and how difficult it is to live like a branch of the True Vine, because I thought of it as something I had to accomplish—shall I not now begin to look upon it as the most blessed and joyful thing under heaven? Shall I not believe that, now I once am in Him, He Himself will keep me and enable me to abide? On my part, abiding is nothing but the acceptance of my position, the consent to be kept there, the surrender of faith to the strong Vine still to hold the feeble branch. Yes, I will, I do abide in Thee, blessed Lord Jesus.[20]

ANDREW MURRAY IN ABIDE IN CHRIST

If you want to bear fruit, see that the inner life is perfectly right, that your relationship to Christ Jesus is clear and close. Begin each day with Him in the morning, to know in truth that you are abiding in Him and he in you. Christ tells us that nothing less will do. It is not your willing and running, it is not by your might or strength, but—by my Spirit, saith the Lord (Zechariah 4:6). Meet each new engagement, undertake every new work, with your ears and heart open to the Master's voice, He that abideth in me…beareth much fruit. You see to the abiding; He will see to the fruit, for He will give it in you and through you. O my brethren, it is Christ who must do all! The Vine provides the sap, the life, and the strength. The branch waits, rests, receives, and bears the fruit. Oh, the blessedness of being only branches, through whom the Spirit flows and brings God's life to men! I pray you, take time and ask the Holy Spirit to help you to realize the unspeakably solemn place you occupy in the mind of God. He has planted you into His Son with the calling and the power to bear much fruit. Accept that place. Look always to God, and to Christ, and joyfully expect to be what God has planned to make you—a fruitful branch.[21]

ANDREW MURRAY IN THE TRUE VINE

ENJOY HIS PRESENCE

Is your life rich and full in the Lord Jesus Christ? Is it productive for Him? Are you living where God's action is, in the Vine, Jesus Christ? Are you satisfied in Him? Do you see that He is everything you need for every circumstance of life? If not, will you draw near to Him and draw upon Him as the source for all the you are and all that you do. Identify those things that pull you away from Christ and develop those habits in your life that will help you remain in vital contact with Christ. Will you say no to many things, so that you can say yes to the very best things in the Lord Jesus Christ? Remember, a branch can do nothing in and of itself. It is only as you remain in vital contact with the Lord Jesus Christ that you can bear fruit. And in Him, you will not just bear fruit. You will bear much fruit! Then you will live a productive life, honoring and glorifying Him. Close your time with the Lord by writing a prayer in your journal expressing your desire for Him as the True Vine, and source of everything you need for every circumstance of life.

REST IN HIS LOVE

"But the fruit of the Spirit is love, joy, peace, patience, kindness, goodness, faithfulness, gentleness, self-control; against such things there is no law" (Galatians 5:22-23).

DEVOTIONAL READING
BY ANDREW MURRAY

DEAR FRIEND,

The next two days are your opportunity to spend time reviewing what you learned this week. You may wish to write your thoughts and insights in your journal in the back of this study book. As you think about all that you have learned about the fact that Jesus is everything you need, record in the space provided:

Your most significant insight:

Your favorite quote:

Your favorite verse:

The question is often asked, What is the reason for the weak spiritual lives of so many Christians? This is an excellent question, for it is remarkable how little the church responds to Christ's call, how little the church is what Christ wants her to be. What really is the matter? What actually is needed? Various answers may be given, but there is one answer that includes them all: each believer needs the full revelation of a personal Christ as an indwelling Lord, as a satisfying portion. When the Lord Jesus was here on earth, what was it that distinguished His disciples from other people? The answer is that Jesus took them away from their fishnets and their homes. He gathered them around Himself, and they knew Him. He was their Master; He guarded them, and they followed Him. And what is supposed to make the difference today between Christ's disciples—not those who are just hoping to get to heaven, but Christ's wholehearted disciples—and other people? It is this: fellowship with Jesus every hour of the day. When Christ was on earth, He was able to keep the disciples with Him for three years, day after day. Now that Christ is in heaven, He is able to do what He could not do when He was on earth—to keep in the closest fellowship with every believer throughout the whole world. Praise God for this.[22]

ANDREW MURRAY IN THE SECRET OF SPIRITUAL STRENGTH

Viewer Guide
❧ WEEK FIVE ❧

What A Friend We Have In Jesus

In Week Five of *A Heart on Fire* you learned that Jesus is everything you need. Today we are going to talk about the kind of relationship Jesus wants with you.

"I no longer call you servants, because a servant does not know his master's business. Instead, I call you friends, for everything that I learned from my Father I have made known to you" (John 15:15 NIV).

The Picture of Friendship with Jesus — What does friendship with Jesus mean?

1. You share in His _____.

2. You have a _____ and a mission in life.

3. You can _____ Him for anything.

Practical Application of Friendship with Jesus — How well do you know Jesus?

How can you become intimate with Jesus? The best way is through the habit of daily _____ alone with Him.

Schedule a time. Find a quiet place. Use the PRAYER plan: Prepare Your Heart, Read and Study God's Word, Adore God in Prayer, Yield Yourself to God, Enjoy His Presence, Rest in His Love

My Personal Friendship with Jesus

❧ *Video messages are available on DVDs or as Downloadable M4V Video. Audio messages are available on Audio CDs or as Downloadable MP3 Audio. Visit the Quiet Time Ministries Online Store at www.quiettime.org.*

Week Six

HE IS YOUR LIFE

Colossians 3:4

When Christ, who is our life, is revealed, then you also will be revealed with Him in glory.

COLOSSIANS 3:4

YOU ARE UNITED WITH CHRIST

For if we have become united with Him in the likeness of His death,
certainly we shall also be in the likeness of His resurrection.

ROMANS 6:5

PREPARE YOUR HEART

You have learned many powerful truths about the Lord Jesus Christ in these quiet times. But there is much more treasure to be discovered. There are secrets in the Christian life known only to those who will take the time to find the golden nuggets of truth in God's Word. These are profound truths that take time to absorb and years to live out in your life. Many men and women of God throughout the years have discovered these secrets in God's Word and have articulated them in profound ways in the books they have written. And yet, these truths are so deep that they are almost impossible to communicate. They simply must be stated and then taken into the heart and mind where the Holy Spirit can communicate them to your soul and spirit. These truths relate to your intimate relationship with Christ.

How are we joined with Christ in a real and vital relationship? Christ has accomplished much on your behalf and, as a result, has united you with His life. It is your union with Christ that allows you to be saved from eternal death, obtain forgiveness of sins, and then be with Him forever in eternity.

This week you are going to look at your union with Christ in intimate detail. These are powerful truths that are the secrets to a victorious Christian life. They are rarely taught because they are so little understood. The saints of old knew and understood their union with Christ and the ramifications of their life in Him. These saints included Andrew Murray, F.B. Meyer, Alan Redpath, Hannah Whitall Smith, Amy Carmichael, Ruth Paxson, Dwight L. Moody, A.W. Tozer, A.B. Simpson, R.A. Torrey, G. Campbell Morgan, and William Newell. You are in for a treat as you will have the opportunity to read some of their writings about the victorious Christian life.

J. Hudson Taylor, founder of the China Inland Mission, speaks of a time when he was extremely frustrated in his ministry. He had many responsibilities but felt defeated in his Christian life. One day he received a letter from another missionary, John McCarthy. In this letter Mr. McCarthy wrote of a life that depended not on self, but on Christ. He described a life free from struggle and filled instead with trust, love, rest and complete joy. He spoke of a surrender and satisfaction that J. Hudson Taylor had never before known. What J. Hudson Taylor realized in that moment when he read that letter was that he had been relying on his own resources to live his life. He had been completely unaware that the affairs of his life were Christ's concern and that Christ and His resources were present and ready to handle everything that came his way. He experienced a new awareness of his union with Christ; that Christ lived in him and worked through him every moment of the day. He realized his responsibility was to trust and rest. It was the Lord's work, not his. The realization of these truths made a radical difference in the life and ministry of J. Hudson Taylor. He accomplished more in Christ than he ever would have on his own. This is what happens when you realize that you are united with Christ and He is your life.

> An empty shell lay by the sea;
> The waves rolled up, and all forgot
> To think of that which mattered not;
> They only saw the sea.
>
> So be it, Lord; let this Thy shell
> Be lost in glory of the sea;
> And as the waves sweep over me,
> Let all forget the shell.[1]

AMY CARMICHAEL IN MOUNTAIN BREEZES

READ AND STUDY GOD'S WORD

1. Paul wrote a defense of the gospel of Jesus Christ that is unparalleled in depth or truth. It is found in the letter to the Roman church. Romans is one of the richest books in the Bible. In Romans, Paul lays out in legal fashion the truths about righteousness. It is these truths that literally transformed Martin Luther's life and led to the Reformation. How is it that a man or woman may be made righteous? How is it that salvation is a free gift of God's grace? These were questions that Paul dealt with. In his argument for grace, the unmerited favor of God, he deals with a huge question that immediately comes to mind. If there is grace for your sin, then does living a holy life really matter? In Paul's defense of the gospel, you will learn some very important truths. Read Romans 6:1-14 and record everything that you learn about yourself and Jesus Christ. Make special note of all that is true because you are "united with Christ." Pay attention to timing (what has already taken place and what is already true). Be sure to personalize everything as you write

it out i.e. *I have died to sin* (verse 2), *I have been baptized into Christ Jesus* (verse 3), *I walk in newness of life* (verse 4)

Romans 6:1-14

2. Read the following verses and record what you learn about your union with Christ. Be sure to personalize your responses.

Romans 5:8-10

Romans 7:4

Romans 8:1

Romans 8:38-39

1 Corinthians 6:17-20

2 Corinthians 5:14-21

Galatians 2:20

Colossians 3:3-4

3. Think about what God is saying in these verses. You died with Christ and now you have been raised to new life in Him. In light of all these truths, described in your own words your new life and what it means to have a relationship with Jesus Christ.

ADORE GOD IN PRAYER

Take some time now to talk with God about all that you are learning about your life in Christ. Ask Him to continue opening your eyes that you may behold wonderful truth in His Word.

YIELD YOURSELF TO GOD

> To be joined in life with the Risen Christ, and thus daily, hourly, to walk, is a wonder not conceived of by many of us. But it is the blessed portion of all true Christians. They shared Christ's death, and now are saved by (or in) His Life –as we read in Chapter 5:10. But not only saved: we walk here on earth by appropriating faith, in the blessedness of His heavenly newness of resurrection life...We reap the exact effect of what Christ did. Did Christ bear our sins in His own body on the tree? He did. Then we bear them no more. Was Christ made to be sin on our behalf, and did He die unto sin? Truly so. Then Christ's relation to sin becomes ours...It is the consciousness of being sinful that keeps back saints from that glorious life Paul lived. Paul had absolutely no sense of bondage before God; but goes on in blessed triumph! Why? He knew he had been justified from all guilt by the blood of Christ; and he knew that he was also justified, cleared, from the thing sin itself: and therefore (though walking in an, as yet, unredeemed body), he was wholly heavenly in his standing, life and relations with God! He knew he was as really justified from sin itself as from sins. The conscious presence of sin in his flesh only reminded him that he was in Christ;--that sin had been condemned judicially, as connected with flesh, at the cross; and that he was justified as to sin; because he had died with Christ, and his former relationship to sin had wholly ceased! Its presence gave him no thought of condemnation, but only eagered his longing for the redemption body. Justified from sin—because, he that hath died is justified from sin. Glorious fact! May we have faith to enter into it as did Paul.
>
> WILLIAM NEWELL IN ROMANS, VERSE BY VERSE

But words fail me here! All that I can say is but a faint picture of the blessed reality. For far more glorious than it would be to have Christ a dweller in the house or in the heart, is it to be brought into such a real and actual union with Him as to be one with Him—one will, one purpose, one interest, one life. Human words cannot express such a glory as this. And yet it ought to be expressed, and our souls ought to be made so unutterably hungry to realize it, that day or night we shall not be able to rest without it. Do you understand the words one with Christ? Do you catch the slightest glimpse of their marvelous meaning? Does not your whole soul begin to exult over such a wondrous destiny? It seems too wonderful to be true that such poor, weak, foolish beings as we are should be created for such an end as this; and yet it is a blessed reality.[2]

HANNAH WHITALL SMITH IN THE CHRISTIAN'S SECRET OF A HAPPY LIFE

ENJOY HIS PRESENCE

Do you see that when Jesus died, you died? It is a fact that has occurred in the past. Why is it so important that you understand that you have been united with Christ in His death? Because then you can be united with Him in His life. Then, He can be your life. His victory on the cross has become yours as well. What is true of Him now makes available to you the Resource beyond all resources that you can draw upon today. All of this is true because you died with Christ and now you walk in newness of life—His life! Do you realize today that it is no longer your life, but His life? Do you see that because you are united with Him you are identified with Him in every way? What does that mean to you today and what difference will that make in how you live your life? How does this change your view of sin? How does it influence the way you approach those responsibilities and privileges that God has entrusted to you? As you close your quiet time, write a prayer expressing all that is on your heart.

REST IN HIS LOVE

"Therefore, my brethren, you also were made to die to the Law through the body of Christ, so that you might be joined to another, to Him who was raised from the dead, in order that we might bear fruit for God" (Romans 7:4).

YOUR LIFE IS HIDDEN WITH CHRIST

For you have died and your life is hidden with Christ in God.
COLOSSIANS 3:3

PREPARE YOUR HEART

Ian Thomas became a Christian at the age of thirteen. Two years later he decided to devote the rest of his life in service to the Lord. For the next few years, he filled his life with much activity. In the midst of all of his service to the Lord, he felt as though he was ineffective. He felt like no matter what he did, nothing happened in his ministry. He felt less effective and powerful no matter how hard he worked. He became more and more frustrated. One night he fell to his knees, weeping. He prayed, "Lord I love You, but I just cannot do it anymore." As he was praying, Scripture began flooding his mind. "When Christ, who is our life, is revealed, then you also will be revealed with Him in glory" (Colossians 3:4). "To live is Christ" (Philippians 1:21). "I am the way, the truth, and the life" (John 14:6). "For if while we were enemies we were reconciled to God through the death of His Son, more , having been reconciled, we shall be saved by His life" (Romans 5:10). He kept thinking about life—new life. Then he thought again of the words, "Christ, who is our life" (Colossians 3:4). A huge burden lifted off of him. He realized it was not his life, but Christ's life. He said that it seemed as though the Lord was telling him that he had been busy trying to do for God what only God could do through him. He needed to accept and act upon the life of Christ in him. That night the Lord showed Ian Thomas that his life was no longer his own, but Christ's. Oh what a powerful, life-transforming truth this is! Today you will look at this truth in God's Word. As you begin your time alone with the Lord, draw near to Him and ask Him to speak to your heart today. Pray these words from the hymn written by Cleland McAfee: "O Jesus, blest Redeemer, sent from the heart of God. Hold us who wait before thee near to the heart of God."

READ AND STUDY GOD'S WORD

1. Turn to Colossians 3:1-17. In this chapter, Paul tells you some powerful truths and then applies them to your life. Write on the next page what you learn is now true about you and what you are to do as a result. Personalize your insights i.e. *I have been raised up with Christ* (verse 1).

Colossians 3:1-17	
What Is True	What I Do As A Result

2. Paul teaches these same truths in Ephesians. Read Ephesians 2:1-10 and write your most significant insight.

3. What is your favorite insight from God's Word today and how will it make a difference in your life?

ADORE GOD IN PRAYER

Jesus, Lord, we look to thee;
let us in thy name agree;
show thyself the Prince of Peace,
bid our strife forever cease.

By thy reconciling love
every stumbling block remove;
each to each unite, endear;
come, and spread thy banner here.

Make us of one heart and mind,
gentle, courteous, and kind,
lowly, meek, in thought and word,
altogether like our Lord.

Let us for each other care,
each the other's burdens bear;
to thy church the pattern give,
show how true believers live.

Free from anger and from pride,
let us thus in God abide;
all the depths of love express,
all the heights of holiness.[3]

CHARLES WESLEY

YIELD YOURSELF TO GOD

God's ultimate purpose in our creation was that we should finally be conformed to the image of Christ. Christ was to be the firstborn among many brethren, and His brethren were to be like Him. All the discipline and training of our lives is with this end in view; and God has implanted in every human heart a longing, however unformed and unexpressed, after the best and highest it knows. Christ is the pattern of what each one of us is to be when finished. We are predestinated to be conformed to His image, in order that He might be the firstborn among many brethren. We are to be partakers of the divine nature with Christ; we are to be filled with the spirit of Christ; we are to share His resurrection life, and to walk as He walked. We are to be one with Him, as He is one with the Father; and the glory God gave to Him, He is to give to us. And when all this is brought to pass, then, and not until then, will God's purpose in our creation be fully accomplished, and we stand forth in his image and after his likeness. Our likeness to His image is an accomplished fact in the mind of God, but we are, so to speak, in the manufactory as yet, and the great master Workman is at work upon us. It doth not yet appear what we shall be: but we know that, when he shall appear, we shall be like him; for we shall see him as he is.[4]

HANNAH WHITALL SMITH IN THE GOD OF ALL COMFORT

Christ must become everything to us not merely in a doctrinal way; He is every aspect of our life. Christ is our completion, our rest, our new beginning, our enjoyment, our joy, our food, our drink, and our satisfaction. Although Christ is universally vast, He is also all the detailed aspects of our practical daily living. Day by day, Jesus is our breath, our life, our everything.

THE SUFFICIENCY OF CHRIST BY AN UNKNOWN CHRISTIAN

ENJOY HIS PRESENCE

Think today about those truths realized by both J. Hudson Taylor (seen this week in Day 1) and Ian Thomas. Have you realized these same truths in your life? It does not mean that God will call you to have a worldwide ministry. But it does mean that you know what it is to be able to say with Paul: For me to live is Christ…(Philippians 1:21). It means that you know Christ to be your life. You look to Him in every situation. It is a place of victory and a place of abundance. Do you know your life to be this way? Write a prayer expressing all that is on your heart today.

All to Jesus I surrender;
all to him I freely give;
I will ever love and trust him,
in his presence daily live.
I surrender all, I surrender all,
all to thee, my blessed Savior,
I surrender all.

J.W. VAN DEVENTER

REST IN HIS LOVE

"For we are His workmanship, created in Christ Jesus for good works, which God prepared beforehand so that we would walk in them" (Ephesians 2:10).

YOU ARE IN CHRIST

Blessed be the God and Father of our Lord Jesus Christ, who has blessed us with every spiritual blessing in the heavenly places in Christ.

EPHESIANS 1:3

PREPARE YOUR HEART

As you study these truths about Christ, your life, you are now going to notice a phrase that is repeated over and over throughout the Word of God. It is made up of two small, but powerful words: *in Christ*. What you understand in these words is that not only are you with Christ, but *in Him*. Ter Steegen included this amazing truth in his hymn when he wrote: "Not beside Him, nay, but in Him, O Beloved are we!" Your blessed union with Him gives you everything that Christ, your Lord, has and all that He is. He is the Resource beyond all resources to give you the highest and the best. Today you will look at this great truth. Ask the Lord now to show you great and wonderful things in His Word as you draw near to Him.

READ AND STUDY GOD'S WORD

1. Paul's letter to Ephesians is a letter to the church of Jesus Christ. That means every word is designed just for you. He wants you to understand who you are in Christ and your high calling as part of the body of Christ. Because he wrote it from prison, it is a testimony to the fact that sometimes the greatest works come from a time of adversity. Read Ephesians 1:1-23 and write everything that is true of you because you are in Christ and you belong to Him. Personalize your insights i.e. God has blessed me with every spiritual blessing in the heavenly places in Christ (verse 3).

Ephesians 1:1-23 What is true because you are in Christ:

Ephesians 1:1-23 What is true because you are in Christ (cont'd):

2. Read the following verses. What else do you learn is true about you because you are in Christ? Be sure to personalize your answers.

Acts 17:28

Romans 8:32

1 Corinthians 1:30-31

Ephesians 2:4-7

Philippians 4:4-7

Philippians 4:19

1 John 5:11-12

Optional Verses: John 16:13, 2 Corinthians 1:19-21, 2 Corinthians 2:14-17, Ephesians 2:19-22, Philippians 3:7-14, Philippians 3:20-21, 2 Peter 1:2-4

3. Keeping in mind what you have seen today, why is it a priceless privilege to know the Lord Jesus Christ?

ADORE GOD IN PRAYER

Pray the words of Paul in Ephesians 3:14-21 as your own prayer today. Personalize these words as you pray, applying them to your own life. "I pray that from His glorious, unlimited resources He will give you mighty inner strength through His Holy Spirit. And I pray that Christ will be more and more at home in your hearts as you trust in Him. May your roots go down deep into the soil of God's marvelous love. And may you have the power to understand, as all God's people should, how wide, how long, how high, and how deep His love really is. May you experience the love of Christ, though it is so great you will never fully understand it. Then you will be filled with the fullness of life and power that comes from God. Now glory be to God! By His mighty power at work within us, He is able to accomplish infinitely more than we would ever dare to ask or hope. May He be given glory in the church and in Christ Jesus forever and ever through endless ages. Amen" (Ephesians 3:16-21 NLT).

YIELD YOURSELF TO GOD

Ages after ages of ever-increasing blessing forever and forever and forever, lie in prospect for believers—for the joint heirs!

WILLIAM R. NEWELL IN ROMANS, VERSE BY VERSE

Nothing comes to us because we are worthy or have any claim other than the worthiness of our Lord Jesus Christ. We are washed in His Blood, we stand in His Merit, we are kept by His Power, we pray in His Name, we shall be received at His Coming to dwell in His Presence.[5]

CHARLES SLEMMING IN HE LEADETH ME

We inherit all things in Christ. We sit down with Him on the throne, and all His riches are ours—all things that are to come in the ages of the future. He has linked His future with us; and never again can Christ possess anything without us. Beloved, if you can say, I am Christ's you can add, I have all things in Him.[6]

A.B. SIMPSON IN THE CHRIST LIFE

To be In Christ determines the Christian's position, privileges and possessions. For to be In Christ is to be where He is, to be what He is and to share what He has. To be In Christ is to be where Christ is. But Christ is in the heavenlies, so that is where the real home of the Christian is. He is a pilgrim on earth, for his real citizenship is in heaven…Your present address is just a stopping place on a journey, yet some of you are planning for your earthly home as though you were going to live here for ever. Your heart is set on earthly things instead of heavenly. If ye then be risen with Christ, seek those things which are above, where Christ sitteth on the right hand of God. Set your affection on things above, not on things on the earth (Colossians 3:1-2)…To be In Christ is to be what Christ is. Christ, the Head of the body, and the Christian who is a member of that body have one life. The blood of the human body is its life. The blood which is now in my head will soon be in my arm. It is the same blood. So the life that is in Christ in the heavenlies is the same life that is in the Christian on earth. Herein is our love made perfect, that we may have boldness in the day of judgment: because as he is, so are we in this world..1 John 4:17. We are so enfolded by the Lord Jesus that God cannot see Christ to-day without seeing us. This moment as God looks at His Son He sees you and me. And what His Son is He sees you and me to be. To be In Christ is to share what Christ has. All that Christ possesses we possess. Every spiritual blessing in Him—joy, peace, victory, power, holiness—is ours here and now. If we are a child of God, then we are His heir and a joint-heir with Christ, so that all the Father has given to His Son, the Son shares with us. Blessed be the God and Father of our Lord Jesus Christ who hath blessed us with every spiritual blessing in the heavenly places in Christ (Ephesians 1:3 Revised Version). He that spared not His own Son, but delivered him up for us all, how shall he not with him also freely give us all things (Romans 8:32). Do you believe that you are a spiritual multimillionaire? Are you living like one?[7]

RUTH PAXSON IN RIVERS OF LIVING WATER

ENJOY HIS PRESENCE

You have probably heard the story about the people who bought tickets for a cruise. While on the cruise, they never ate any of the meals. Finally, someone asked them why they never ate. They said they had only bought the tickets, but had no money for the meals. They were then told that the meals were included in the price of the ticket. You can just imagine how much they ate from that point on. In the same way, because you are in Christ, you are a spiritual multimillionaire.

As you close your time with the Lord, describe in your own words what it means to you that you are in Christ. What is so powerful about that truth? If someone were to ask you what they have now because they are in Christ, what would you tell them? Write out your insights in the space provided. You might close with a prayer of thanksgiving for all that the Lord has given to you.

REST IN HIS LOVE

"He who did not spare His own Son, but delivered Him over for us all, how will He not also with Him freely give us all things" (Romans 8:32).

CHRIST LIVES IN YOU

Christ in you, the hope of glory...
COLOSSIANS 1:27

PREPARE YOUR HEART

There were at least two things that revolutionized the lives of the disciples and moved them from a place of fear to power and conviction. First, Christ rose from the dead and appeared to them. He then ascended to heaven. However, in John 14, Jesus promised that He would come to make His home in them. And He did exactly that. At Pentecost, the disciples were given the Holy Spirit. Because of the indwelling Holy Spirit, Christ was no longer just with them, but in them. Now they had an intimacy with Him and experienced all that was true of Him in a completely new way. S.D. Gordon describes it like this: "...these men learned to live always in the presence of a Jesus whom their outer eyes saw not...He would be with them continually manifesting Himself in rarest power of action, in tenderest personal care, in talking and walking with them. They would see the power plainly at work; then they would say in a soft hush, He is here. They would find new bodily strength, new guidance in perplexity, new peace in the midst of confusion, and they would say to each other in awed tones, He is here: it's the Master's touch. And so it would come to be a habit to anticipate His presence. They would figure Him in, and figure Him in big, as big as He is, in all sorts of circumstances and planning and meeting of difficulties."[8]

The question for you today is: Do you figure Him in big, as big as He is in your life? Do you realize the powerful fact that the Lord Jesus is not only with you, but lives in you? He has made His home in you through the Holy Spirit. This fact makes a huge difference in what can happen in your life. It means that when you go to work, He goes with you. When you cook a meal, He is with you. When you stand up to speak, He is there also. You are never alone. And all that Christ is resides within you so that you are never without resource in any given situation.

Begin your quiet time today asking God to show you in a new way the amazing truth that Christ is in you. Meditate on these words of David from Psalm 18: "He sent from on high, He took me; He drew me out of many waters...He brought me forth also into a broad place; He rescued me, because He delighted in me...You light my lamp; the LORD my God illumines my darkness. For by You I can run upon a troop; and by my God I can leap over a wall...He makes my feet like hinds' feet, and sets me upon my high places. He trains my hands for battle, so that my arms can bend a bow of bronze. You have also given me the shield of Your salvation, and Your right hand upholds me; and Your gentleness makes me great...Therefore I will give thanks to You among the nations, O LORD, and I will sing praises to Your name."

READ AND STUDY GOD'S WORD

1. Paul wrote a letter to the Colossian church to refute a heresy that was being propagated by false teachers. Paul's goal in this letter is to show the supremacy of Jesus Christ. Read Colossians 1:26-27. What do you learn about the mystery?

2. The mystery is that Christ lives in you. Look at the following verses and record what you learn about *Christ in you*. Include your insights about the Holy Spirit.

John 15:11

John 16:12-15

John 17:25-26

1 Corinthians 6:19-20

2 Corinthians 4:6-7

Ephesians 6:10

Philippians 1:19-21

Philippians 4:13

Optional Verses: John 14:16-17 , 1 Corinthians 3:16-17, Galatians 5:16-26 , Philippians 4:4

3. What is your most significant insight about *Christ in you.*

ADORE GOD IN PRAYER

Turn to your Lord now in prayer. Take each area of your life to Him. Give Him all those places where you need His touch, His power, His strength. You may wish to use one of your prayer pages to list each area as you place your life in His hands. Confess any sin that He may bring to your mind. And then, ask Him to fill you with His Holy Spirit. By doing this, you are asking Him to control and empower you today. While you are indwelt with the Holy Spirit once and for all at the time of salvation, you are filled with the Holy Spirit again and again. Paul says in Ephesians 5:18: "Do not get drunk with wine, for that is dissipation, but be filled with the Spirit." That word filled is in the present tense and is a habitual and continuous action. Always be filled with the Spirit. Then, you will walk in the power of the Lord Jesus Christ as He lives in and through you.

YIELD YOURSELF TO GOD

Dear friend, I make the glad announcement to thee that the Lord is in thy heart. Since the day of thy conversion He has been dwelling there, but thou hast lived on in ignorance of it. Every moment during all that time might have passed in the sunshine of His sweet presence, and every step have been taken under His advice. But because thou knew it not, and did not look for Him there, thy life has been lonely and full of failure. But now that I make the announcement to thee, how wilt thou receive it? Art thou glad to have Him? Wilt thou throw wide open every door to welcome Him in? Wilt thou joyfully and thankfully give up the government of thy life into His hands? Wilt thou consult Him about everything, and let Him decide each step for thee, and mark out every path? Wilt thou invite Him into thy innermost chambers, and make Him the sharer in thy most hidden life? Wilt thou say Yes to all His longing for union with thee, and with a glad and eager abandonment hand thyself and all that concerns thee over into His hands? If thou wilt, then shall thy soul begin to know something of the joy of union with Christ.[9]

HANNAH WHITALL SMITH IN THE CHRISTIAN'S SECRET OF A HAPPY LIFE

How can these things be? How can I live such a life in my home where I receive no help or sympathy but rather ridicule, and where I have so long lived a defeated life? How can I live a consistent life in my social circle which is pervaded with worldliness and wickedness and where Christ is never mentioned or even thought of? How can I live a spiritual life in a place of business where all around me are living wholly in the flesh? How can I even live on the highest plane in my church when it is worldly and modernistic, and I am unfed and untaught? Well you cannot live this life, but Christ can. CHRIST IN US can live this life anywhere and everywhere. He did live it on earth in a home where He was misunderstood and maligned; among people who ridiculed, scoffed, opposed and finally crucified Him…In God's reckoning, Christ and the Christian become one in such a way that Christ is both in the heavenlies and upon earth and the Christian is both on earth and in the heavenlies. Christ in the heavenlies is the invisible part of the Christian. The Christian on earth is the visible part of Christ. This is a staggering thought. Its plain import is that you and I are to bring Christ down from heaven to earth that men may see who He is and what He can do in a human life. It is to have Christ's life lived out in us in such fullness that seeing Him in us men are drawn to Him in faith and love.[10]

RUTH PAXSON IN RIVERS OF LIVING WATER

ENJOY HIS PRESENCE

It is a most amazing truth that Christ lives in you. Think of all that this means in your life today. Do you see that it is no longer your life, but His life? He has taken up residence in you by the power of the Holy Spirit. The Lord Jesus Christ lives in you! Those things that you think you face alone, are His to face today. And, by His design, those things will bring great glory to God. Maybe you think you cannot do what He has asked of you. The fact is: you can't, but He can. He is able to do more than you can imagine in and through you. "Now to Him who is able to do far more abundantly beyond all that we ask or think, according to the power that works within us, to Him be the glory in the church and in Christ Jesus to all generations forever and ever. Amen." (Ephesians 3:20-21)

> Enlarge my heart, O Lord I pray
> That I might know
> More of Jesus in this day
> More of Him, more of Him
> Until this earthly life grow dim.
> Then it will be,
> Face to face
> In glory and grace
> My bridegroom I will see
> Then I will ever, always, truly,
> be forever set free.

REST IN HIS LOVE

"I can do all things through Him who strengthens me" (Philippians 4:13).

HOW TO LIVE THE EXCHANGED LIFE

I have been crucified with Christ; and it is no longer I who live, but
Christ lives in me; and the life which I now live in the flesh I live by faith
in the Son of God, who loved me and gave Himself up for me.

GALATIANS 2:20

PREPARE YOUR HEART

Frances Ridley Havergal, a writer of hymns and devotional books, became a Christian at the age of thirteen. As she continued on in her walk with the Lord, she experienced a growing sense of inadequacy and an increasing desire for an abundant life. During this time, she came across a book *All For Jesus*. She read and reread this book as it impressed her in a deep and profound way. She greatly desired the kind of life it described. And so, she ran the truths she read through her mind over and over again, thinking about what they might mean for her. Such persistence and meditation is essential for truth to go from the head to the heart. Spiritual understanding takes time and thought so that you can be quiet enough to hear God speak in His Word. She clearly remembers a particular day when the Lord broke through and gave her a new understanding into His ways. She realized that if the blood of Christ could cleanse her sin, then it surely could keep her from the habit of sin. She then yielded her life to the Lord in a new way, trusting Him to do what He promised. It was quite simple, really. However, the results were amazing in her life. She knew a joy and peace that she had not known before. She had a radiant life, one that all who know Christ intimately will exhibit. "They looked to Him and were radiant, and their faces will never be ashamed" (Psalm 34:5). Do you know the radiant life that comes from Jesus Christ? May the Lord grant it to you with increasing fullness each day.

Begin your quiet time today by meditating on these words:

> Not I, but Christ, be honoured, loved, exalted,
> Not I, but Christ, be seen, be known and heard;
> Not I, but Christ, in ev'ry look and action,
> Not I, but Christ, in ev'ry thought and word.
> Not I, but Christ, in lowly silent labour,
> Not I, but Christ, in humble earnest toil;

Christ, only Christ, no show, no ostentation;
Christ, none but Christ, the gatherer of the spoil.
Christ, only Christ, no idle word e'er falling,
Christ, only Christ, no needless bustling sound;
Christ, only Christ, no self-important bearing,
Christ, only Christ, no trace of I be found.
Not I, but Christ, my every need supplying,
Not I, but Christ, my strength and health to be;
Christ, only Christ, for spirit, soul and body,
Christ, only Christ, live then Thy life in me.
Christ, only Christ, ere long will fill my vision,
Glory excelling soon, full soon I'll see;
Christ, only Christ, my every wish fulfilling,
Christ, only Christ, my all in all to be.
Oh, to be saved from myself, dear Lord,
Oh, to be lost in Thee,
Oh, that it may be no more I,
But Christ that lives in me. Amen and Amen.[11]

ZAC POONEN IN BEAUTY FOR ASHES

READ AND STUDY GOD'S WORD

1. The experience of Christ as your life may be thought of as *the exchanged life*. You experience His life for yours. What an amazing exchange. Instead of your own weakness, you may have His strength. Instead of your own lack of understanding, you may have His wisdom. Instead of your sin, you may have His holiness. Instead of the wrath of God for sin and death, you may have the righteousness of God and eternal life. It is an incredible exchange. Who would refuse it? It is the best offer that can be made and your Lord offers it to you now. And so, the question is, will you make the transaction? What does it involve? Surrender to Him. Faith and trust. One of the most powerful verses on the exchanged life is Galatians 2:20. Turn to this verse now and write it out, word-for-word.

2. Read the following verses and record everything that you learn about faith and the exchanged life.

Isaiah 61:1-3 a prophecy about the Messiah (Jesus)

Romans 8:16-17

2 Corinthians 3:4-5

2 Corinthians 5:7

1 John 3:2-3

Optional Verses: John 10:10, Romans 8:29-30, 1 Corinthians 13:12, 2 Corinthians 3:18 , Ephesians 3:14-19, Ephesians 4:20-5:10

3. What is your most significant insight from your time in God's Word today?

ADORE GOD IN PRAYER

How will you respond to the Lord in light of the magnificent truth that Christ now lives in you? Use these words by Frances Ridley Havergal as your prayer today.:

Take my life, and let it be
consecrated, Lord, to thee.
Take my moments and my days;

let them flow in ceaseless praise.
Take my hands, and let them move
at the impulse of thy love.
Take my feet, and let them be
swift and beautiful for thee.

Take my voice, and let me sing
always, only, for my King.
Take my lips, and let them be
filled with messages from thee.
Take my silver and my gold;
not a mite would I withhold.
Take my intellect, and use
every power as thou shalt choose.

Take my will, and make it thine;
it shall be no longer mine.
Take my heart, it is thine own;
it shall be thy royal throne.
Take my love, my Lord, I pour
at thy feet its treasure-store.
Take myself, and I will be
ever, only, all for thee.

FRANCES RIDLEY HAVERGAL (1836-1879)

YIELD YOURSELF TO GOD

Always alongside is One standing close up, putting all His limitless power at our
disposal, in our action. All He did in living and dying and rising up out of death
was done on our behalf. And now all the tremendous result of His victory is at our
command. All the power native in Him is for our use…We may count on Him.
And as we do we shall cast nets into hopeless waters and get a great haul. We shall
find His presence anticipating all our personal needs. We shall rejoice to serve
and—if so it prove to be—to suffer for the One we love with tenderest devotion.
And we shall look eagerly forward to seeing Him who is always in touch with us,

here and now, to seeing Him with these outer eyes of ours, coming in glory with His resistless power…[12]

S.D. GORDON IN QUIET TALKS ON JOHN'S GOSPEL

Can we not say a willing Yes to our Lord? It is a very simple transaction, and yet very real. The steps are but three: first, we must be convinced that the Scriptures teach this glorious indwelling of God; then we must surrender our whole selves to Him to be possessed by Him; and finally, we must believe that He has taken possession, and is dwelling in us. We must begin to reckon ourselves dead, and to reckon Christ as our only life. We must maintain this attitude of soul unwaveringly. It will help us to say I am crucified with Christ: nevertheless I live, yet not I, but Christ liveth in me, over and over, day and night, until it becomes the habitual breathing of our souls. We must put off our self-life by faith continually, and put on the life of Christ; and we must do this, not only by faith, but practically as well. We must continually put self to death in all the details of daily life, and must let Christ instead live and work in us. I mean we must never do the selfish thing, but always the Christlike thing. We must let this become, by its constant repetition, the attitude of our whole being. And as surely as we do, we shall come at last to understand something of what it means to be made one with Christ as He and the Father are one. Christ left all to be joined to us; shall we not also leave all to be joined to Him, in this Divine union which transcends words, but for which our Lord prayed when He said, "Neither pray I for these alone, but for them also which shall believe on me through their words that they all may be one; as thou, Father, art in me, and I in thee, that they also may be one in us"[13]?

HANNAH WHITALL SMITH IN THE CHRISTIAN'S SECRET OF A HAPPY LIFE

It is not difficult for man to live the Christian life, somebody once said, It is a sheer impossibility! A sheer impossibility, that is, without CHRIST—but for all that He says, you have all that He is, and that is all that it takes![14]

W. IAN THOMAS IN THE MYSTERY OF GODLINESS

Faith, we are told, calls those things which be not as though they were; and, in so calling them, brings them into being. Therefore, although we cannot see any tangible sign of change when by faith we put off the old man, which is corrupt according to the deceitful lusts, and by faith put on the new man which after God is created in righteousness and true holiness, yet nevertheless, it has really been done, and faith has accomplished it. I cannot explain this theologically, but I can fearlessly assert that it is a tremendous practical reality; and that those souls who abandon the self-life, and give themselves up to the Lord to be fully possessed by Him, do find that He takes possession of the inner springs of their being, and works there to will and to do His good pleasure…Are we so conformed to the image of Christ that men in seeing us see a glimpse of Him also?[15]

HANNAH WHITALL SMITH IN THE GOD OF ALL COMFORT

ENJOY HIS PRESENCE

What you have in Christ is yours whether you realize it or not. If you are a millionaire, the money is yours whether you choose to believe it or not. However, if you know you are a millionaire, chances are you will begin to spend the money. There comes at a point in time in your walk with the Lord a realization that you are in Christ and He is in you. You see it. You know it. And then, you never see yourself or your life in the same way again. Life is never again viewed outside the realm of Christ, but in Him. Your life will take on a new dimension and you will live as you have never lived before. You will dare to do mighty things in the strength of the Lord. You will realize the truth of the phrase: I can't, but He can! As Paul said: I can do all things through Christ who strengthens me. What is your response to all that you have learned in this great truth that Christ is your life? Close by writing a prayer to the Lord expressing all that is on your heart.

REST IN HIS LOVE

"He will give beauty for ashes, joy instead of mourning, praise instead of despair" (Isaiah 61:3 NLT)

DEVOTIONAL READING
BY ALAN REDPATH

DEAR FRIEND,

The next two days are your opportunity to spend time reviewing what you learned this week. You may wish to write your thoughts and insights in your journal in the back of this study book. As you think about all that you have learned about Christ as your life, record in the space provided:

Your most significant insight:

Your favorite quote:

Your favorite verse:

Meditate on the words of this hymn by Horatio Bonar (1857):

Thy works, not mine, O Christ,
Speak gladness to this heart;
They tell me all is done,
They bid my fear depart.
To whom save Thee, who canst alone
For sin atone, Lord, shall I flee?
Thy wounds, not mine, O Christ,
Can heal my bruised soul;
Thy stripes, not mine, contain
The balm that makes me whole.

To whom save Thee, who canst alone
For sin atone, Lord, shall I flee?
Thy cross, not mine, O Christ,
Has borne the awe-full load
Of sins that none could bear
But the incarnate God.
To whom save Thee, who canst alone
For sin atone, Lord, shall I flee?
Thy death, not mine, O Christ,
Has paid the ransom due;
Ten thousand deaths like mine
Would have been all too few.
To whom save Thee, who canst alone
For sin atone, Lord, shall I flee?
Thy righteousness, O Christ,
Alone can cover me;
No righteousness avails
Save that which is of Thee.
To whom save Thee, who canst alone
For sin atone, Lord, shall I flee

Think about these words by Alan Redpath in *Victorious Christian Living*: "Are you committed one hundred per cent to living a holy life? Have you determined to put away all revealed sin? Have you determined to ally yourself by faith with the Christ of absolute authority? If you have, once again the Church of the Lord Jesus Christ can take up the sword and, in the language of the Old Testament, brandish it and say, The sword of the Lord and of Gideon. "I will build my church, said the Lord Jesus, and the gates of hell shall not prevail against it" (Matthew 16:18). An ordinary girl, sitting at a typewriter in her office and thinking she is not able to do much about the Lord's work, can, if she is linked with the Lord in heaven, give testimony that is irresistible. A man who works in a factory five days a week, amid obscene and blasphemous company and almost in despair that nothing ever seems to happen for the Lord, may realize that faith is not only looking back to Calvary but also looking up to the throne, and so begin to derive heavenly power and to count for God. To an educated boy or girl, treating to teach a little handful of youngsters in Sunday school and wondering how it can be done, may come a moment in experience when he or she is linked with the living Christ on His throne, and God begins to work and the Jerichos begin to fall. To a simple housewife whose husband has refused for years to accept Christ, and whose home has been divided, may come one day the realization that her faith is in an omnipotent Lord, and that faith linked to omnipotence becomes mighty and powerful. Then God begins to do what He could not do for a lifetime, and the man is saved. All that God asks from us is to take the Lord Jesus Christ into the heart of the church so that every member of it may be linked with the throne. If we are made captive by a living Christ, then God begins to work. Revival comes, and lives are blessed. So souls are saved, and the church moves on like a mighty army!"[16]

There's a Man in the glory
Whose Life is for me,
He's pure and He's holy,
Triumphant and free.
He's wise and He's loving,
Tender is He;
And His Life in the Glory
My life must be.

There's a Man in the Glory
Whose Life is for me,
He overcame Satan;
From bondage He's free.
In life He is reigning,
Kingly is He;
And His Life in the Glory
My life must be.

There's a Man in the Glory
Whose Life is for me,
In Him is no sickness:
No weakness has He,
He's strong and in vigour,

Buoyant is He;
And His Life in the Glory
My life may be.

There's a Man in the Glory
Whose Life is for me.
His peace is abiding;
Patient is He.
He's joyful and radiant,
Expecting to see
His Life in the Glory
Lived out in me.[17]

RUTH PAXSON IN RIVERS OF LIVING WATER

Viewer Guide
WEKE SIX
WEEK SIX

The Life-Changing Power Of Jesus Christ

In Week Six of *A Heart On Fire*, you had the opportunity to study what it really means to know Christ and be united with Him. How will knowing Him change your life? That's what I want to discuss with you today. So grab your Bibles, and let's study God's Word together.

"Therefore, I urge you, brethren, by the mercies of God, to present your bodies a living and holy sacrifice, acceptable to God, which is your spiritual service of worship. And do not be conformed to this world, but be transformed by the renewing of your mind, so that you may prove what the will of God is, that which is good and acceptable and perfect" (Romans 12:1-2).

What kind of change does God want to make in your life?

1. A _____change.

2. A _____change.

3. A _____change.

4. A _____change.

5. A _____change.

Are you growing in your relationship with Christ?

So often we just want the circumstances of our lives changed. But what we don't realize is that God is more concerned with transforming _____ than our circumstances. And often, he will use the circumstances of our lives as tools to bring about the transformation that He desires in us.

"For the eyes of the LORD move to and fro throughout the earth that He may strongly support those whose heart is completely His" (2 Chronicles 16:9)

❧   *Video messages are available on DVDs or as Downloadable M4V Video. Audio messages are available on Audio CDs or as Downloadable MP3 Audio. Visit the Quiet Time Ministries Online Store at www.quiettime.org.*

HE IS YOUR INTERCESSOR

Hebrews 7:25

Therefore He is able also to save forever those who draw near to God through Him, since He always lives to make intercession for them.

HEBREWS 7:25

FOR GOD THE FATHER

*Therefore, holy brethren, partakers of a heavenly calling, consider Jesus, the Apostle
and High Priest of our confession; He was faithful to Him who appointed Him*

HEBREWS 3:1-2

PREPARE YOUR HEART

And now it is your privilege to walk on more holy ground as you gaze at another facet of
the character and person of your Lord Jesus Christ. He is your great High Priest and your
Intercessor. The writer of Hebrews tells us that "He always lives to make intercession for you"
(Hebrews 7:25). Oh, what an amazing truth this is. As your Intercessor, He carries you into the
very throne room of God. F.B. Meyer says that "He stands for us with God, and for God with us."[1]
You need to know today that Jesus is for you. You are never alone and He is intimately involved
with you. He intercedes for your temptations, sins, weaknesses, and needs. He mediates a new
covenant and ushers in a new kingdom. All these truths and more are yours to discover in your
quiet times this week.

You are going to look at realities this week that will revolutionize your life. An inner revolution
begins when your mind and heart connect the statements of fact in God's Word with a realization
that they are true. It is that moment when you leap out of your chair and shout with joy, "It really
is true!" You are so convinced that you begin "writing checks" on the promises of God, counting on their truth. If you had a million dollars in your checking account yet never spent any of
it, then it really is of no use to you. The moment you begin to write checks, you begin to benefit
from what is in the account. The bottom line is that you can count on the promises of God. Write
the check—act on God's promises. He who promised is faithful (Hebrews 10:25). Not only that,
"for as many as are the promises of God, in Him they are yes; therefore also through Him is our
Amen to the glory of God through us" (2 Corinthians 1:20).

"Consider Jesus" is the exhortation of Hebrews 3:1. This word was one used by the astrono-
mers who would gaze with great concentration at the sky to discover as much as possible about
the stars. In the same way, your goal is to contemplate with patience and perseverance the beauty
of your Lord as Apostle and High Priest. These names of Jesus reveal His work on our behalf. As
Apostle, He goes to men on behalf of God and as High Priest, He goes to God on behalf of men.

He performs these functions as an accomplishment of the will of the Father. You can count on Him for He is faithful. Today you are going to begin to look at how Jesus is your intercessor. You need to know this as a reality. And as you count on this promise, you will be ushered into the very throne room of God. Begin your time with the Lord meditating on these words by Gerhard Tersteegen (1697-1769):

> God reveals His presence:
> Let us now adore Him,
> And with awe appear before Him.
> God is in His temple:
> All within keep silence,
> Prostrate lie with deepest reverence.
> Him alone
> God we own,
> Him our God and Saviour:
> Praise His Name forever!

READ AND STUDY GOD'S WORD

1. This week you are going to have the opportunity to spend some time in the letter to the Hebrews. The author of this letter is unknown. Some say it was Paul or possibly Apollos. It was someone who was a brilliant thinker and very familiar with the Old Testament. Hebrews was written to Jews and its purpose is to answer the question: *What is the relationship of Christ and Christianity to Judaism?* This was extremely relevant as Judaism was the religion with the one true God. The Epistle (letter) of Hebrews deals with the relationship of Christ to the Jewish religious ordinances, offerings, priesthood, and the temple. And what is the answer in Hebrews? Jesus is better. Not only is He better, He is the best. You will notice the repeated word "better" throughout Hebrews. He is better than angels, better than Moses, ministers in a better sanctuary, and mediates a better covenant. Jesus is seen in Hebrews as our High Priest. As such, He is your intercessor. In Hebrews, you see that Jesus functions as your intercessor for many reasons. Today you are going to see that He is an intercessor for God the Father. He is doing what the Father has asked Him to do.

As you begin your study this week, you are going to take an overview journey through Hebrews looking at various passages. Read these verses in Hebrews and write your insights related to who Jesus is and what He does and has done:

Hebrews 1:1-4

Hebrews 2:9

Hebrews 2:17-18

Hebrews 7:24-28

Hebrews 8:1-6

Hebrews 9:15

Hebrews 10:14

Optional Verses: Hebrews 3:1-6, 4:14, 5:1-10, 6:19-20

2. Isaiah 53:11-12 tells us that the Messiah (Jesus) would "justify the many," "bear their iniquities," and intercede for the transgressors. With this in mind and considering what you've learned in Hebrews, why is Jesus, as your High Priest, better than the Old Testament priests?

3. Optional: Hebrews 3:1-6 compares the ministry of Jesus with that of Moses. According to Exodus 40:16, Moses did all that the Lord commanded him. He was faithful to the Lord. He went to God on behalf of the people. Read Numbers 14:11-20 and record what you learn from the intercession of Moses for the people of Israel.

4. Optional: In the Old Testament, the High Priest would make atonement for the sins of the people through animal sacrifices on the altar. The blood would satisfy God's requirement of a penalty of death to be paid for sin, but only temporarily. Sacrifices needed to be made continually. Look at the following verses and record what you learn about the Old Testament function of the priest. Exodus 40:1-16, Numbers 15:28, Leviticus 1

ADORE GOD IN PRAYER

Will you draw near to Jesus, your great High Priest? In Hebrews 10:22 you are encouraged to "draw near with a sincere heart in full assurance of faith." Because Jesus was faithful, you can draw near no matter what you have done. "If we confess our sins, He is faithful and righteous to forgive us our sins and to cleanse us from all unrighteousness" (1 John 1:9). Confession means saying the same that God says about your sin. This means that when you draw near to God, you need to call those things that offend God "sin". As Corrie Ten Boom used to say, "God never cleanses excuses, only sin." Will you bring your sin to Him today? He lives that your sin might be forgiven and that you might be cleansed, pure and holy. Don't be afraid. He loves you more than life itself. He proved it by going all the way to the cross to die for you. Now He lives to intercede for you in every way, even in prayer.

YIELD YOURSELF TO GOD

There never was a beginning to the priestliness of our Saviour's heart. There is no date in heaven's calendar for the uprising within him of mercy and pity, and of the intention to stand as the Advocate and Intercessor for our race. Before the mountains were brought forth, or the heavens and earth were made, there was already in his thoughts the germ of that marvelous drama which is slowly unfolding before the gaze of the universe. He was priest, as well as the Lamb slain, from before the foundation of the world. Love is eternal. Sacrifice is one of the root principles of the being of God. Priesthood is part of the texture of the nature of the Second Person in the adorable Trinity. There need be no fear, therefore, that he will ever desert his office; or lay it aside for some other purpose; or cease to have compassion on the ignorant and erring, the tempted and fallen.[2]

F.B. MEYER IN THE WAY INTO THE HOLIEST

Our Lord's life in heaven is the life of one who has been brought back from the death which he endured when he gave himself as a sacrifice for his people's sins. In the language of the Apocalypse, it is as the Lamb once slain that he exercises world dominion from the heavenly throne (Revelation 5:6-14). The appearance in God's presence of the Crucified One constitutes his perpetual and prevalent intercession. His once-completed self-offering is utterly acceptable and efficacious; his contact with the Father is immediate and unbroken; his priestly ministry on his people's behalf is never ending, and therefore the salvation which he secures to them is absolute.[3]

F.F. BRUCE IN THE EPISTLE TO THE HEBREWS

As Son, Christ alone was heir of all that God had. All the life of the Father was in Him. God could have no union or fellowship with any creature but through His beloved Son or as far as the life and spirit and image of the Son was seen in it. Therefore no one could be our High Priest but the Son of God. If our salvation was not to be a merely legal one—external and, I may say, artificial—but an entrance anew into the very life of God, with the restoration of the divine nature we had lost in paradise, it was the Son of God alone who could impart this to us. He had the life of God to give; He was able to give it; He could only give it by taking us into living fellowship with Himself. The priesthood of Christ is the God-devised channel through which the ever-blessed Son could make us partakers of Himself, and with Himself of all the life and glory He hath from and in the Father. And this now is our confidence and safety—that it was the Father who appointed the Son High Priest. It is the love of the God against whom we had sinned that gave the Son. It is the will and the power of this God that ordained and worked out the great salvation. It is in God Himself our salvation has its origin, its life, its power. It is God drawing nigh to communicate Himself to us in His Son.[4]

ANDREW MURRAY IN THE HOLIEST OF ALL

ENJOY HIS PRESENCE

Will you close today by pouring out your heart to the Lord in gratitude that He is so much, so big, and immeasurably more than you can imagine? You may wish to write a brief prayer expressing your love for Him.

Jesus, I Consider
Words cannot express,
Or my tongue confess,
The gratitude of heart -
That I've been made a part,
Of Your divine family:
Heaven's own economy.
All my sins forgiven,
Access freely given,
To see my Father's face
And glory in His grace.

Lord Jesus Christ, the Author
Whose place upon the altar,
Obtained life for eternity;
Intercedes with all authority.
Prayers taken and perfected,
Then offered and accepted.
So, Lord Jesus, I consider.
Focus fixed! The race, a winner.
I'll lay my crown before Thee,
For You secured my victory.[5]

CONNI HUDSON

REST IN HIS LOVE

"Every priest stands daily ministering and offering time after time the same sacrifices which can never take away sins; but He, having offered one sacrifice for sins for all time, SAT DOWN AT THE RIGHT HAND OF GOD" (Hebrews 10:11-12).

FOR YOUR SINS AND TEMPTATIONS

Therefore, He had to be made like His brethren in all things, so that He might become a merciful and faithful high priest in things pertaining to God, to make propitiation for the sins of the people. For since He Himself was tempted in that which He has suffered, He is able to come to the aid of those who are tempted.

HEBREWS 2:17-18

PREPARE YOUR HEART

Samuel Logan Brengle was Commissioner of the Salvation Army. He experienced a season in life of deep hunger for holiness. He felt as though he was his own worst enemy. He became painfully aware of the purity of Jesus and his own sin. He began to hate himself for his sin. One day he came across 1 John 1:9: "If we confess our sins, He is faithful and righteous to forgive us our sins and to cleanse us from all unrighteousness." This one verse helped him realized that the blood of Christ cleansed him from all his sins.

Do you realize the truth of Christ's payment and cleansing for your sin? If you will write the check and claim the promise you will walk in victory in your life. Most try to handle sin by hanging on to guilt. They figure that if they hang on to the sin and pay for it with guilt, after awhile they will feel better about their sin. Your feeling of guilt does not appease God for your sin. Only your great High Priest Jesus can intercede for your sin. You must accept that and deal with sin only one way. Run to the Lord with it. And do it immediately. Don't wait. Accept His payment for your sin. Receive His forgiveness. He delights to have you run to Him in this way. As you confess your sin to Him, He is faithful. He will forgive your sin and cleanse you from all unrighteousness. His Blood shed on the cross did everything on your behalf. It purchased your pardon, satisfied the requirement of God, and it makes you holy today. There's power in the blood of the Lord Jesus Christ.

Ask God to quiet your heart today and to open your eyes that you might behold wonderful things in His Word. Write a prayer today giving the Lord everything that is troubling your heart. Ask Him to lighten those burdens, so that you might run the race and fix your eyes on Him.

READ AND STUDY GOD'S WORD

1. As you continue on in your journey to discover all that Jesus is as your intercessor, turn to Hebrews 2:17-18. What do you learn about Jesus in these verses?

2. Hebrews 2:17-18 says that Jesus suffered when He was tempted, and is a merciful and faithful high priest. In Hebrews 4:15 we see that He sympathizes with our weaknesses because He was tempted in every way, yet without sin. Read the following verses and write your insights related to the temptation and suffering of Jesus.

Matthew 4:1

Matthew 27:45-50

Mark 14:32-42, 48-50

Optional Verses: Luke 22:39-46, Luke 22:54-62

3. Throughout Scripture, we see that we have an enemy who tries to keep us from standing firm and who wants to discourage our faith (see Ephesians 6:10-13, 1 Peter 5:8-11). However, you have an intercessor, Jesus, Who prays for you. Write your insights as to what Jesus prays as you examine the following passages of Scripture.

Luke 22:31-32

John 17:15-19

4. What comfort does it bring to you to know that the Lord Jesus sympathizes with your weaknesses, intercedes for you, and is praying for you today?

ADORE GOD IN PRAYER

Think about all you have learned about Jesus. Think about how He knows what it is to be tempted, to suffer, and to be abandoned by those He loves. He knows what it is to be weak and to feel forsaken by God. There are things that burden your heart even now. Will you bring these to Jesus, who ever lives to make intercession for you? Perhaps there are those in your life who are struggling right now, maybe even wrestling with a sin. Will you pray for them as well? You may wish to use your prayer pages to record your requests.

YIELD YOURSELF TO GOD

Our warfare is not against flesh and blood, but against principalities and powers. One day He, our High Priest, after the garden, the Cross, and the tomb, rose in triumph and spoiled our enemy. He repulsed every attack of Satan, and He rose, our victorious, conquering, coming King. Hallelujah! And to all that pass through the waters He said, I will be with thee, and the river shall not overflow thee. The floods, the opposition of principalities and powers to the child of God, can never get past what our triumphant Lord Jesus conquered.[6]

ALAN REDPATH IN VICTORIOUS CHRISTIAN LIVING

Eyes may light on these words, weary with weeping, of those who have been reduced well-nigh to despair through the greatness and virulence of their sins. Not only does the record of the past seem too black to be forgiven, but old habits are perpetually reasserting themselves; ridiculing the most steadfast resolutions, and smiting the inner life of the soul down to the ground…But the greatness of our sin is always less than the greatness of God's grace. Where the one abounds, the other much more abounds. If we go down to the bottoms of the mountains and touch the heart of the deep, deeper than all is the redeeming mercy of God. The love and grace and power of Jesus are more than our unutterable necessities. Only trust him, he is able to save unto the uttermost (Hebrews 7:25); and he is as willing as able.[7]

F.B. MEYER IN THE WAY INTO THE HOLIEST

Glory be to God for the wondrous picture of what our Lord Jesus is. A priest must be God's representative with men. But he cannot be this, without being himself a man himself encompassed with weaknesses, and so identified with and representing men with God. This was why Jesus was made a little lower than the angels…Jesus could not ascend the throne as Priest, until He had first, in the school of personal experience, learnt to sympathize and to bear gently with the feeblest. And let our weakness and ignorance henceforth, instead of discouraging and keeping us back, be the motive and the pleas which lead us to come boldly to Him for help, who can bear gently with the ignorant and erring. In the pursuit of holiness our ignorance is often our greatest source of failure. We cannot fully understand what is taught of the rest of God, and the power of faith, of dwelling within the veil or of Christ dwelling in our heart. Things appear too high for us, utterly beyond our reach. If we but knew to trust Jesus, not only as He who made propitiation for our sins, but as one who has been specially chosen and trained and prepared, and then elevated to the throne of God, to be the Leader of the ignorant and erring, bearing gently with their every weakness! Let us this day afresh accept this Savior, as God here revealed Him to us, and rejoice that all our ignorance need not be a barrier in the way to God, because Jesus takes it into His care.[8]

ANDREW MURRAY IN THE HOLIEST OF ALL

O sufferers, tempted ones, desolate and not comforted, lean your heads against the breast of the God-Man, whose feet have trodden each inch of your thorny path; and whose experiences of the power of evil well qualify him to strengthen you to stand, to lift you up if you have fallen, to speak such words as will heal the ache of the freshly gaping wound. If he were impassive, and had never wept or fought in the Garden shadows, or cried out forsaken on the cross, we had not felt him so near as we can do now in all hours of bitter grief. O matchless Saviour, on whom God our Father has laid our help, we can dispense with human sympathy, with priestly help, with the solace and stay of many a holy service; but thou art indispensable to us, in thy life, and death, and resurrection, and brotherhood, and sympathizing intercession at the throne of God.[9]

F.B. MEYER IN THE WAY INTO THE HOLIEST

ENJOY HIS PRESENCE

Do you see Jesus interceding for you even in the darkest times of your life? You are never alone in your weakness or temptation. Jesus is always there interceding for you. Think of Him as your greatest ally, your champion, the one who fights on your behalf, and who stands with you no matter what enemy attempts to assail you. And when you sin, you can count on His blood to cleanse you of it. Boldly draw near and confess your sin and receive forgiveness, knowing that He ever lives to do exactly that. Close your time alone with God by meditating on these words by William Cowper (1731-1800).

There is a fountain filled with blood
drawn from Emmanuel's veins;
and sinners plunged beneath that flood
lose all their guilty stains.
Lose all their guilty stains,
lose all their guilty stains;
and sinners plunged beneath that flood
lose all their guilty stains.
The dying thief rejoiced to see
that fountain in his day;
and there may I, though vile as he,
wash all my sins away.
Wash all my sins away,
wash all my sins away;
and there may I, though vile as he,
wash all my sins away.

Dear dying Lamb, thy precious blood
shall never lose its power
till all the ransomed church of God
be saved, to sin no more.

Be saved, to sin no more,
be saved, to sin no more;
till all the ransomed church of God
be saved, to sin no more.

E'er since, by faith, I saw the stream
thy flowing wounds supply,
redeeming love has been my theme,
and shall be till I die.
And shall be till I die,
and shall be till I die;
redeeming love has been my theme,
and shall be till I die.

Then in a nobler, sweeter song,
I'll sing thy power to save,
when this poor lisping, stammering tongue
lies silent in the grave.
Lies silent in the grave,
lies silent in the grave;
when this poor lisping, stammering tongue
lies silent in the grave.

REST IN HIS LOVE

"For it was fitting for us to have such a high priest, holy, innocent, undefiled, separated from sinners and exalted above the heavens; who does not need daily, like those high priests, to offer up sacrifices, first for His own sins and then for the sins of the people, because this He did once for all when He offered up Himself" (Hebrews 7:26-27).

FOR YOUR TIME OF NEED

For we do not have a high priest who cannot sympathize with our weaknesses, but one who has been tempted in all things as we are, yet without sin. Therefore let us draw near with confidence to the throne of grace, so that we may receive mercy and find grace to help in time of need.

HEBREWS 4:15-16

PREPARE YOUR HEART

Those who have accomplished the most for the sake of God's kingdom have been the ones who have endured the most pain and adversity. They have been enabled, by the grace of God, to be more than conquerors through Him who loved us (Romans 8:37). This has been especially true of many of the hymn writers. Fanny Crosby, who wrote over eight thousand hymns, was blind for almost her entire life. Annie Johnson Flint, who wrote over six thousand hymns, was an orphan, lived with crippling arthritis, and then was stricken with cancer. And yet, Annie knew what it was to draw near to the throne of grace. In fact, you might say she was intimate with His grace. She wrote the following words:

> He giveth more grace as the burdens grow greater,
> He sendeth more strength when the labors increase,
> To added afflictions He addeth His mercy,
> To multiplied trials His multiplied peace.[10]

Do you know His grace today? Have you run to His throne of grace to find His mercy and grace to help you in your time of need? Ask God to speak to you as you draw near to Him today.

READ AND STUDY GOD'S WORD

1. One powerful truth that you discover about Jesus your intercessor is that He is always available with help for your every need. Turn to Hebrews 4:13-16 and record everything you learn about the Lord and what He encourages you to do in your time of need.

2. The way is open to the throne of grace. This is an incredible truth made possible because of what your High Priest has done. In the Old Testament tabernacle a curtain (veil) separated the Holy Place from the Most Holy Place. The ark of the covenant was placed in the Most Holy Place (Exodus 26:30-33). Only the High Priest could enter the Holy of Holies and he could enter only once a year on the Day of Atonement (Leviticus 16).[11] Later, the temple, built with the same specifications, replaced the tabernacle. According to Edersheim, the veil that separated the Holy Place from the Most Holy Place in the temple was 60 feet long, 20 feet wide, and as thick as the palm of a hand. It was so heavy that it needed approximately 300 priests to manipulate it.[12]

With this in mind, read Mark 15:33-39 and record what happened when Jesus died on the cross.

4. What did Jesus' death on the cross accomplish and what was the significance of the veil into the Most Holy Place torn in two from top to bottom? The Most Holy Place in the temple was the place where God dwelt and was only entered once a year by the high priest when he sacrificed for the people of Israel. Note that the veil was torn from top to bottom—only God could do this significant and powerful work. Read the following verses and record your insights about what Jesus accomplished as your intercessor, your great and merciful high priest:

Hebrews 9:11-14

Hebrews 9:24-28

Hebrews 10:18-22

Optional Verses: Hebrews 4:14, 8:1-2

5. According to Hebrews 4:16, when you run to God you will receive mercy and grace. Mercy is *eleos* in the Greek and means "special and immediate regard to the misery which is the consequence of sins."[13] Grace is *charis* and means "unearned and unmerited favor; absolute freeness of the lovingkindness of God to men finding its only motive in the bounty and freeheartedness of the Giver."[14] What do you learn about mercy and grace in the following verses?

Ephesians 2:4-9

1 Peter 5:10

6. Optional: What does grace in action from the throne of God look like? Look at Acts 7:54-60 and note how Stephen found grace in his time of need.

ADORE GOD IN PRAYER

Run to the Lord's throne of grace now. Take each need that you have and lay it at His feet. You may wish to use your prayer pages to record your requests. As you draw near to the Lord in prayer, pray through these words by Horatio Bonar (1857):

Thy way, not mine, O Lord,
However dark it be.
Lead me by Thine own hand;
Choose Thou the path for me.
Smooth let it be or rough,
It will be still the best;
Winding or straight, it leads
Right onward to Thy rest.
I dare not choose my lot;
I would not if I might.
Choose Thou for me, my God;
So shall I walk aright.
The kingdom that I seek
Is Thine; so let the way

That leads to it be Thine
Else I must surely stray
Take Thou my cup and it
With joy or sorrow fill,
As best to Thee may seem;
Choose Thou my good and ill.
Choose Thou for me my friends,
My sickness or my health;
Choose Thou my cares for me,
My poverty or wealth.
Not mine, not mine, the choice,
In things or great or small;
Be Thou my Guide, my Strength,
My Wisdom, and my All.

YIELD YOURSELF TO GOD

In Christ we are presented by our Great High Priest before the throne in our prayers and in our worship, and we are accepted for His sake, even as He Himself is accepted. He hands over the petition in your name, and puts His name on the back; and your prayers go to the Father as if He were asking. He is in His very person and character your Representative.[15]

A.B. SIMPSON IN THE CHRIST LIFE

The only difference between nature and grace is this, that what the trees and the flowers do unconsciously, as they drink in the blessing of the light, is to be with us a voluntary and a loving acceptance. Faith, simple faith in God's Word and love, is to be the opening of the eyes, the opening of the heart, to receive and enjoy the unspeakable glory of His grace. And just as the trees, day by day, and month by month, stand and grow into beauty and fruitfulness, just welcoming whatever sunshine the sun may give, so it is the very highest exercise of our Christian life just to abide in the light of God, and let it, and let Him, fill us with the life and the brightness it brings.[16]

ANDREW MURRAY IN WAITING ON GOD

Fellow-laborers in His vineyard, it is quite evident that our Master desires us to ask, and to ask much. He tells us we glorify God by doing so! Nothing is beyond the scope of prayer which is not beyond the will of God…Let us get a fresh vision of Christ in all His glory, and a fresh glimpse of all the riches of His glory which He places at our disposal, and of all the mighty power given unto Him. Then let us get a fresh vision of the world and all its needs. (And the world was never so needy as it is today.) Why, the wonder is not that we pray so little, but that we can ever get up from our knees if we realize our own needs; the needs of our home and our loved ones; the needs of our pastor and the Church; the needs of our city—of our country…All these needs can be met by the riches of God in Christ Jesus.[17]

AN UNKNOWN CHRISTIAN IN THE KNEELING CHRISTIAN

Is your place a small place?
Tend it with care!—
He set you there.
Is your place a large place?
Guard it with care!
He set you there.
Whate'er your place, it is
Not yours alone, but His.
He set you there.[18]

JOHN OXENHAM IN SPRINGS IN THE VALLEY

If instead of being a poor man you had been rich, if instead of being a lone woman you had had one to call you wife, and little children to clutch your dress and call you mother; if instead of being tied to the office-stool you had been a minister or missionary, you think that you would have been a better, a sweeter character. But I want you to understand that God chose for you your lot in life out of myriads that were open to Him, because just where you are you might realize your noblest possibilities. Otherwise God would have made you different from what you are. But your soul, born into His kingdom, was a matter of care and thought to Him, how best He might nurture you; and He chose your lot with its irritations, its difficulties, all the agony that eats out your nature. Though men and women do not guess it, He chose it just as it is, because in it, if you will let Him, He can realize the fairest life within your reach.[19]

F.B. MEYER IN THE CHRIST LIFE FOR YOUR LIFE

ENJOY HIS PRESENCE

What are your needs today? Will you realize that they are not liabilities but actually the platform upon which the Lord desires to do a mighty work. Is He worried? Is He anxious? Is He wondering what is He going to do? Not at all. He is waiting for you to draw near to the throne of grace that you might find help in time of need. He is merciful and He is mighty, absolutely able to handle all that comes your way today. Nothing is so great, that He is not greater. Give all your worries and cares to God, for he cares about what happens to you (1 Peter 5:7 NLT). How do you need God's mercy and grace today? Write a prayer to the Lord, expressing all that is on your heart.

God hath not promised skies always blue
Flower strewn pathways,
All our lives through;
God hath not promised sun without rain
Joy without sorrow
Peace without pain.

But God hath promised
Strength for the day
Rest for the labour,
Light for the way
Grace for the trials,
Help from above
Unfailing sympathy
Undying love.[20]

ANNIE JOHNSON FLINT

REST IN HIS LOVE

"In His kindness God called you to His eternal glory by means of Jesus Christ. After you have suffered a little while, He will restore, support, and strengthen you, and He will place you on a firm foundation. All power is His forever and ever" (1 Peter 5:10-11 NLT).

FOR THE NEW COVENANT

But now He has obtained a more excellent ministry, by as much as He is also the mediator of a better covenant, which has been enacted on better promises.

HEBREWS 8:6

PREPARE YOUR HEART

In his classic book, *Pilgrim's Progress*, John Bunyan describes the plight of a man, clothed with rags and a great burden on his back. The burden became so heavy that this man would do anything to get rid of it. His plight is descriptive of the entire human race. The burden man carries is sin and its penalty. Without a savior to lift the burden, mankind will be crushed by the burden.

Nowhere is this burden seen more clearly than among the people of Israel before Jesus came to earth. Year after year, they made their way to the temple in Jerusalem to make offerings for their sins. Can you just imagine trudging along the road with the knowledge that you would have to go again and again? There was no real sense of peace or reconciliation with God. And there was no ability to live a righteous life in the company of God. There was no true intimate experience of God for there was no permanent indwelling of the Holy Spirit. There was the promise from God of something better that was still to come. But it was only a promise, not an experience. At least not yet.

God gave the Law to Moses on Mount Sinai. This law was given to the people of Israel as the stipulation of their relationship with God. It was known as the Old Covenant and it was holy, righteous and good. The problem was that the people could not keep it because of their sin. Paul tells us in Romans that no one is righteous and that no one seeks God (Romans 3:11-12). This is the description of the depravity of man. He concludes in Romans 3:20 (NIV): "Therefore no one will be declared righteous in his sight by observing the law, rather, through the law we become conscious of sin." How true this is. The natural tendency of men and women is to break the law. In James 2:10 we see that "whoever keeps the whole law and yet stumbles in one point, he has become guilty of all." Sounds like a hopeless situation, but it is not. There is one reason why it is not hopeless: Jesus is your Intercessor and mediates a New Covenant. According to Hebrews 8:6-7, now He has obtained a more excellent ministry, by as much as He is also the mediator of a better covenant, which has been enacted on better promises. For if the first covenant had been faultless, there would have been no occasion sought for a second. The writer of Hebrews goes on to show that the fault was in man, and so the Lord promised a new covenant that would make the old one obsolete (Hebrews 8:13).

Oh happy day it was when the veil of the temple was rent in two from top to bottom and the way was made clear to the presence of God. That same day the New Covenant was enacted. And its promises are true for all who say yes to it and receive Jesus Christ as Savior and Lord.

Today is a day to say "thank you Lord" for doing what you could never do and making the way clear to know God and experience an eternal, intimate relationship with Him. Today is a day to throw off any burden of sin that may be weighing you down and enter into the liberation of the easy, gracious relationship with God that is yours in Jesus Christ. Will you begin your time with the Lord in solitude, thinking on these truths, and then telling the Lord how much you love Him?

READ AND STUDY GOD'S WORD

1. 1. Jeremiah has been called the Weeping Prophet because of the sorrow and suffering he endured as God's servant among the people of God. Perhaps that is why God gave him one of the brightest lights of promise in all of the Old Testament: the new covenant. Read Jeremiah 31:31-34 and record everything you learn about the new covenant.

2. Read the following verses in Hebrews and record your most significant insights about the old covenant (the Law) and the new covenant.

Old Covenant (Law)	New Covenant (Grace)
Hebrews 8:6	
Hebrews 8:13	

Old Covenant (Law)	New Covenant (Grace)
Hebrews 9:1, 7-8, 13-15	
Hebrews 10:1, 8-10, 15-18	

3. The promise from God of the new covenant in Jeremiah 31:33-34 says that "God will put His laws in your mind and write them on your heart. He will be your God and you will belong to Him. You will know Him, He will forgive your wickedness, and will never again remember your sins" (NLT). This is such an incredible promise. How is it that God can put His laws in your mind and write them on your heart? How can all of this actually take place? First, because of the work of your intercessor, Jesus Christ, and then, because of the work of the Holy Spirit. Read Ezekiel 36:26-27 and record what you learn.

4. God gives us His Holy Spirit as part of the new covenant. Through the Holy Spirit, we are placed in Christ and He in us. This is how we are united with Christ. This is how His law is written in our hearts. This is how all that is Christ's becomes ours. Read through these verses and underline those words and phrases that are most significant to you.

"If the Spirit of him who raised Jesus from the dead is living in you, He who raised Christ from the dead will also give life to your mortal bodies through His Spirit, who lives in you" (Romans 8:11 NIV)

"You show that you are a letter from Christ, the result of our ministry, written not with ink but with the Spirit of the living God, not on tablets of stone but on tablets of human hearts…He has made us competent as ministers of a new covenant— not of the letter but of the Spirit; for the letter kills, but the Spirit gives life…will not the ministry of the Spirit be even more glorious? If the ministry that condemns men is glorious, how much more glorious is the ministry that brings righteousness" (2 Corinthians 3:3-6, 8-9 NIV).

ADORE GOD IN PRAYER

But I have seen a fiery flame
Take to his pure and burning heart
Mere dust of earth, to it impart
His virtue, till that dust became
Transparent loveliness of flame.

O Fire of God, Thou fervent Flame,
Thy dust of earth in Thee would fall,
And so be lost beyond recall,
Transformed by Thee, its very name
Forgotten in Thine own, O Flame.[21]

AMY CARMICHAEL IN TOWARD JERUSALEM

YIELD YOURSELF TO GOD

The soul that receives the Holy Spirit in all His fullness will find the providence of God keeping pace with His inward blessing, and the grace that we have experienced in our heart will reflect it in all our outward life. The King that reigns supreme upon the throne of the heart will sway His scepter around the whole circle of our life, and bring into subjection everything that hurts or hinders us…The blessings of God's providence are inseparably connected with the indwelling of His Spirit and the experience of His sanctifying grace. It is only to those who love God and are the called according to His purpose (Romans 8:28) that all things work together for good. They know that they work together for good. It is not a struggle to believe it. It is not a desperate effort to count it. When we walk with Him in holy trust and obedience, the inmost consciousness of our spiritual being bears witness to the promise, and we know without doubt or fear that all things are ours, for we are Christ's and Christ is God's.[22]

A.B. SIMPSON IN THE HOLY SPIRIT

Let us look up to the Mediator of the covenant, our High Priest upon the throne in the heavens. When He was with His disciples on earth, the law was not yet put into their hearts. How often they failed in humility and love and boldness. But when He sat down upon the throne, He sent down the Holy Spirit from heaven in their hearts, and all was new. They were full of humility and love and great boldness. The law of God was in their hearts as the power of a life that knew, and loved, and did His will. Christ dwelt in their hearts by faith. The power of the endless life from the throne of God had taken possession of them. Oh, let us not doubt. Let us plead God's promise, I will make a new covenant. Let us trust God's Son, the surety of the covenant, and receive God's Spirit—we shall be brought into the covenant, and into the sanctuary together, and have grace to continue, to abide continually.[23]

ANDREW MURRAY IN THE HOLIEST OF ALL

ENJOY HIS PRESENCE

What is the most profound truth you have learned today? Close by writing a prayer to the Lord, thanking Him for who He is and for all that He has shown you about Himself and His awesome plan for you.

REST IN HIS LOVE

"But when the Holy Spirit controls our lives, he will produce this kind of fruit in us: love, joy, peace, patience, kindness, goodness, faithfulness, gentleness, and self-control. Here there is no conflict with the law. Those who belong to Christ Jesus have nailed the passions and desires of their sinful nature to his cross and crucified them there. If we are living now by the Holy Spirit, let us follow the Holy Spirit's leading in every part of our lives" (Galatians 5:22-23 NLT).

FOR THE UNSHAKEABLE KINGDOM

Therefore, since we receive a kingdom which cannot be shaken, let us show gratitude,
by which we may offer to God an acceptable service with reverence and awe.

HEBREWS 12:28

PREPARE YOUR HEART

One of the favorite fairy tales of all time is Cinderella. And the moral of the story is that dreams can come true. Cinderella is a girl who had very few, if any, resources of her own. One night she was transformed with beautiful clothes, and arrived at a dance hosted by the prince. He was overwhelmed with her beauty and they danced. The prince fell in love with Cinderella. Just before midnight, she ran away, knowing that when the clock struck twelve midnight, her clothes would change back to rags, and she would be who she was before. But the prince loved her and would not give up until he found her. All that he had was a glass slipper worn by his one true love. And so he searched far and wide throughout the land, trying the glass slipper on one girl after another. Finally, one day he slipped the glass slipper on the foot of the least likely of all, a young girl who does all the hard work in a house and sits for warmth in a corner of the chimney among the cinders. She had been treated harshly by her stepmother and stepsisters. But the slipper fit confirming her identity, and the prince rescued her from her harsh life, married her, and gave her a home in his kingdom. And the story ends the way we wish all stories should end: they lived happily ever after.

That is the fairy tale. But the fairy tail is but a shadow of our own story. For our Prince, the Lord Jesus Christ, has accomplished everything necessary to move us from the domain of darkness to His kingdom. The writer of Hebrews tells us that we are given "a kingdom which cannot be shaken" (Hebrews 12:28). What a promise especially in a world where there is nothing to count on and everything changes! There is never a day in this world where there is not a threat of danger or war or trial. Imagine a kingdom which cannot be shaken. That kingdom is now ours because of the work of our Lord Jesus Christ who is our High Priest, our intercessor. Ask Him now to speak to you as you draw near and spend quiet time alone with Him.

READ AND STUDY GOD'S WORD

1. The writer of Hebrews tells us that "since we are receiving a kingdom that cannot be shaken, let us be thankful, and so worship God acceptably with reverence and awe" (Hebrews 12:28). worship of God will increase the more we know about His kingdom. Jesus taught often about the kingdom of God while on earth. Read the following verses and record what you learn about the kingdom:

Matthew 6:33

Matthew 13:44-46

Luke 17:20-21

John 18:36-37

3. According to the promise of God in Colossians 1:13 you have been rescued from the domain of darkness and transferred to the kingdom of His beloved Son. Now, there is another truth that you need to know about what the Lord has accomplished related to the kingdom. Read Revelation 1:6 and record what you learn about the new responsibility that the Lord has given you as part of His kingdom.

4. You are a member of the kingdom of God and you have been assigned the service of a priest. A priest goes to men about God and to God about men. He has given you the task to tell others about Christ and then to intercede on their behalf in prayer and supplication. Look at the following verses and record what you learn about your new responsibilities:

2 Corinthians 5:20

Ephesians 6:18

5. Optional: Jesus was your example of a prayer warrior. What do you learn about his prayer life in Luke 5:15-16? How can you apply His example to your own life?

ADORE GOD IN PRAYER

What is your response to God as you learn about His unshakeable kingdom and your service to Him in the kingdom as a priest? Will you talk to Him now about your responsibility as an ambassador for Christ and an intercessor? Will you pray for those in your life today? You may wish to use your prayer pages to record your requests for those in your life.

YIELD YOURSELF TO GOD

> He shakes all things, that the material, the sensuous, and the temporal may pass away; leaving the essential and eternal to stand out in more than former beauty. But not a grain of pure metal shall be lost in the fires; not a fragment of heaven's masonry shall crumble beneath the shock…This world of change and earthquake is not our rest or home. These await us where God lives, in the city which hath foundations, and in the land where the storm rages not, but the sea of glass lies peacefully at the foot of the throne of God. We may well brace ourselves to fortitude and patience, to reverence and Godly fear; since we have that in ourselves and yonder which partakes of the nature of God, and neither thieving time can steal it, nor moth corrupt, nor change affect. It is out of a spirit like this that we are able to offer service that pleases God…when once we breathe the Spirit of the Eternal and Infinite, our hand becomes steadier, our heart quieter, and we learn to receive his grace. We do not agonize for it; we claim and use it, and we serve God with acceptance, through the merits of Jesus Christ our Lord.[24]
>
> F. B. MEYER IN THE WAY INTO THE HOLIEST

The best and most faithful intercessors I have met learned the holy art of intercession only after many trials or great suffering. All that some of them could do at last was to lie in bed, scarcely able to whisk a fly away from their faces…But how they could pray! Though they lay unseen by men, nevertheless they were centers of spiritual power, and by their simple and persevering prayers they were the chief supporters of the Christian work which was being done in their neighborhood, their community, their country and even to the ends of the earth.[25]

O'HALLESBY IN PRAYER

Christian, to all this you are come. Just as sure as you are come to God in the Holiest, to dwell with Him, you are come to all this, and dwell in the midst of it. God hath brought you to it by the Holy Spirit, and will, by the Holy Spirit, reveal it in your heart, so that you know the things which are freely given you of God. Can it be, that any are content to sleep on, while the call is heard: You are come to the heavenly Jerusalem—enter in and dwell here. There is no other choice—can it be that any will prefer to live under Sinai and its bondage? Can it be that any will count the price too great, and, because they love the world, refuse, with Abraham and Moses, to go out and live by faith, in this city of God. God forbid that it should be so with us. Let Zion, the city of God, with its heavenly joy, and its beauty of holiness, and its eternal life power, be the place of our abode. The Holy Spirit, sent down when Jesus had entered and opened the gates for us, brings down into our hearts the very life and light of heaven, brings us into the experience of it all.[26]

ANDREW MURRAY IN THE HOLIEST OF ALL

ENJOY HIS PRESENCE

You have had the opportunity to look at many aspects of the character of the Lord Jesus Christ this week. Each facet of His character is a profound revelation of the One with whom you are united. But the sum total of who He is can never be truly calculated because one cannot add together His infinite attributes. The only response for you when you see the beauty of His Person is worship, as you find your entire life defined in Him. Will you now just bow before Him in silence and behold His beauty?

REST IN HIS LOVE

"For He rescued us from the domain of darkness, and transferred us to the kingdom of His beloved Son" (Colossians 1:13).

DEVOTIONAL READING
BY HENRY GARIEPY

DEAR FRIEND,

The next two days are your opportunity to spend time reviewing what you learned this week. You may wish to write your thoughts and insights in your journal in the back of this study book. As you think about all that you have learned about Jesus as your Intercessor, what were your most meaningful discoveries?

Your most significant insight:

Your favorite quote:

Your favorite verse:

One of the primary functions of the high priest was intercession for the people. On his shoulders were 2 onyx stones with the names of the 12 tribes inscribed on them. Also, on his breastplate were 12 stones with the names of the 12 tribes. Israel was represented on the shoulders of his strength and the heart of his love. Christ, our Great High Priest, on the shoulders of His omnipotence and on His heart of infinite love carries our names and our needs into the presence of God.[27]

HENRY GARIEPY IN 100 PORTRAITS OF CHRIST

In all their afflictions He is afflicted, for He is touched with a feeling of our infirmities. This golden truth becomes most precious to the soul, when in the midst of losses and crosses, by the Holy Spirit's influence, the power of it is felt in the soul. A confident belief in the fact that Jesus is not an unconcerned spectator of our tribulation, and a confident assurance that He is in the furnace with us, will furnish a downy pillow for our aching head. When the hours limp tardily along, how sweet to reflect that He has felt the weariness of time when sorrows multiplied! When the spirit is wounded by reproach and slander, how comforting to remember that He also once said, Reproach has broken Mine heart. And, above all, how abundantly full of consolation is the thought that now, even now, He feels for us, and is a living Head, sympathizing in every pang of His wounded body. The certainty that Jesus knows and feels all that we endure is one of the dainties with which afflicted souls are comforted. More especially is this a cheering thought when our good is evil spoken of, our motives misrepresented, and our zeal condemned. Then, in absence of all other balms, this acts as a sovereign remedy for decay of spirit. Give us Christ with us, and we can afford to smile in the face of our foes…We can be content to be unappreciated here, so long as Christ understand us, and has a fellow-feeling for us. It is for Him we labour. One of His smiles outweighs all other commendation. To Him we look for our reward; and oh! is it not enough that He has promised it at His coming? It will not be long to wait. Do our hearts crave human fellowship and sympathy? We surely have it in our great High Priest.[28]

CHARLES HADDON SPURGEON IN THE SAINT AND HIS SAVIOUR

Viewer Guide

≈◎ WEEK SEVEN ◎≈

Do You Love Jesus?

In Week Seven of *A Heart On Fire*, we studied all that Jesus has accomplished as our Intercessor. And now, what is your response? Do you love Him? That's what I want to talk about today open the Word of God together. So grab your Bible, these notes, and let's study God's Word.

"There He is able to save forever those who draw near to God through Him, since He always lives to make intercession for them" (Hebrews 7:25).

My Jesus I love Thee
I know Thou art mine.
For thee all the follies of sin I resign.
My gracious Redeemer,
My Savior art Thou.
If ever I loved Thee my Jesus tis now.

"Above all else, guard your heart. For everything you do flows from it" (Proverbs 4:23 NIV).

The main message in Hebrews is that Jesus is _____.

Three Aspects of the Character of Christ

1. Jesus is _____.

2. Jesus is _____.

   a. He _____ in the presence of God for us.

   b. He _____ all accusations against you.

   c. He makes our prayers and service pleasing and _____ to God.

---

d. He _____for us.

e. His intercession on our behalf is not only continual but _____.

3. Jesus is _____.

Your Response — Hebrews 4:14-16

1. Hold _____your confession. Take God at His Word.

2. Draw near to your Lord with _____.

Oh how I love Jesus!
1. Because He is my _____.
2. Because He did what it took so that I could be _____.
3. Because He first _____me.
4. Because He _____me to Himself.
5. Because He is intimately _____with me.
6. Because He goes to God on _____behalf.
7. Because He _____for me.
8. Because He goes _____me.
9. Because He is more _____than my greatest enemy.
10. Because He is _____, then who can be against me.
11. Because He _____to me in His Word.
12. Because He _____the Father to me.
13. Because He _____me when I am down, lonely, hurt, and afraid.
14. Because He _____ with me even when no one else does.
15. Because He draws _____to me when I draw near to Him.
16. Because He prays the _____for me.

The result: You will receive mercy and find grace to help in time of need. Hebrews 4:16

⇜❀ *Video messages are available on DVDs or as Downloadable M4V Video. Audio messages are available on Audio CDs or as Downloadable MP3 Audio. Visit the Quiet Time Ministries Online Store at www.quiettime.org.*

HE IS YOUR BRIDEGROOM

Revelation 19:7

Let us rejoice and be glad and give the glory to Him, for the marriage of the Lamb has come, and His bride has made herself ready.

REVELATION 19:7

YOU WILL MARRY THE ONE WHO SAVED YOU

Let us rejoice and be glad and give the glory to Him, for the marriage of the Lamb has come and His bride has made herself ready."

Revelation 19:7 niv

PREPARE YOUR HEART

You have spent considerable time looking at the Lord Jesus Christ. You've seen Him from many angles. But there is one view that surpasses them all. Jesus is your Bridegroom. This is the view of Jesus as the Person of Eternity. It is the view of Him that was afforded John on the isle of Patmos and was given to us in written form in the Revelation. Revelation is the last book of the Bible. To many, Revelation seems so difficult and impossible to understand, that there are some who will not even read it. It's almost as though the last book of the Bible remains a closed book. Today is the day to end that idea, at least for you. Revelation is one of the most incredible books of the Bible. Yes, it does have some unusual pictures and descriptions. But if you understand the context, it will make much more sense to you.

Revelation is an apocalypse. An apocalypse is a type of literature that has a lot of symbolism in it. Its goal is to leave an impression on your mind. That is why the imagery is so vivid. In addition, it is important to note that this revelation is also a letter. Chapters 2-3 contain letters from Jesus Christ to the seven churches in western Asia Minor. These churches had problems similar to the churches of today. Revelation is also a prophecy, given by Jesus to tell His people the rest of the story. In other words, this life is not all there is nor is it the best there is. There is something incredible to look forward to that will serve as an anchor for your soul. Merrill C. Tenney says it best: "For nearly nineteen centuries the book of Revelation has been both an inspiration and a mystery to the Christian church. In hours of darkness it has given courage to its readers, enabling them to endure persecution and death for the sake of Christ. In periods of ease and prosperity it has been the battleground of exegetes who have endeavored to fashion its strange pageant into a consistent eschatology."[1] It is best to think of Revelation as the Lord's love letter to the church in difficult times. The Lord wanted His church to have hope to hold in their hearts when the way seemed impossible. One of the high points of Revelation is the picture Jesus gives of Himself. It is grand and glorious. You will look at Him in Revelation this week. It is holy ground. And so, following the example of Moses, when he was in the presence of God at the burning bush, you must remove your shoes, and come near in reverence and humility, to behold the Lord in all His glory. As you draw near, you will behold Him, and you will have touched the edge of heaven.

There is a day in the future that will not be like any other day that has ever been. It is the day of the marriage of the Lamb and His Bride, the Church. The invitation has already been sent. You have it in written form in the Word of God. The Lamb, Jesus Christ, is looking forward to and is preparing for the day when He will receive you to Himself so that you can be with Him where He is (John 14:3). This is not a theoretical truth, but one that is absolute and experiential, one to take into your heart and count on to give great hope in the most difficult of times. Jesus, your Bridegroom, is really what life is all about. All of eternity, all of heaven is fixed on Him. It is only this small world with its own earthly pursuits that has missed the point. But this is not so with you. He fills your gaze and your world in such a way as to overshadow all earthly pursuits. Anticipate with excitement seeing His face, knowing Him, living with Him, and enjoying everything about Him! Imagine One who loves you completely, who is intensely interested in you, who wants only the very best for you. It is incomprehensible, yet absolute reality. You are the one who brings the smile to His face. Is He the one who lights up your life, brings the sparkle to your eyes, and the lilt to your step?

As you begin your quiet time, pray that the Lord Jesus will so fill your mind with a vision of Himself in His glory that you will be filled with a tremendous anticipation to see Him, face to face.

READ AND STUDY GOD'S WORD

1. Today as you begin your time in God's Word, as a form of context in Revelation, read Revelation 1:1-3 and record what you learn about this revelation.

2. Jesus reveals in this revelation to John that there is going to be a marriage in heaven. Read Revelation 19:7-9 and record what you learn about the marriage and the Bride.

3. This marriage relationship is also described in other areas of the New Testament. Read the following passages and record what you learn about the relationship between Christ and the Church.

John 3:27-30

Ephesians 5:25-27

4. Revelation 19 talks about the marriage of the Lamb. In this, you see the name of Jesus as He is known in heaven. Your Bridegroom is the Lamb of God. In this name of Jesus you see His fulfillment of God's redemptive plan for all mankind through the supreme sacrifice of Himself as the unblemished Lamb. This title of Christ, the Lamb of God, is used twenty-eight times in Revelation.[2] As you look at the throne room of God where the Lamb is seen in Revelation, you need to take note of one very important thing. The Lamb of God is not meekly lying on an altar. No, He is standing. And all of heaven worships the Lamb. See it for yourself. Turn to Revelation 5:1-14 and record your favorite insight about the Lamb, keeping in mind that this is the One who is your Bridegroom.

5. Read Revelation 21:22-23 and underline those truths about the Lamb who is your Bridegroom, the One with whom you are united for all eternity. (Optional Verses: Revelation 7:9-17, Revelation 12:10-11, Revelation 13:8, Revelation 17:14)

> I did not see a temple in the city, because the Lord God Almighty and the Lamb are its temple. The city does not need the sun or the moon to shine on it, for the glory of God gives it light, and the Lamb is its lamp.

ADORE GOD IN PRAYER

O Lamb of God, still keep me
Near to thy wounded side!
'Tis only there in safety
And peace I can abide.
What foes and snares surround me!
What lusts and fears within!
The grace that sought and found me
Alone can keep me clean.
'Tis only in thee hiding,
I feel my life secure;
Only in thee abiding,
The conflict can endure:
Thine arm the victory gaineth
O'er every hurtful foe;
Thy love my heart sustaineth
In all its care and woe.
Soon shall my eyes behold thee,
With rapture, face to face;
One half hath not been told me
Of all thy power and grace;
Thy beauty, Lord, and glory,
The wonders of thy love,
Shall be the endless story
Of all thy saints above.
Amen.

FREDERICK C. MAKER 1889

YIELD YOURSELF TO GOD

O, blessed day! Would God it had dawned, when these temples should be left, because the whole world should be a temple for God. But whatever may be the splendors of that day,—and truly here is a temptation to let our imagination revel—however bright may be the walls set with chalcedony and amethyst, however splendid the gates which are of one pearl, whatever may be the magnificence set forth by the streets of gold, this we know, that the sum and substance, the light and glory of the whole will be the person of our Lord Jesus Christ; for the glory of God did lighten it, and the Lamb is the light thereof. Now, I want the Christian to meditate over this. In the highest, holiest, and happiest era that shall ever dawn upon this poor earth, Christ is to be her light. When she puts on her wedding garments, and adorns herself as a bride is adorned with jewels, Christ is to be her glory and her beauty. There shall be no earrings in her ears made with other gold than that which cometh from his mine of love; there shall be no crown set upon her brow fashioned by any other hand than his hands of wisdom and of grace. She sits to reign, but it shall be upon his throne; she feeds, but it shall be upon his bread; she triumphs, but it shall be because of the might which ever belongs to him who is the Rock of Ages. Come then, Christian, contemplate for a moment thy beloved Lord. Jesus, in a millennial age, shall be the light and the glory of the city of the New Jerusalem. Observe, then, that Jesus makes the light of the millennium, because his presence will be that which distinguishes that age from the present.[3]

CHARLES HADDON SPURGEON IN "THE LAMB: THE LIGHT"

Are you a bride of the Lamb? His bride carries a wonderful secret in her heart. She has a blessed hope. She lives in expectation of the fulfillment of her deepest longings. She knows that eternal joy and happiness will be hers. This is why the bride needs little else in this life. The test of whether I am a true bride of Jesus is this: How important to me is the love of others? To what extent do I look to my career for satisfaction? Do I covet prestige and status? Do health, talents, and popularity mean more to me than Jesus? The true bride of Jesus is focused on Him in her innermost being rather than on the things of this world. Her Bridegroom is her life, the joy of her heart. Supremely happy in His love, she is enthralled by her heavenly Bridegroom, spending herself for Him, eagerly awaiting His coming, and carrying in her heart this one name: Jesus.[4]

BASILEA SCHLINK IN MY ALL FOR HIM

ENJOY HIS PRESENCE

Think about the following words by William Newell. Are your earthly relationships, even marriage, but a whisper of what you have with Christ? What does it mean to you today that you are joined with the Lamb of God, the Lord Jesus Christ for all eternity? Close by talking with your Bridegroom about your love for Him.

> The bliss of the marriage of the Lamb is without limit. It is the PERSONAL DELIGHT of Him who created all things!...Christ also loved the church and GAVE HIMSELF up for it. He values His Bride as Himself. And upon her, He lavishes His personal affection, without limit constantly, and forevermore!...Here then is a marital love, a tenderness, an appreciation, and a delight, that will grow forever and forever. Oh, wonder of wonders, that such a record can be written! Christ will never change in His affections! What must the ages hold for the wife of the Lamb! And the love of that Bride, the wife of the Lamb, will correspond to that of her husband—unceasing, increasing, forever and forever! Have you known a husband and wife whose love deepened as the years went by, whose satisfaction with each other was such as to keep them together constantly, of their own mutual will; whom neither society or business, nor outside pleasures could separate? Let such a happy marital existence be a whisper to you of what Christ and the Church will enjoy more and yet more forevermore![5]
>
> WILLIAM R. NEWELL IN REVELATION VERSE BY VERSE

REST IN HIS LOVE

"Christ also loved the church and gave Himself up for her, so that He might sanctify her, having cleansed her by the washing of water with the word, that He might present to Himself the church in all her glory, having no spot or wrinkle or any such thing; but that she would be holy and blameless" (Ephesians 5:25-27).

YOU WILL SEE HIS FACE

...they will see His face
REVELATION 22:4

PREPARE YOUR HEART

Everyone knows what it is like to be away from home. You are away from everything familiar, especially the company of those you love. What a great day it is when you see the faces of your family, your loved ones. The smiles and the light in their eyes tells you that you are home. There is a contentment and sense of security that is almost unparalleled.

Someday, you are going to have the ultimate fulfillment of that which you have taken by faith all these years. You will see the face of Christ. What a day that will be! Your faith will become sight. Paul says for now we see in a mirror dimly, but then face to face; now I know in part, but then I will know fully just as I also have been fully known (1 Corinthians 13:12). There is no question that the Lord Jesus Christ can be seen on every page of your Bible. And the Holy Spirit gives you His Presence in a real and intimate way. However, it is not the same as seeing Him face to face. That is what you have to look forward to in eternity.

As you begin your quiet time, write a prayer, telling the Lord what it will mean to you to see Him face to face. Ask Him to reveal Himself to you today.

READ AND STUDY GOD'S WORD

1. John, the beloved disciple of Christ, was exiled to the isle of Patmos because of his faith in Christ. It is thought that he probably was the last surviving apostle of the original twelve who had walked with Jesus. His brother James was martyred early on by Herod Agrippa (Acts 12) and Paul and Peter were martyred under Nero in AD 64-65. In later years, John lived in Ephesus and ministered there. In AD 95 the Roman emperor, Domitian, was in power. It was under his reign that John was exiled to Patmos. Domitian meant it for evil, but it was from that place that the

Lord Jesus gave the most complete picture of Himself in glory in the form of the Revelation to John. Read Revelation 1:9-11 and record the circumstances surrounding the Revelation to John:

2. Now John turns to see who is speaking to him. Little did he know what awaited him. Read Revelation 1:12-20 and record everything John saw. What stands out the most to you in this vision of Jesus?

3. Look at the following verses and record what you learn about the future view of Jesus that awaits you:

   1 Corinthians 13:12

   1 John 3:2

ADORE GOD IN PRAYER

   Draw near to the Lord in prayer using the words of this beloved hymn. If you know the melody, you might sing it to Him.

My Jesus, I love Thee, I know Thou art mine;

For Thee all the follies of sin I resign.

My gracious Redeemer, my Savior art Thou;

If ever I loved Thee, my Jesus, 'tis now.

I love Thee because Thou has first loved me,

And purchased my pardon on Calvary's tree.

I love Thee for wearing the thorns on Thy brow;

If ever I loved Thee, my Jesus, 'tis now.

I'll love Thee in life, I will love Thee in death,

And praise Thee as long as Thou lendest me breath;

And say when the death dew lies cold on my brow,

If ever I loved Thee, my Jesus, 'tis now.

In mansions of glory and endless delight,

I'll ever adore Thee in heaven so bright;

I'll sing with the glittering crown on my brow;

If ever I loved Thee, my Jesus, 'tis now.

WILLIAM FEATHERSTON 1864

YIELD YOURSELF TO GOD

This is the sum and substance of heaven, this is the joyful hope of all believers. It is their delight to see Him now in the ordinances by faith. They love to behold Him in communion and in prayer; but there in heaven they shall have an open and unclouded vision, and thus seeing, Him as He is, shall be made completely like Him. Likeness to God—what can we wish for more? And a sight of God—what can we desire better? Some read the passage, Yet I shall see God in my flesh, and find here an allusion to Christ, as the Word made flesh, and that glorious beholding of Him which shall be the splendour of the latter days. Whether so or not it is certain that Christ shall be the object of our eternal vision; nor shall we ever want any joy beyond that of seeing Him. Think not that this will be a narrow sphere for the mind to dwell in. It is but one source of delight, but that source is infinite. All His attributes shall be subjects for contemplation, and as He is infinite under each aspect, there is no fear of exhaustion. His works, His gifts, His love to us, and His glory in all His purposes, and in all His actions, these shall make a theme which will be ever new.[6]

CHARLES HADDON SPURGEON IN MORNING AND EVENING

ENJOY HIS PRESENCE

What are you looking forward to the most when you see the face of Christ? Close your time today by writing your thoughts in your journal about this most amazing fact about eternity.

I love the windows of thy grace,
Through which my Lord is seen,
And long to meet my Saviour's face
Without a glass between.

Oh that the happy hour were come
To change my faith to sight!
I shall behold my Lord at home
In a diviner light.

Haste, my Beloved, and remove
These interposing days;
Then shall my passions all be love,
And all my powers be praise.[7]

ISAAC WATTS IN THE PSALMS AND HYMNS OF ISAAC WATTS

REST IN HIS LOVE

"We do know that when He comes we will be like Him, for we will see Him as He really is" (1 John 3:2 NLT).

HE WILL GIVE YOU HIS NAME

His name will be on their foreheads.
REVELATION 22:4

PREPARE YOUR HEART

Who are you identified with in life? When you think of yourself, who do you think about? While this is a serious question, it becomes even more critical when your life is on the line. Beginning with the First Century Church, lives were on the line because of their identification with Jesus Christ. Wherever believers have gone, if they identify with Christ in a serious way, then as Christ shines in them, persecution may result. The Lord Jesus Christ has enemies. And your identification with Him will bring the attention of Christ's enemies. However, greater is He who is in you than He who is in the world (1 John 4:4 NASB). And so, you need not fear, but instead stand strong in the Lord. It is a distinctive, incredible privilege to bear the name Christian. You are His. And you will never know more than in eternity, when His name is on your forehead, how knowing Him is such a priceless privilege. May it cause your heart to burn with such passion that everyone around you know you are His.

As a preparation of heart, meditate on these words as a prayer to the Lord. Underline your favorite phrases in this prayer.

> Thou God of all grace,
> Thou hast given me a saviour,
> Produce in me a faith to live by him,
> To make him all my desire,
> All my hope,
> All my glory.
> May I enter him as my refuge,
> Build on him as my foundation,
> Walk in him as my way,
> Follow him as my guide,
> Conform to him as my example,
> Receive his instructions as my prophet,

Rely on his intercession as my high priest,
Obey him as my king.
May I never be ashamed of him or his words,
But joyfully bear his reproach,
Never displease him by unholy or imprudent conduct,
Never count it a glory if I take it patiently
When buffeted for a fault,
Never make the multitude my model,
Never delay when thy Word invites me to advance.
May thy dear Son preserve me from this present evil world,
So that its smiles never allure,
Nor its frowns terrify,
Nor its vices defile,
Nor its errors delude me.
May I feel that I am a stranger and a pilgrim on earth,
Declaring plainly that I seek a country,
My title to it becoming daily more clear,
My meetness for it more perfect,
My foretastes of it more abundant;
And whatsoever I do may it be done in the Saviour's name.[8]

THE VALLEY OF VISION: A COLLECTION OF PURITAN PRAYERS & DEVOTIONS

READ AND STUDY GOD'S WORD

1. What will it be like when you enter Paradise and enjoy eternal life with your Lord? Read Revelation 22:1-5. Record everything you learn about eternity with your Lord.

2. One of the profound truths you learn is that the name of your Lord will be on your forehead (Revelation 22:4). This name is a sign of ownership and also identity—it shows whose you are. This is especially powerful in light of the fact that many prior to the coming of Christ will choose to deny Christ and take the mark of the beast, identifying themselves with the antichrist. Those who love Jesus Christ want only to belong to Him. To have the name of Christ means first, that you belong to Him. Read 1 Corinthians 6:17-20 and write out what you learn about belonging to Him.

3. What a privilege to have the Lord's name on our foreheads. There is much truth in God's Word about the name of Jesus. In fact, He has many names. Read the following verses and record what you learn about the name of Christ. Personalize your answers.

Philippians 2:9-11

Colossians 3:17

4. A name in the Bible represents the character of the person. In the case of Jesus, His names reveal His character—who He is, what He does, and what He says. Now we belong to our Lord, represent Him, and are being conformed to His likeness (Romans 8:29). With that in mind, what do you think it means to do everything in the name of the Lord Jesus?

5. Optional: Revelation is filled with many names of Jesus that reveal His character. Look at the following verses just to see a few of these powerful names. Record your insights as you meditate on each verse and write what you think is significant about each name. Revelation 3:14, Revelation 22:13, Revelation 22:16

ADORE GOD IN PRAYER

What is on your heart today that you would like to talk about with the Lord? Take your requests to Him and talk freely and openly with Him. Who is in your life that does not know the name of Jesus? Will you pray for them today that somehow, some way, their eyes will be opened to the truth of Jesus Christ?

YIELD YOURSELF TO GOD

The primary signification of the name borne thus upon the forehead is, so to speak, ownership; that it marks out those who have it as belonging to Christ. And this conveys much; for to be His is really the sum of eternal blessedness, inasmuch as it brings us into everlasting association with Him, both now and also in heaven itself…name expresses the truth of the Person; and hence we regard it here that full likeness to Christ is displayed on every redeemed brow. That all believers will be conformed to the image of God's Son, we learn from another scripture (Romans 8:29); and here we are allowed to behold it actually accomplished. What joy, we may be permitted to say, it will be to the Lord Himself to see, as He surveys the unnumbered hosts of His glorified saints, His own likeness beaming from every face, Himself mirrored and reflected in all the redeemed! It helps us to enter more fully into the words of the prophet: He shall see of the travail of His soul, and be satisfied. Then indeed Christ will fill the scene. Old things will have forever passed away, and all things have been made new; for then, not to faith as now, but in actuality, Christ will be Everything to all His own, and this in full and unclouded display. To Him be all the praise now and throughout eternity!

There in the sweetness of His love repose,
His love unknown!
All else forever lost—forgotten all
That else can be;
In rapture undisturbed, O Lord, to fall,
And worship Thee.[9]

EDWARD DENNETT IN THE NAME ABOVE EVERY NAME

ENJOY HIS PRESENCE

What does it mean to you today to belong to Jesus Christ and reflect His image, His character? That is what it will mean to have His name on your forehead. Have you taken the name *Christian*? If so, do others, by your actions, know that you belong to Him? Will you proclaim Him today in everything you do?

O my Lord! I do thank Thee for the glorious assurance that while I am engaged with Thee, in my work of beholding Thy glory, the Holy Spirit is engaged with me, in His work of changing me into that image, and of laying of Thy glory on me. Lord! Grant me to behold Thy glory aright. Moses had been forty days with Thee when Thy glory shone upon Him. I acknowledge that my communion with Thee has been too short and passing, that I have taken too little time to come under the full impression of what Thine image is. Lord! Teach me this. Draw me, in these my meditations too, to surrender myself to contemplate and adore, until my soul at every line of that image may exclaim: This is glorious! This is the glory of God! O my God, show me Thy glory…O my Lord, as often as I gaze upon Thine image and Thine example, I would do it in the faith that Thy Holy Spirit will fill me, will take entire possession of me, and so work Thy likeness in me, that the world may see in me somewhat of Thy glory. In this faith I will venture to take Thy precious word, FROM GLORY TO GLORY, as my watch-word, to be to me the promise of a grace that grows richer every day, of a blessing that is ever ready to surpass itself, and to make what has been given only the pledge of the better that is to come. Precious Saviour! Gazing on Thee it shall indeed be so, From glory to glory. Amen.[10]

ANDREW MURRAY IN LIKE CHRIST

REST IN HIS LOVE

"God raised him up to the heights of heaven and gave him a name that is above every other name, so that at the name of Jesus every knee will bow, in heaven and on earth and under earth, and every tongue will confess that Jesus Christ is Lord, to the glory of God the Father" (Philippians 2:9-10).

YOU WILL REIGN WITH HIM

They will reign forever and ever...
REVELATION 22:5

PREPARE YOUR HEART

What must it be like to come into a massive inheritance, one that moves you from a shack to a palace? You see, if you belong to Jesus Christ by trusting in Him, then you stand to inherit everything that is His. He is the King of Kings and you are His Bride. Now here is the paradox or, you might say, the challenge for you. During your brief stay on earth (brief compared to eternity), it does not always seem like reality. Your life is a by faith experience of what you know as fact in the Word of God. You can see, obviously, why it is imperative that you know what is in His Word. Studying His Word is the most important thing you can do in order to live like the royalty you are because you are united to Jesus Christ.

While we are on earth, we often experience warfare. The enemy of God, Satan, has blinded the eyes of so many in this world. We are called, as royalty in the kingdom of God, to tell others about the true King. It is as though we are engaged in a campaign of sabotage. Imagine how frustrated the enemy is when your Bible is open and you are studying the plan of your King. Imagine how much the enemy would love to keep you from any contact or communication with the Captain of your salvation. Imagine how the enemy would be delighted if you tried to fight alone rather than joining the ranks of the army of the Lord. If you think about it this way, perhaps then you will get serious, truly serious, about living the life you are meant to live, as royalty who will reign with Jesus Christ in eternity. He has a job for you to do now. Paul says, "We are His workmanship, created in Christ Jesus for good works, which God prepared beforehand so that we would walk in them" (Ephesians 2:10). God has an overall plan and you are a part of it. Today, your goal in your quiet time is to know what you stand to inherit as someone who will reign with Him in heaven. How exciting it will be when you step into glory to inherit all that is yours.

READ AND STUDY GOD'S WORD

1. Read Revelation 22:3-5 and record what you learn about God's bondservants.

2. Revelation 22:5 truly is a "revelation" for you discover that in eternity you will "reign forever and ever." You are royalty because of your union with Jesus Christ. Because of that, you have an inheritance and an incredible future planned for you. Read the following verses and record what you learn:

Matthew 25:34

Ephesians 1:13-14, 18

Colossians 3:23-24

1 Peter 1:3-9

Revelation 21:1-7

3. You belong to the kingdom of heaven, there is an inheritance reserved for you, and you will reign forever and ever. How then should you live during your time on earth? Think of these verses and passages of Scripture as God's blueprint for action for you, His orders from heaven for you as He carries out His plan in the world. Read the following verses and record what you learn:

1 Corinthians 15:58

2 Corinthians 5:18-20

Ephesians 5:15-16

Colossians 3:12-24

1 Thessalonians 5:12-17

2 Timothy 2:15

4. What verse challenges you the most today? How can you begin to apply what you have learned to your life?

ADORE GOD IN PRAYER

What area of your life is challenged the most today? Will you talk to your King, your Lord about it? And then, will you thank Him for all that you are going to inherit and that you are going to reign forever and ever in eternity with Him?

YIELD YOURSELF TO GOD

There is a price to be paid. Are you willing to pay it? Cancel every responsibility in your life other than what you believe to be God's will for you. Deliberately refuse any engagement that will keep you from meditation on His Word. We are living in an age which has lost the art of being silent with an open Bible and waiting for God to speak. Practice holiness, beginning today! If you are guilty of seeking position for position's sake, resign, or alone with God, confess your sin and get right with Him. Then, through the church, through all its leadership will be expressed heavenly light, heavenly authority, heavenly power, and the river of God will surely flow through each of us in great blessing to others.[11]

ALAN REDPATH IN VICTORIOUS CHRISTIAN LIVING

It is a great boon for a company of pilgrims to have a Greatheart; for an army to have a captain; for an exodus to have a Moses. Courageous, sagacious, and strong leaders are God's good gifts to men. And it is only what we might have expected that God has placed such a One as the efficient Leader at the head of the long line of pilgrims, whom he is engaged in bringing to glory. The toils seem lighter and the distance shorter; laggards quicken their pace; wandering ones are recalled from by-paths by the presence and voice of the Leader, who marches, efficient, royal, and divine, in the van. O heirs of glory, weary of the long and toilsome march, remember that ye are part of a great host: and that the Prince, at the head of the column, has long since entered the city; though he is back again, passing as an inspiration along the ranks as they are toiling on.[12]

F.B. MEYER IN THE WAY INTO THE HOLIEST

Now it shall be the day of light and the victory of Emmanuel, and the sounding of his praise both in earth and heaven. Contemplate this thought; and though I speak of it so feebly, yet it may ravish your hearts with transport that Christ is the Sun of that long-expected, that blessed day; that Christ shall be the highest mountain of all the hills of joy, the widest river of all the streams of delight; that whatever there may be of magnificence and of triumph, Christ shall be the centre and soul of it all. Oh to be present, and to see him in his own light, the King of kings and Lord of lords![13]

CHARLES HADDON SPURGEON IN "THE LAMB: THE LIGHT"

ENJOY HIS PRESENCE

What is the most important truth you have learned today? How will it make a difference in your life? In what way has what you have learned about your future with Christ make your heart burn today for Him? Write out your thoughts.

REST IN HIS LOVE

"No eye has seen, no ear has heard, and no mind has imagined what God has prepared for those who love Him" (1 Corinthians 2:9 NLT).

HE IS COMING SOON

He who testifies to these things says, "Yes, I am coming quickly." Amen. Come, Lord Jesus.
REVELATION 22:20

PREPARE YOUR HEART

They stood on a hillside at Bethany. The One they had known and loved for three years, the Lord Jesus Christ, lifted up His hands and blessed them. While He blessed them, according to Luke "He parted from them and was carried up into heaven." More details are given by Luke in Acts. As Jesus was taken up into heaven, all who were there gazed intently into the sky, barely able to contain or comprehend the myriad of events that had occurred in the last three days. While they were looking up into the sky, two men in white clothing stood beside them. They said, "Men of Galilee, why do you stand looking into the sky? This Jesus, who has been taken up from you into heaven, will come in just the same way as you have watched Him go into heaven" (Acts 1:11).

Anticipating the return of Christ brings to mind the familiar words that we have heard in the story of Sleeping Beauty. After Aurora pricked her finger and fell into a deep sleep, she could only be wakened with a kiss by her one true love, the Prince. And so, the familiar refrain was: someday your Prince will come.

And that is our refrain as well. Someday our Prince will come. The Lord Jesus promised that when He left the earth, He was going to prepare a place for us. He then said: When everything is ready, I will come and get you, so that you will always be with me where I am (John 14:3). Those are powerful words. Jesus is coming again! Think about that and bank your life on it. As you do, your heart will burn in such a way that it will be on fire. On fire for Jesus Christ.

You have learned much about the priceless privilege of knowing Christ. You have walked on the road to Emmaus and experienced the burning heart that comes from walking with Jesus. You have seen just how priceless it is to know Christ as you receive Him, love Him, and follow Him. You have looked at the day when God became man and dwelt among us. And then, you have seen that Jesus is everything you need, He is your life, He is your intercessor, and He is your Bridegroom. And now, as you leave this study, it is fitting on the last day, that you look at what has been called the blessed hope, the appearing of your Lord Jesus Christ (Titus 2:13). What will that day be like and what should you do until He comes? That is the subject of your time with the Lord today.

289

In preparation for your time alone with the Lord, will you be still and know that He is God today (Psalm 46:10)? Think about everything you have learned in this book of quiet times. And then, thank Him for what He has shown you about Himself during the time you have spent looking at the priceless privilege of knowing Him.

READ AND STUDY GOD'S WORD

1. One of the great promises throughout Scripture is that Jesus will come again. This is a great event that is one of your great hopes and joys in life. Jesus talked about it Himself to His disciples. Look at the following passages in the gospels and write what you learn about His return and what He wants you to do until He comes.

Matthew 24:42-47

Matthew 25:13, 21

2. His Second Coming is seen in more detail in Revelation 19. Read Revelation 19:11-16. How is the Lord Jesus described in this passage of Scripture? Write out your overall impression of this event when heaven stands open and a white horse is seen with a rider who is called "Faithful and True."

3. What is the Lord Jesus' final message to John as the Revelation comes to a close? Read Revelation 22:12, 20-21 and write what you learn from His Words.

4. The Lord desires that you serve Him until He comes. In Revelation 19:7-8 you see that the bride is clothed with fine linen representing the "righteous acts of the saints." He wants you to be alert and be ready. He could come again at any time. One of the exhortations from Christ to His disciples was this: Follow Me, and I will make you fishers of men (Matthew 4:19). His plan is discipleship. That means to pour what you have learned into a few faithful men and women who will be able to pour what they have learned into others. And the ripple effect of discipleship goes on and on. It is the principle of multiplication, not addition. The question for you is: who are you pouring your life into right now? Who is going to come after you and reap the results of your brief stay on earth? Who will read those same books you are reading? Who will know to do what you are doing in serving the Lord? Who will know to pray and study God's Word as you have learned to do? It may be your children. It may be some close friends. It is imperative that you resolve to live a life that counts for the Lord Jesus Christ. He will show you His plan for you as you invest in the priceless privilege of knowing Him. As you think about what has been said here, what are your thoughts and how are you challenged today?

5. Close your time in the Word of God by reading through Paul's familiar words in Philippians 3:7-14. In what way do these words mean so much more now that you have spent this time looking at the character of your Lord Jesus Christ?

ADORE GOD IN PRAYER

Have we not seen Thy shining garment's hem
Floating at dawn across the golden skies;
Though thin blue veils at noon, bright majesties;
Seen starry hosts delight to gem
Thy splendor that shall be Thy diadem?

O Immanence, that knows no far nor near,
But as the air we breathe is with us here,
Our Breath of Life, O Lord, we worship Thee.

Worship and laud and praise Thee evermore;
Look up in wonder, and behold a door
Opened in heaven, and One set on a throne:
Stretch out a hand, and touch Thine own,
O Christ, our King, our Lord whom we adore.[14]

AMY CARMICHAEL IN MOUNTAIN BREEZES

YIELD YOURSELF TO GOD

The coming of the Lord is an event which transcends the thought and imagination of man. It is not so much a movement in space as a revelation of him who is there, a transcendent deed in which grace and judgment are combined as truly as they are in the cross of Christ. In the context of the Revelation it is important as focusing hope on a Person, on him who alone can perform what needs above all things else, namely, redemption from the powers which destroy the world and judgment upon the agents of destruction. This message the Church of John's time sorely needed for its encouragement in faith and obedience, as indeed the Church of all ages needs it. For the scene on earth takes on a different aspect when viewed in the light of the coming of the Lord. If the glory of that event has power to transform present living and inspire continuance in well doing to the end, the Church can afford patiently to wait to learn the nature of the great unveiling. The day itself will declare it.[15]

G. R. BEASLEY-MURRAY IN REVELATION

May God Almighty hasten the consummation, and may we, with passionate, steady-burning, unquenchable ardour, strive to know and to imitate Christ! Let us deliberately crown Him Lord of all. In practice and in speculation, in intellect and in affection, in the family circle, in the social throng, in the political enterprise, in the inmost recesses of our being, in the slightest outgoing of our activity, let Him reign perpetually, unreservedly, supremely![16]

PETER BAYNE IN THE TESTIMONY OF CHRIST TO CHRISTIANITY

For the Christian the future is not measured in terms of what but in terms of whom. Time, events, and trends are all secondary to the disclosure of the Person who is the Son of God, the King of men, and the Redeemer of all creation.[17]

MERRILL C. TENNEY IN INTERPRETING REVELATION

The greatest opportunity
that God has ever given me
was not when that suggestion came
to show an easy road to fame
was not the day when fortune smiled
and claimed me, for a time, her child;
nor yet the chance that I must hold
to turn some talent into gold;
the greatest one of all, I say,
Is now, always here—today.
Today, my opportunity
Is just as great as I can see;
It is my privilege to live,
To learn, to earn, receive, and give;
To do the little task assigned,
And smile the while, nor leave behind
Regrets or flaws in what I build;
But do what work as God has willed
And see in the small part I play
My opportunity—today.[18]

QUOTES FROM THE QUIET HOUR

Wherever she goes, the bride of Jesus reflects something of heaven's radiance. Aflame with love for her Bridegroom, she sparks off fires in the hearts of others. Such is the nature of the bride, for no one is a bride of Jesus who does not have a burning love and zeal for the kingdom of God. Yet the zeal of the bride does not come from herself; like everyone else, she is a sinful human being. However, she lives in union with Him who is ablaze with love and who has become her Bridegroom. With Him she treads the path of self-denial, which leads to spiritual life and to a foretaste of heaven. At His side she shares in this life. In obedience she has let go of everything else to walk with Him who is her all and all. This is why she does not have to rely on self, talent, personality, resources, or opportunities. She reckons exclusively with Him and with the power of His love. Jesus is the very fire of God, the Light of the world, a furnace of love. As such He cannot fail to inflame the heart of His bride.[19]

BASILEA SCHLINK IN *MY ALL FOR HIM*

ENJOY HIS PRESENCE

There can be a sense of sadness leaving a study such as this one. You have gained such a vivid picture of your Lord. However, there is no sadness here. For this study is merely a springboard to the rest of your adventure with the Lord. You may re-read quotes and notes that you made. But the real experience, the focus of your life, is your relationship with the Lord Jesus Christ. It is a moment by moment intimacy with this One you have come to know in more detail than you could ever imagine. Life is all about Him. And there is so much more to know. "No eye has seen, no ear has heard, and no mind has imagined what God has prepared for those who love him" (1 Corinthians 2:9 NLT). Even John said at the end of his gospel "if all the other things Jesus did were written down, the whole world could not contain the books" (John 21:25 NLT). We have only scratched the surface. You have a faint outline, a mere overview. Now, you have the great joy and challenge to know Him more. Live in the Word of God and ask Him to show Himself to you. You can know Him, and then you can know Him even more. Your intimacy with Jesus Christ can increase in depth to a point unimaginable to you right now.

There have been a few who have known the intimacy with Jesus that John the Beloved enjoyed. How did they come to know Him to such depth? Because Jesus was all they wanted in life. They had set aside the playthings of the world and sacrificed all for that one thing, the highest and the best—to know Jesus Christ.

There is nothing in this world that can compare to Jesus. Nothing. Things may look good, but have you noticed? Once you get that thing you thought you could not live without, the excitement fades away. Not so with Jesus. The joy, the peace, the profound sense of comfort and security only increases, and will do so until that one bright day when you see Him face to face. Oh what a day that will be. To look into His eyes. And those eyes will be familiar for you will have come to know Him so well because you have walked with Him here. There will be a knowing that happens between the two of you; a knowing that says "We made it. We got through all those things on earth."

Then you will experience what you have anticipated. You will have all eternity to enjoy and share and serve with your Lord. What rapture of the soul awaits you in eternity. LOOK TO YOUR REWARD. When you fix your eyes on Jesus, the troubles, the trials will fade. They don't disappear, but they simply are not the main thing. Jesus is the main thing in your life. Don't ever forget it. Bank your life on it. Remind yourself of it. Day by day, moment by moment, fix your eyes on Him. And always look to the sky. It could be any day now. The skies will be rolled back like a scroll, the trump shall resound, the Lord will descend, and the moment will be here. He will return. And that will be bring an end to life as we know it on earth. Your faith will be sight. And everything will be as it should be. It will be well, it will be well with your soul.

> Oh Lord, haste the day when my faith shall be sight
> The sky rolled back like a scroll
> The trump shall resound
> The Lord will descend
> It is well it is well with my soul.
>
> HORATIO SPAFFORD

REST IN HIS LOVE

"Don't be troubled. You trust God, now trust in me. There are many rooms in my Father's home, and I am going to prepare a place for you. If this were not so, I would tell you plainly. When everything is ready, I will come and get you, so that you will always be with me where I am" (John 14:1-3 NLT).

DEVOTIONAL READING
BY ANNE R. COUSIN

DEAR FRIEND,

The next two days are your opportunity to spend time reviewing what you have learned this week. You may wish to write your thoughts and insights in your journal in the back of this study book. As you think about all that you have learned about Jesus as your Bridegroom, record your most meaningful discoveries in the space provided:

Your most significant insight:

Your favorite quote:

Your favorite verse:

Turn to page 18 (in the Introduction) to the letter you wrote to the Lord at the beginning of this study. Read through the words you wrote. How has the Lord answered your prayer?

What is the most important truth you have learned in A Heart On Fire?

What was your favorite week of quiet times and why?

What was your favorite aspect of the priceless privilege of knowing Christ? What is your favorite view of Him?

How has this time in God's Word helped you have a heart on fire?

As you close this time of study on the character of Christ, meditate on these words by Anne R. Cousin (1824-1906) :

In Immanuel's Land

The sands of time are sinking,
The dawn of Heaven breaks,
The summer morn I've sighed for,
The fair sweet morn awakes:
Dark, dark hath been the midnight,
But dayspring is at hand,
And glory—glory dwelleth
In Immanuel's land.

There the Red Rose of Sharon
Unfolds its heartsome bloom,
And fills the air of Heaven
With ravishing perfume:—
Oh! to behold it blossom,
While by its fragrance fann'd
Where glory—glory dwelleth
In Immanuel's land.

The King there in His beauty,
Without a veil, is seen:
It were a well-spent journey,

Though seven deaths lay between.
The Lamb, with His fair army,
Doth on Mount Zion stand,
And glory—glory dwelleth
In Immanuel's land.

Oh! Christ He is the Fountain,
The deep sweet well of love!
The streams on earth I've tasted,
More deep I'll drink above:
There, to an ocean fullness,
His mercy doth expand,
And glory—glory dwelleth
In Immanuel's land.

I have wrestled on toward Heaven,
'Gainst storm, and wind, and tide:—
Now, like a weary traveler,
That leaneth on his guide,
Amid the shades of evening,
While sinks life's ling'ring sand,
I hail the glory dawning
From Immanuel's land.

Deep water cross'd life's pathway,
The hedge of thorns was sharp;
Now these lie all behind me—
Oh! for a well-tuned harp!
Oh! to join Hallelujah
With yon triumphant band,
Who sing, where glory dwelleth,
In Immanuel's land.

With mercy and with judgment
My web of time He wove,

And aye the dews of sorrow
Were lustered with His love.
I'll bless the hand that guided,
I'll bless the heart that plann'd,
When throned where glory dwelleth
In Immanuel's land.

The Bride eyes not her garment,
But her dear Bridegroom's face;
I will not gaze at glory,
But on my King of Grace—
Not at the crown He giveth,
But on His pierced hand:
The Lamb is all the glory
Of Immanuel's land.

I have borne scorn and hatred,
I have borne wrong and shame,
Earth's proud ones have reproach'd me,
For Christ's thrice blessed name:—
Where God His seal set fairest
They've stamp'd their foulest brand;
But judgment shines like noonday
In Immanuel's land.

They've summoned me before them,
But there I may not come,—
My Lord says, Come up hither,
My Lord says, Welcome Home!
My kingly King, at His white throne,
My presence doth command,
Where glory—glory dwelleth
In Immanuel's land.[20]

Viewer Guide

When Your Heart Burns On Fire

In Week Eight of *A Heart On Fire* we studied the promises from Revelation about our eternal relationship with Christ. Today we are going to look at this One who is our eternal companion in heaven. And how shall we respond? Our hearts will burn on fire for Him as we gaze upon the One who will be with us forever.

"Worthy is the Lamb that was slain to receive power and riches and wisdom and might and honor and glory and blessing" (Revelation 5:12).

The View of Jesus in Revelation 5

1. Jesus is _____ to open the Book.

2. Jesus is the _____ from the tribe of Judah.

3. Jesus is the Root of _____.

4. Jesus is the _____.

5. Jesus is the _____.

6. Jesus has _____ horns, eye, and Spirits of God.

7. He is known in heaven for the _____ He did on your behalf.

8. He advances with _____ to carry out what He is called to do.

9. Jesus is adored and _____ by all of heaven.

How do hearts on fire burn brightly for Jesus during their brief stay on earth?

1. Give yourself _____to the work of the Lord.

2. As Christ's ambassador, share His gospel _____with others.

3. Make the most of your _____.

4. Be _____with the Spirit.

5. _____as one of God's chosen, holy, and dearly-loved people.

6. _____on what you are learning to others.

7. Draw near to God and His Word in _____each day.

8. Cultivate a life of _____.

9. Fix your eyes on _____ the author and perfecter of your faith.

10. _____the race and never give up.

꙳   *Video messages are available on DVDs or as Downloadable M4V Video. Audio messages are available on Audio CDs or as Downloadable MP3 Audio. Visit the Quiet Time Ministries Online Store at www.quiettime.org.*

NOW THAT YOU HAVE COMPLETED THESE QUIET TIMES

You have spent eight weeks consistently drawing near to God in quiet time with Him. That time alone with Him does not need to come to an end. What is the next step? To continue your pursuit of God, you might consider other books from the Quiet Times for the Heart series, including *Pilgrimage of the Heart, Revive My Heart, A Heart that Dances,* and *A Heart To See Forever.* A Quiet Time Experience series includes books of quiet times with titles such as *A Heart that Hopes in God, Run Before the Wind, Trusting in the Names of God,* and *Passionate Prayer.* To learn more about quiet time, read signature books from the A 30-Day Journey series such as *Six Secrets to a Powerful Quiet Time* and *Knowing and Loving the Bible.* Leader's Kits with DVD messages and Leader's Guides are available for each book. Learn more about quiet time from Catherine's many books, *Enriching Your Quiet Time* quarterly magazine, and The Quiet Time Notebook™. Quiet Time Ministries Online has many resources to encourage you in your quiet time with God. Find daily encouragement from Cath's Blog and view A Walk In Grace™, the devotional photojournal featuring Catherine's own photography at www.quiettime.org. Join hundreds of other women online to study God's Word and grow in God's grace at Ministry For Women (www.ministryfor-women.com). Resources may be ordered online from Quiet Time Ministries at www.quiettime.org or by calling Quiet Time Ministries. For more information, you may contact:

Quiet Time Ministries
P.O. Box 14007
Palm Desert, California 92255
(800) 925-6458, (760) 772-2357
E-mail: catherine@quiettime.org
Website: www.quiettime.org

About the Author

Catherine Martin is a summa cum laude graduate of Bethel Theological Seminary with a Master of Arts degree in Theological Studies. She is founder and president of Quiet Time Ministries, director of women's ministries at Southwest Community Church in Indian Wells, California, and adjunct faculty member of Biola University. She is the author of *Six Secrets to a Powerful Quiet Time, Knowing and Loving the Bible, Walking with the God Who Cares, Set my Heart on Fire, Trusting in the Names of God, Passionate Prayer, Quiet Time Moments for Women,* and *Drawing Strength from the Names of God* published by Harvest House Publishers, and *Pilgrimage of the Heart, Revive My Heart!* and *A Heart That Dances,* published by NavPress. She has also written The Quiet Time Notebook™, *A Heart on Fire, A Heart to See Forever,* and *A Heart That Hopes in God,* published by Quiet Time Ministries. She is senior editor for *Enriching Your Quiet Time* quarterly magazine. As a popular speaker at retreats and conferences, Catherine challenges others to seek God and love Him with all of their heart, soul, mind, and strength. For more information about Catherine, visit www.quiettime.org and www.ministryforwomen.com

About Quiet Time Ministries

Quiet Time Ministries is a nonprofit religious organization under Section 501(c)(3) of the Internal Revenue Code. Cash donations are tax deductible as charitable contributions. We count on prayerful donors like you, partners with Quiet Time Ministries pursuing our goals of the furtherance of the Gospel of Jesus Christ and teaching devotion to God and His Word. Visit us online at www.quiettime.org to view special funding opportunities and current ministry projects. Your prayerful donations bring countless project to life!

Quiet Time Ministries | P.O. Box 14007 | Palm Desert, California 92255
1.800.925.6458 | catherine@quiettime.org | www.quiettime.org | www.ministryforwomen.com

APPENDIX

❧ DISCUSSION QUESTIONS ❧

Introduction

Begin your class with prayer and then welcome everyone to this new book of quiet times. Have the people in your group share their names and what brought them to the study. Make sure each person in your group has a book. Also, gather contact information for all participants in your group including name, address, phone number, and e-mail. That way you can keep in touch and encourage those in your group.

Familiarize your group with the layout of the book. Each week consists of five days of quiet times, as well as a devotional reading and response for days 6 and 7. Each day follows the PRAYER quiet time plan:

Prepare Your Heart

Read and Study God's Word

Adore God in Prayer

Yield Yourself to God

Enjoy His Presence

Rest in His Love

Journal and prayer pages are included in the back of the book. Note that the quiet times offer devotional reading, Bible study, prayer, and practical application. Some days are longer than others so be sure to encourage your group to study at their own pace. Days 6-7 are for catching up, review, etc. This is a concentrated, intentional journey to discover the priceless privilege of knowing Christ and have a heart on fire for Him. Encourage your group to interact with the study, underline significant insights, and write comments in the margins. Encourage your group to read the Introduction sometime the first day. Also point out that the Introduction includes a place where they will write a letter to the Lord. Encourage them to draw near to God each day and ask Him to speak to their hearts.

You can determine how to organize your group sessions, but here's one idea: Discuss the week of quiet times together in the first hour, break for ten minutes, and then watch the message on the companion DVD. There are nine messages for *A Heart On Fire*—one for the introduction and one for each week. You might also share with your group a summary of how to prepare for their quiet time by setting aside a time each day and a place. Consider sharing how time alone with the Lord has made a difference in your own life. Let your class know about the Quiet Time Ministries website at www.quiettime.org and also Ministry For Women at www.ministryforwomen.com.

Another option is to divide each week (completing the study in 16 weeks) by discussing Days 1–3 one week and Days 4–7 another week. This allows your group to journey through each quiet time at a slower pace.

Pray for one another by offering a way to record and exchange prayer requests. Some groups like to pass around a basket with cards that people can use to record prayer requests. Then, people take a request out of the basket and pray for someone during the week. Others like to use three by five cards and then exchange cards on a weekly basis.

Close this introductory class with prayer, take a short break, and then show the companion DVD message.

Week One: The Burning Heart

Your goal today with your group is that they would begin to catch a glimpse into how a heart burns on fire for Jesus Christ. This week lays the foundation for everything as we take the journey on the Emmaus Road where Jesus opens up the Scripture and explains everything concerning Himself. We will continue this journey on the Emmaus Road and go to different areas in the Bible allowing the Lord Jesus to open up the Word to us concerning Himself. As a result, our hearts will begin to burn for Him: on fire for Jesus Christ.

DAY 1: The Defining Moment

You might begin this first week of discussion with a brief overview of what everyone studied. You might say something like: *This week we are looking at how our hearts catch on fire for Jesus.*

1. Open your discussion with prayer. Ask any new members of your group to introduce themselves. Share the goal of these quiet times: to learn about the priceless privilege of knowing Christ and have our hearts catch on fire for Him. Ask your group what it meant to them to begin a new study like *A Heart On Fire*.

2. What do you hope will happen as you engage in these quiet times with the Lord?

3. In the Introduction, Catherine talked about the Ripple Effect. Can someone explain the Ripple Effect? All of us are a product of God's ripple effect. Who has had a profound impact in your life in helping you grow in your intimate relationship with the Lord? What was it about them that meant the most to you?

4. You began your study in Day 1 by looking at the events that occurred in the last days of Jesus. To refresh our memories (or to put us in context) let's answer question 2: what are the significant events described in Luke 22-23? Now, back to question 1:

As you read about all that happened, what do you think it must have been like to be one of Jesus' disciples during this time?

5. As you read Luke 22-23, what was most significant to you about Jesus?

6. What was the significance of Jesus' death on the cross?

7. What did you learn from the devotional reading in Day 1

DAY 2: The Road to Emmaus

1. What do you think it would have been like to have gone to the tomb of Jesus three days after He was crucified? What would your response have been?

2. And now we come to the two disciples walking on the road back to Emmaus. Describe what happened.

3. What was most significant to you in this event on the road to Emmaus?

4. What caused their hearts to burn?

5. Why do you think they did not recognize Jesus at first?

6. Share your favorite insight from the devotional reading.

DAY 3: When Your Heart Begins to Burn

1. In Day 3 you saw how The Message translates Luke 24:32 *Didn't we feel on fire as he conversed with us on the road, as he opened up the Scriptures for us?* What do you think it means to be on fire for Jesus Christ?

2. Is there a person you have known in your life with a heart on fire for Jesus Christ?

3. What did you learn about the words of Christ from the verses you studied?

4. Andrew Murray said that the disciples got burning hearts through the way the Lord opened the Scriptures up to them. Can you think of a time when the Word of God has influenced you in a profound way

5. Share your insights from the devotional reading.

DAY 4: Recognizing Jesus

1. In Day 4 you studied the meanings of some of the Greek words in Luke 24:31. How did this help you in understanding what happened. What do you think the men now understood about Jesus?

2. Knowing Jesus will change your life forever. What did you learn about knowing Christ from the verses you read in question 3?

3. After reading the quotes and studying these passages of Scripture, what do you think it means to know Christ?

DAY 5: Hearts Set Aflame for Christ

1. In Day 5 you had the opportunity to read what happened following the disciples' realization that Jesus had, in fact, risen from the dead. You looked at a number of different experiences they had with Jesus following His resurrection. What did the disciples see and learn about Jesus in Luke 24:31-53?

2. What were the last moments with Jesus like for the disciples before He ascended into heaven? What did you learn from Acts 1:1-11

3. How did the power of the Holy Spirit make a difference in Peter?

4. What was your most significant insight from Day 5.

DAYS 6 AND 7: Devotional Reading by Annie Johnson Flint

1. What was your favorite verse, insight, or quote from your quiet times this week?

2. What was your favorite phrase from the poem by Annie Johnson Flint?

3. Close your time together in prayer asking the Lord to give everyone in your group a heart on fire.

Week Two: The Priceless Privilege

Your goal this week in your discussion is to help your group understand the many responses they will have as they begin to gaze upon the character of Jesus Christ. What are those responses? They will know Him, receive and believe Him, ask and seek Him, love Him, and follow Him.

The more we learn to respond in these ways, the more we will experience the Lord Jesus for ourselves. Then our hearts will burn for Him: on fire for Jesus Christ.

DAY 1: Know Him

1. Open your discussion with prayer. In this first day we see one of the most important biblical truths we can ever understand—to know Jesus Christ. What will it take to know Him? That is what we will discuss today. You had the opportunity to live in Philippians 3:8 this week. What does this statement tell you about Paul the Apostle?

2. How does Philippians 3:8 give you a glimpse into Paul's relationship with Christ?

3. You read Philippians 3:8 in many translations. What did that kind of study, called a translation study, mean to you? How did it help you understand Philippians 3:8?

4. What was your favorite translation and why?

5. What was your favorite phrase and why?

6. How did your time with the Lord in Day 1 motivate you to make knowing Christ a priority in life?

7. Did you have a favorite quote in Day 1?

DAY 2: Receive and Believe Him

1. Another response you and I must have as we meet and begin to know Jesus is to Receive and Believe. What does it mean to receive Jesus? What is involved in receiving Him?

2. Belief in Jesus means a complete dependence on Him. Jesus was constantly asking those who heard Him teach to make a decision, revealing their real trust in Him. What kinds of things did He desire from those He taught according to the verses you looked at in Day Two?

3. Did the Lord move you to any specific decisions this week as you spent time with Him?

4. What was your favorite quote in the devotional reading in Day 2?

DAY 3: Ask and Seek Him

1. What did you learn about the importance of prayer in your time with the Lord in Day 3?

2. What was the most important truth you learned about prayer from the verses of Day 3?

3. What was the most important truth you learned about prayer from the devotional readings in Day 3

DAY 4: Love Him

1. What did you learn about your love for the Lord in John 14?

2. In John 21:15-19 you read a conversation between Peter and Jesus. What did you learn about the priority of love for Jesus?

3. From your study of the verses and devotional readings, what was most significant to you about what it means to love Jesus?

DAY 5: Follow Him

1. One of the most important decisions you will ever make is to follow Jesus. What does it mean to follow Jesus?

2. What qualities do you think will be seen in the life of someone who follows Jesus?

3. What did you learn about discipleship from Jesus in the gospels?

4. What did you learn about discipleship from the early Church in Acts 4?

5. How did the devotional reading help you understand what it means to follow Jesus? What was favorite quote in the devotional reading?

DAYS 6 AND 7: Devotional Reading by Charles Haddon Spurgeon

1. What was your favorite verse, insight, or quote from your quiet times this week?

2. What did you learn from the excerpt by Spurgeon in Days 6-7?

3. How did your quiet times make a difference in your life this week?

4. Why is knowing Christ such a priceless privilege?

5. Close in prayer.

Week Three: The Divine Romance

The goal of your discussion this week is to understand the romance deep in the heart of the Lord. When the Lord Jesus was walking with the disciples on the road to Emmaus, the text tells us that He began with Moses and the Prophets and explained to them what was said in all the Scriptures concerning Himself. That means that He explained passages in the Old Testament since the New Testament was not yet written at that time. The text also says that as He opened the Scriptures to them, their hearts began to burn. This week you had the opportunity to examine and think about passages in the Old Testament that speak of Jesus. In fact, perhaps these were some of the very same passages He shared with those two men on the road to Emmaus that day. Let's pray that our hearts will burn as theirs did.

DAY 1: Chosen As His Beloved

1. Open your discussion with prayer. Week Three begins with John 3:16. How do you see the great romance between God and His people in John 3:16: "For God so loved the world that He gave His only begotten Son, that whoever believes in Him will not perish, but have everlasting life?"

2. What did you learn about God's choice of His people in the Deuteronomy passages?

3. Have someone in your group read the brief summary of the history of Israel in question 2. This provides the explanation of Israel's exile and sets the stage for the rest of the study. What did you see in Zechariah about the heart of God for His people?

4. What did you learn about God's choice of you and His love for you in the verses you read from the New Testament?

5. What does it mean to be chosen by God?

6. What was your favorite quote in the devotional reading?

DAY 2: The Great Dilemma

1. The title of Day 2 is The Great Dilemma. What is the great dilemma from the human side and from God's side?(see Prepare your Heart)?

2. What did learn in Isaiah that helps you understand man's need and God's love and action on man's behalf?

3. What did you learn from your study in Jeremiah?

4. Paul offers more explanation in Romans. What did you learn from the verses in Romans?

5. What was most significant to you in the devotional reading?

6. Share any personal thoughts about how you saw the love, devotion, and faithfulness of your Lord as you spent time with Him.

DAY 3: The Anointed One

1. In Day 3, you had the opportunity to see that God's answer to the Great Dilemma was a plan that He unfolded over time to His people through the lives and words of His prophets. What impressed you the most as you read through many of these different prophecies?

2. Share a significant insight about the One who was the promised Messiah.

3. If you were able to read the verses in the Optional Study, did you learn about Jesus and how He fulfilled prophecy?

4. What did it take for the Second Person of the Trinity to come to the earth and go to the cross? What did you learn from Philippians 2:5-11?

5. How did the devotional reading help you understand in more depth what Jesus did on your behalf?

DAY 4: The Proof of God's Amazing Love

1. In Day 4 what did you learn from Isaiah 53 about the Great Rescue accomplished by Jesus Christ? And what did you learn about the promised Messiah?

2. When Jesus cried out, "It is finished," what do you think He meant by those words?

3. As you thought about Jesus' death on the cross in Romans 5, what was the most important phrase or sentence to you in this passage?

4. What is your favorite truth from Romans 8:31-39?

5. How did the devotional readings in Day Four help you understand the work of Jesus on your behalf?

6. If you were to describe to someone what Jesus has done for them, what would you say?

DAY 5: Together Forever

1. In Day 5, you had the opportunity to read a passage from *Pilgrim's Progress.* What do you think it will be like to be in Paradise with your Lord? (Prepare your Heart)

2. What do we have to look forward to according to the verses you read in questions 1 and 2 of Day 5 in Read and Study God's Word?

3. What did you learn about your relationship with the Lord from the New Testament verses?

4. What was your favorite quote from the devotional reading in Day 5?

DAYS 6 AND 7: Devotional Reading by Charles Haddon Spurgeon

1. In Days 6-7 you had the opportunity to read from Charles Haddon Spurgeon. What was your favorite truth from his writing?

2. What was your favorite verse, insight, or quote from your quiet times this week?

3. How would you describe the divine romance? What does it mean to you and how have you experienced this romance in your own relationship with the Lord?

4. How is this study impacting your life and your relationship with the Lord?

5. Then close in prayer. You might want to use the prayer on Day 3 (Adore God in Prayer).

Week Four: When God Became Man

You have been looking at what it means to have a heart on fire. We walked on the road to Emmaus. Then we looked at what a priceless privilege it is to know Christ. Last week you saw the divine romance in God's plan to rescue His people and the promise of His Messiah. Then, following Zechariah, we saw that there would be 400 years of silence before that promise would be realized. We thought about the question in the Old Testament: "How is God going to fulfill His promise for the One who would give himself as a guilt offering for God the Father?" This week we looked at the time when God fulfilled His promise and became man. Now you are going to see the Lord Jesus in a way you may not have seen Him before. He is the fulfillment of all the promises of God.

DAY 1: We Want To See Jesus

1. Open your discussion with prayer. As you began your time in Day 1, what was the most significant truth you learned in the Prepare Your Heart section? What is the most important thing you learned about truth?

2. John records an event in John 12:20-33. What did the Greeks want specifically, and how did Jesus respond to this?

3. What did you learn about spiritual sight and how to see Jesus?

DAY 2: He Was in the Beginning

1. In Day 2 you looked at the eternal nature of Jesus Christ. In John 1 you learned some powerful truths about Jesus. What was your favorite truth?

2. As you read through Genesis (and Job—Optional), what were your most significant insights as you thought about creation?

3. What did you learn about Jesus in Colossians 1:15-20?

4. What was your favorite insight from the devotional reading in Day 2?

DAY 3: He Dwelt Among Us

1. In Day 3 you looked at the fact that Jesus, the Word, became flesh and dwelt among us. We looked at events in Scripture about Jesus' life in the flesh. What was your favorite insight from these verses?

2. What did you learn about Jesus as the Son of Man?

3. What was your most significant insight from the devotional reading?

DAY 4: The Great Attraction

1. In Day 4, you looked at the reaction of the world when Jesus was present. How did people respond to Him according to John 12:19 (Prepare Your Heart).

2. What did you learn about Jesus from the verses you read in the gospels?

3. Why do you think people were drawn to Jesus? What was attractive about Him. Why did people want to be close to Him?

DAY 5: Is He Who He Claimed to Be?

1. From your reading in Matthew and Mark, what did you see about Jesus' claims about Himself? What did others around Him understand Him to be saying about Himself?

2. What did Paul say about Christ in Colossians 1:13-20?

3. What was your favorite devotional reading in Day 5?

4. Who do you say Jesus is?

DAYS 6 AND 7: Devotional Reading by Josh McDowell and Bill Wilson

1. On Days 6-7 you had the opportunity to read from Josh McDowell and Bill Wilson. What were your favorite truths from their writings?

2. Did you have a favorite quote, insight, or verse from your study in Week Four?

3. How did your quiet times this week impact your relationship with the Lord?

4. Close in prayer. (You might want to sing the hymn, *Turn Your Eyes Upon Jesus*, from Day 1, Enjoy His Presence).

Week Five: He is Everything You Need

One of the great truths that will cause your heart to burn for Christ is to realize that He is everything you need. That was the subject of your quiet times this week.

DAY 1: For Life and Light

1. Open your discussion with prayer. In speaking with the Jews, Jesus said something very radical. He said "Truly, truly I say to you, before Abraham was born, I am" (John 8:58). Why was that such a radical statement and what was He really saying?

2. What did you learn about God in Exodus 3?

3. This week we had the opportunity to look at the 7 I AM's that Jesus claimed related to His character. In Day 1 we looked at two of them. In John 6:35 what did you learn about Jesus? What "I AM' statement did He make? What stood out to you and spoke to your heart in this verse? Why is it important for us to know that Jesus is the bread of life? What does He want us to understand in revealing Himself this way?

4. What did Jesus claim about Himself in John 8:12?

5. If you had time to look at the optional verses, what did you learn about light?

6. What does it mean to you that Jesus is the light?

7. What was your favorite insight from the devotional reading in Day 1?

DAY 2: For Comfort and Security

1. In Day 2 you looked at how Jesus is your comfort and security. What was your favorite verse or phrase in Psalm 23?

2. What did Jesus reveal about Himself in John 10:7-10 and John 10:11-14?

3. As you read the verse in Day 2, what was your favorite insight related to Jesus as your Shepherd?

4. How did the quotes help you understand the great value of Jesus as your Shepherd?

DAY 3: For Hope that Anchors the Soul

1. In Day 3 you looked at the hope found in Jesus. Who does He claim to be in John 11:25?

2. What did you learn about the resurrection in 1 Corinthians 15?

3. What were some truths in the verses you studied that give you hope as an anchor for your soul?

4. What was your favorite quote about heaven in Day 3?

DAY 4: For Your Relationship with God

1. In Day 4 who does Jesus say He is in John 14:6?

2. What is Jesus saying in John 14:6?

3. What did you learn about truth in the verses in question 2 of Read and Study God's Word?

DAY 5: For a Fruitful and Satisfying Life

1. In Day 5, you read John 15. Who does Jesus say that He is?

2. What does Jesus want from you as the branch?

3. What do you think it means to abide in Christ?

4. As you read through many truths about who Jesus is, what do you need most from Him today?

5. If you abide in Christ you will bear much fruit. What did you learn about fruit?

6. How did the quotes help you understand what it means to abide in Christ?

DAYS 6 AND 7: Devotional Reading by Andrew Murray

1. What was your favorite verse, insight, or quote from your quiet times this week?

2. What did you learn from the excerpt by Andrew Murray?

3. Close your time together in prayer.

Week Six: He Is Your Life

Over the last five weeks of quiet times you have looked at many truths about Jesus Christ. These are truths that will make a heart begin to catch on fire for the Lord. Now, we are going to look at a deep life changing truth about the Lord this week. It is the fact that because of what the

Lord has done, and because of your union with Him, now He is your life. It sounds like a simple statement, but there is so much more than meets the eye in understanding this truth. There are many things that are now possible because He is your life and we want to talk about it together.

DAY 1: You Are United with Christ

1. Open your discussion with prayer. As you read Prepare Your Heart in Day 1, what do you think happened to Hudson Taylor that so changed his life?

2. What was your most significant insight in Romans 6:1-14?

3. What is now true because you are united with Christ?

4. What did you learn about your union with Christ from the verses in question 2 of Read and Study God's Word?

5. Describe in your own words your new life and what it means to have a relationship with Christ.

6. How did the quotes help you understand what it means to be united with Christ?

DAY 2: Your Life is Hidden with Christ

1. In Day 2, what did you learn is true about you now according to Colossians 3:1-17?

2. How are you to live according to Colossians 3:1-17 as a result of what is true?

3. What was your most significant insight in Ephesians 2:1-10?

4. What was most significant to you in the devotional reading?

DAY 3: You Are in Christ

1. In Day 3 you had the opportunity to look at what it means to be in Christ. According to Ephesians 1:1-23 what is true about you?

2. What did you learn from the verses in question 2 in Read and Study God's Word?

3. What truth meant the most to you from the verses or devotional reading on Day 3 about being in Christ?

DAY 4: Christ Lives in You

1. In Day 4 you looked at the fact that Christ lives in you. What does Paul call "a mystery" in Colossians 1:24-27?

2. Why do you think the fact that Christ lives in you is a mystery? (biblical mystery is defined as "something that was once hidden but later revealed.").

3. What did you learn about Christ in you from the verses in question 2 of Read and Study God's Word?

4. How did the devotional reading help you understand this truth that Christ is in you?

DAY 5: How to Live the Exchanged Life

1. Paul said in Galatians 2:20 that "I have been crucified with Christ; and it is no longer I who live, but Christ lives in me; and the life which I now live in the flesh I live by faith in the Son of God, who loved me and gave Himself up for me." This verse is descriptive of the exchanged life. What does it means to experience the exchanged life (see question 1 in Read and Study God's Word).

2. How did the verses you read help you understand the exchanged life?

3. What was your favorite quote in the devotional reading?

DAYS 6 AND 7: Devotional Reading by Alan Redpath

1. What was your favorite verse, insight, or quote from your quiet times this week?

2. What did you learn from the excerpt by Alan Redpath?

3. How do these truths from this week's quiet times help you realize that knowing Christ really is a priceless privilege? How do these truths set your heart on fire?

4. Close in prayer.

Week Seven: He is Your Intercessor

In our study of Jesus we are now going to look at truths that can truly revolutionize your life. This week you spent a good deal of time in Hebrews and saw the powerful truth that Jesus is your Great High Priest and He is your Intercessor.

DAY 1: For God the Father

1. Open your discussion with prayer. You might begin by reading the first paragraph in Day 1, Prepare Your Heart, as an introduction. As you read through the Hebrews' passages, what did you learn about Jesus?

2. How is Jesus better than the Old Testament priests?

3. What comfort does it bring you to know that Jesus is your intercessor?

4. How did the devotional readings help you understand Jesus as your High Priest? What was most significant to you?

DAY 2: For Your Sins and Temptations

1. Read Hebrews 2:17-18. What did you learn about Jesus from these verses?

2. Jesus is your Intercessor when you sin or are tempted. How is it that Jesus can sympathize with your weakness and temptation? What did you learn from His life?

3. You learned that you have an enemy who wants to discourage your faith and keep you from standing firm. But Jesus is your intercessor and prays for you. What did you learn about Jesus' prayers for you?

4. What did you learn from the devotional reading?

DAY 3: For Your Time of Need

1. In Day 3 you learned that Jesus is available in your time of need. What was your most important insight from Hebrews 4:13-16?

2. Why was the temple veil rent in two when Jesus died on the cross, and what did that mean for you?

3. What did you learn about mercy and grace from Ephesians 2:4-9 and 1 Peter 5:10?

4. Optional: How was Stephen an example of receiving grace and mercy in time of need?

5. What was your favorite quote from your quiet time in Day 3?

DAY 4: For the New Covenant

1. In Day 4 what did you learn about the difference between the Old and New Covenant? Why is the New Covenant so much better?

2. Why is the Holy Spirit such a blessed, wonderful gift from God in your life?

3. What encouraged you in the devotional reading?

DAY 5: For the Unshakeable Kingdom

1. In Day 5 you saw that one of the great blessings of God as a result of Jesus interceding for you is that you are now a member of an unshakeable kingdom. What did you learn about the kingdom that meant the most to you this week?

2. What did you learn about your responsibilities as a member of the kingdom?

3. How did the Lord speak to you about serving Him as a result of your study?

4. What was your favorite quote in the devotional reading?

DAYS 6 AND 7: Devotional Reading by Henry Gariepy

1. What was your favorite verse, insight, or quote from your quiet times this week?

2. What were your favorite insights from the devotional reading by Henry Gariepy?

3. How will what you are learning change the way you live your life? How are you being transformed as a result of these quiet times. And how is your heart being set on fire?

4. Close your time together in prayer.

Week Eight: He is Your Bridegroom

It's hard to believe that this is our last week of discussion. In leading this last discussion it will be important for you to summarize what you have looked at in the last 8 weeks to refresh their memories of their time in the Word. You might begin by saying something like the following: We have spent the last 8 weeks concentrating on Jesus. We have walked with Him on the road to Emmaus. And then we have looked at Paul's exhortations in his letters and his convictions about Jesus. We saw that the substance of our relationship with Jesus is a divine romance. And then, as we looked at the "I AM's" in John we thought about how Jesus is everything we need for every circumstance of life. We learned a powerful truth that we are "in Christ" and that we can live an exchanged life – it is no longer I who lives but Christ lives in me. Last week we lived in Hebrews and learned that Jesus intercedes for us. Now, in Week Eight we have looked at the great truth that Jesus is our Bridegroom. .

DAY 1: You Will Marry the One Who Saved You

1. Open your discussion with prayer. We spent a good deal of time in Revelation. How many of you have studied Revelation before? How many of you are apprehensive about Revelation? What did you learn about the background of Revelation?

2. What did you learn from Revelation 1:1-3?

3. What did you learn in your quiet time about your relationship with Christ (see questions 2-3 in Read and Study God's Word).

4. You saw in your study that Jesus is known as the Lamb of God in heaven. You were able to go right into the throne room as you looked at Revelation 5:1-14. What did you learn about Jesus, the Lamb of God?

5. What did you learn from Revelation 21:22-23 about Jesus as the Lamb?

6. How did the quotes help you appreciate your relationship with Jesus your Bridegroom?

DAY 2: You Will See His Face

1. In Day 2, we saw that John the Beloved disciple of Jesus was given the privilege of an exalted view of Jesus that the other disciples did not see. In Revelation 1, what were the circumstances surrounding this revelation and then, what did he see?

2. What did you learn about the future view of Jesus that awaits you?

3. What does it mean to you that you will see the face of the Lord? If He walked in here right now, what would it mean to you to see Him face to face?

DAY 3: He Will Give You His Name

1. In Day 3, we saw that there is going to come a day when you will enter Paradise and enjoy eternal life with your Lord. What did you learn about this time from reading Revelation 22:1-5?

2. To have the name of Christ means that you belong to Him and that you will be conformed to His image. What did you learn from 1 Corinthians 6:17-20?

3. What did you learn about the name of Christ?

4. How did the devotional reading in Day 3 encourage you?

DAY 4: You Will Reign With Him

1. In Day 4, you learned that you have a job now and you also have responsibilities in heaven. What did you learn about God's bondservants in Revelation 22:3-5?

2. What did you learn about your inheritance in Christ from the verses in question 2 of Read and Study God's Word?

3. How are you to live now according to the verses you read?

4. What was your favorite quote in Day 4?

DAY 5: He is Coming Soon

1. You have spent some time looking at who Jesus is. And now, in Day 5, you saw the powerful truth that Jesus is coming again. What did you learn about His 2nd coming in Matthew 24 and 25?

2. What is your overall impression of the return of Christ in Revelation 19:11-16?

3. What are we to do until He comes? What challenged you the most in all that you learned?

4. How does the fact that Jesus is coming again encourage you?

5. What encouraged you the most in the devotional reading?

DAYS 6 AND 7: Devotional Reading by Anne R. Cousin

1. What was your favorite insight, quote, or verse from your quiet times in Week Eight?

2. What will you take with you from *A Heart On Fire*? How has this study changed your life? What will you always remember? How was your heart set on fire?

3. What was your favorite week of quiet times?

4. What was your favorite part of the study?

5. What was your favorite truth about Jesus?

6. How did these quiet times impact your relationship with Jesus and help you grow closer to Him?

7. At the beginning of your study, you wrote a letter to the Lord in the Introduction section. How did God answer and respond to all that you wrote in that letter?

8. Have different members of the group share their favorite phrase or stanza from Immanuel's Land in Week Eight, Days 6 and 7. Then close in prayer together.

NOTES

WEEK 1

1. Amy Carmichael, *Toward Jerusalem* (Fort Washington: Christian Literature Crusade 1936) p. 17. Used by permission.

2. Andrew Murray, *The Holiest of All* (London: Nisbet & Co. Ltd.) p. 326.

3. Alan Redpath, *The Life of Victory* (Great Britain: Christian Focus Publications, 2000) April 9 reading. Used by permission of Mrs. Marjorie Redpath.

4. Corrie ten Boom, *Don't Wrestle, Just Nestle* (Old Tappen: Fleming H. Revell Company, a division of Baker Book House Company © 1960) p. 17.

5. A. B. Bruce, *The Training of the Twelve*, p. 500.

6. Donald Grey Barnhouse, "The Day-By-Day Christian Life" Herbert F. Stevenson ed., *Keswick's Authentic Voice* (London: Marshall, Morgan & Scott 1959) pp. 380-381.

7. C. Austin Miles, *In The Garden* The Rodeheaver Company, a division of Word Inc. © 1912. In the public domain.

8. Arthur Bennett ed., *The Valley of Vision: A Collection of Puritan Prayers and Devotions* (Carlisle: The Banner of Truth Trust, 1975) p. 17. Used by permission.

9. A.T. Pierson, *George Muller of Bristol* (New York: Fleming H. Revell Company) p. 140.

10. Charles Haddon Spurgeon, *Morning and Evening*, January 18, Evening selection.

11. A.B. Bruce, *The Training of the Twelve*, pp. 503-505.

12. Andrew Murray, *The Secret of Spiritual Strength* (New Kensington: Whitaker House © 1997) p. 24. Used by permission.

13. Amy Carmichael, *Thou Givest, They Gather* (Fort Washington: Christian Literature Crusade 1977) pp. 13-14. Used by permission.

14. Brennan Manning, *The Lion and the Lamb* (Grand Rapids: Chosen Books a division of Baker Book House 1987) p. 34. Used by permission.

15. A.H. Strong, *Strong's Exhaustive Concordance*, p. 31.

16. Kenneth S. Wuest, *Word Studies in the Greek New Testament, Volume 1* (Grand Rapids: Wm. B. Eerdmans Publishing Company 1973) p. 111. Used by permission.

17. Kenneth S. Wuest, *Word Studies in the Greek New Testament, Volume 1* (Grand Rapids: Wm. B. Eerdmans Publishing Company 1973) p. 133. Used by permission.

18. Spiros Zodhiates, *The Complete Word Study Dictionary: New Testament* (Chattanooga: AMG Publishers 1993) p. 372. Strong's Number 1097. Used by permission.

19. Spiros Zodhiates, *The Complete Word Study Dictionary: New Testament* (Chattanooga: AMG Publishers 1993) p. 437. Strong's Number 1272. Used by permission..

20. F.B. Meyer, Reprinted from *Daily Prayers* Copyright © 1995 by Harold Shaw Publishers, WaterBrook Press, Colorado Springs, CO. All Rights Reserved, p. 57.

21. Andrew Murray, *The Secret of Spiritual Strength* (New Kensington: Whitaker House © 1997) p. 28. Used by permission.

22. Norval Geldenhuys, *Commentary on the Gospel of Luke* from *The New International Commentary on the New Testament* (Grand Rapids: Wm. B. Eerdmans Publishing Company 1975) p. 635. Used by permission.

23. A.B. Simpson, *The Christ in the Bible Commentary Volume Four* (Camp Hill: Christian Publications 1993) p. 347. Used by permission.

24. A.W. Tozer, *That Incredible Christian* (Camp Hill: Christian Publications 1964) p. 67.

25. Joan Winmill Brown, *Corrie, The Lives She's Touched* (Old Tappan: Fleming H. Revell Company 1979) p. 69. Used by permission.

26. Joan Winmill Brown, *Corrie, The Lives She's Touched* (Old Tappan: Fleming H. Revell Company 1979) p. 11. Used by permission.

27. Joan Winmill Brown, *Corrie, The Lives She's Touched* (Old Tappan: Fleming H. Revell Company 1979) p. 155. Used by permission.

28. Charles Haddon Spurgeon, *Morning and Evening*, May 25, Evening selection.

29. A.B. Simpson, *The Christ in the Bible Commentary Volume Four* (Camp Hill: Christian Publications 1993) p. 348. Used by permission.

30. A.B. Simpson, *The Christ in the Bible Commentary Volume Four* (Camp Hill: Christian Publications 1993) p. 349. Used by permission.

31. Annie Johnson Flint, "His Lamp" (Toronto: Evangelical Publishers).

WEEK 2

1. John F. Walvoord, *Jesus Christ Our Lord* (Chicago: Moody Press 1969) p. 8. Used by permission.

2. G. Campbell Morgan, *The Crises of Christ* (Old Tappan: Fleming H. Revell Publishing Company 1936) p. 7. Used by permission of the G. Campbell Morgan Estate.

3. *The Amplified Bible* (Grand Rapids: Zondervan Publishing House © 1965).

4. Kenneth Wuest, *The New Testament: An Expanded Translation* (Grand Rapids: Wm. B. Eerdmans Publishing Company 1988) p. 465. Used by permission.

5. Catherine Marshall ed., *The Prayers of Peter Marshall* (Grand Rapids: Chosen Books, a division of Baker Book House Company 1982) p. 13. Used by permission.

6. Kenneth Wuest, *Word Studies of the Greek New Testament Volume 2* (Grand Rapids: Wm. B. Eerdmans Publishing Company 1942) p. 91. Used by permission.

7. Peter Bayne, *The Testimony of Christ in Christianity* © 1862 as quoted in *The Crises of the Christ* by G. Campbell Morgan.

8. *The Amplified Bible* Philippians 3:8 (Grand Rapids: Zondervan Publishing House © 1965).

9. Gipsy Smith, *As Jesus Passed By* © 1905 written in the flyleaf.

10. Spiros Zodhiates, *The Complete Word Study Dictionary: New Testament* (Chattanooga: AMG Publishers 1993) p. 1108. Strong's Numbers 3880, 2983. Used by permission.

11. Spiros Zodhiates, *The Complete Word Study Dictionary: New Testament*, p. 1160. Strong's Number 4100. Used by permission.

12. Gipsy Smith, *As Jesus Passed By*, pp. 20-21.

13. A.W. Tozer, *The Root of the Righteous* (Camp Hill: Christian Publications 1955) pp. 49-51. Used by permission.

14. F.B. Meyer, *The Christ Life For Your Life* (Chicago: Moody Press) pp. 60-61.

15. Corrie ten Boom, *Each New Day* (Grand Rapids: Fleming H. Revell Company a division of Baker Book House Company 1977) p. 80. Used by permission.

16. Donald Whitney, *Spiritual Disciplines for the Christian Life* (Colorado Springs: NavPress © 1991) p. 63. Used by permission of Navpress - www.navpress.com. All rights reserved.

17. Arthur T. Pierson, *George Mueller of Bristol* (Old Tappan: Fleming H. Revell Company) pp. 93-97.

18. Henri Nouwen, *The Way of the Heart* (New York: Ballantine Books a division of Random House 1981) pp. 63-69.

19. Amy Carmichael, *Mountain Breezes: The Collected Poems of Amy Carmichael* (Fort Washington: Christian Literature Crusade 1999) p. 20. Used by permission.

20. A.W. Tozer, *The Christian Book of Mystical Verse* (Camp Hill: Christian Publications 1963) pp. 66-67. Used by permission.

21. John Flavel, *Christ Altogether Lovely*, Application. For complete text, go to www.ccel.org.

22. Charles Haddon Spurgeon, *The Saint and His Saviour* (Pasadena: Pilgrim Publications 1970) pp. 185-187.

23. Constance Hudson © 2002 written during the pilot class of *A Heart On Fire*. Used by permission.

24. F.B. Meyer, Reprinted from *Daily Prayers* Copyright © 1995 by Harold Shaw Publishers, WaterBrook Press, Colorado Springs, CO. All Rights Reserved, p. 42.

25. Taken from *My Utmost For His Highest* by Oswald Chambers, © 1935 by Dodd Mead & Co., renewed © 1963 by the Oswald Chambers

Publications Assn. Ltd. Used by permission of Discovery House Publishers, Box 3566, Grand Rapids, MI 49501. All rights reserved, p. 128, May 7 selection.

26. Taken from *My Utmost For His Highest* by Oswald Chambers, © 1935 by Dodd Mead & Co., renewed © 1963 by the Oswald Chambers Publications Assn. Ltd. Used by permission of Discovery House Publishers, Box 3566, Grand Rapids, MI 49501. All rights reserved, p. 184, July 2 selection.

27. Charles Haddon Spurgeon, *Morning and Evening*, May 8 Evening.

WEEK 3

1. A.W. Tozer, *The Christian Book of Mystical Verse* (Camp Hill: Christian Publications 1963) pp. 106-107. Used by permission.

2. Used with permission from *I Promise You A Crown* by David Hazard © 1995 Bethany House Publishers. All rights reserved. p. 47.

3. J.I. Packer, *Keep in Step with the Spirit* (Grand Rapids: Fleming H. Revell a division of Baker Book House Company 1984) p. 34. Used by permission.

4. William Newell, *Romans Verse by Verse*, pp. 121-122.

5. F.B. Meyer, *The Christ Life For Your Life* (Chicago: Moody Press) p. 64.

6. Walter C. Kaiser, Jr., *Back Toward The Future* (Grand Rapids: Baker Book House 1989) pp. 69-79. Used by permission.

7. Josh McDowell, *Evidence That Demands a Verdict* (Nashville: Thomas Nelson Publishers 1992). Much thanks to Josh McDowell and his research in *Evidence That Demands a Verdict* on Jesus' fulfillment of Messianic prophecies.

8. Josh McDowell, *Evidence That Demands a Verdict* (Nashville: Thomas Nelson Publishers 1992) p. 175.

9. Arthur Bennett ed., *The Valley of Vision: A Collection of Puritan Prayers and Devotions* (Carlisle: The Banner of Truth Trust, 1975) pp. 44-45. Used by permission.

10. G. Campbell Morgan, *The Crises of Christ* (Old Tappan: Fleming H. Revell Publishing Company 1936) pp. 87-88. Used by permission of the G. Campbell Morgan Estate.

11. E. Stanley Jones, *The Divine Yes* (Nashville: Abingdon Press 1975) pp. 21-22. Used by permission.

12. Herbert F. Stevenson ed., *Keswick's Authentic Voice*, "The Master Is Come" by Rev. Charles A. Fox, M.A., p. 156.

13. Lewis Sperry Chafer, *Salvation* (Grand Rapids: Zondervan Publishing House 1917, 1965, 1978) p. 50.

14. Herbert F. Stevenson ed., *Keswick's Authentic Voice*, "A Summons To Newness of Life" by Rev. Alexander Smellie, M.A., D.D. (Holburn: Marshall, Morgan & Scott 1959).

15. Gipsy Smith, *As Jesus Passed By and Other Addresses*, pp. 193-194.

16. William R. Newell, *Revelation* (Chicago: Moody Press 1935) pp. 346-347.

17. Charles Haddon Spurgeon, *Spurgeon's Sermons Volume 15*, pp. 205-207.

18. Charles Haddon Spurgeon, *Spurgeon's Sermons Volume 9*, pp. 328-332.

WEEK 4

1. Amy Carmichael, *Toward Jerusalem* (Fort Washington: Christian Literature Crusade 1936) p. 115. Used by permission.

2. J.I. Packer, *Keep in Step with the Spirit* (Grand Rapids: Fleming H. Revell a division of Baker Book House Company 1984) pp. 47, 66. Used by permission.

3. Charles Haddon Spurgeon, *Morning and Evening*, November 16 Evening.

4. Ron Rhodes, *Christ Before the Manger* (Grand Rapids: Baker Book House © 1992) p. 57. Used by permission.

5. A.W. Tozer, *Christ the Eternal Son* (Camp Hill: Christian Publications 1982) pp. 35-36. Used by permission.

6. Ron Rhodes, *Christ Before the Manger* (Grand Rapids: Baker Book House © 1992) pp. 58-59. Used by permission.

7. Amy Carmichael, *Toward Jerusalem* (Fort Washington: Christian Literature Crusade 1936) p. 84. Used by permission.

8. Merrill F. Unger, *Unger's Bible Dictionary* (Chicago: Moody Press 1977) p. 1038.

9. A.W. Tozer, *Christ the Eternal Son* (Camp Hill: Christian Publications 1982) pp. 31-32.

10. A.W. Tozer, *The Christian Book of Mystical Verse* "The Man Divine" by T.P. (Camp Hill: Christian Publications 1963) pp. 105-106.

11. *Catholic Encyclopedia* 1917 www.newadvent.org/cathen/14661a.htm.

12. F.B. Meyer, Reprinted from *Daily Prayers* Copyright © 1995 by Harold Shaw Publishers, WaterBrook Press, Colorado Springs, CO. All Rights Reserved, p. 56.

13. Brennan Manning, *The Lion and the Lamb* (Grand Rapids: Chosen Books a division of Baker Book House 1987) p. 128. Used by permission.

14. Thomas à Kempis, *Of The Imitation of Christ* (New Kensington: Whitaker House © 1981) pp. 75-76. Used by permission of the publisher and available at local Christian bookstores everywhere.

15. John S.B. Monsell, *Parish Musings*, p. 78.

16. G. Campbell Morgan, *The Teaching of Christ*, (Grand Rapids: Fleming H. Revell 1913) pp. 42-43. Used by permission of the G. Campbell Morgan Estate.

17. A.W. Tozer, *I Talk Back To The Devil* (Camp Hill: Christian Publications 1972) pp. 133-135. Used by permission.

18. Josh McDowell and Bill Wilson, *He Walked Among Us*, (Nashville: Thomas Nelson Publishers 1988) pp. 335-336.

WEEK 5

1. For more information on Yahweh, it is recommended that you read *Trusting in the Names of God—A 30 Day Journey* by Catherine Martin (Eugene: Harvest House Publishers 2008) and *Trusting in the Names of God—A Quiet Time Experience* (Eugene: Harvest House Publishers 2008).

2. A.W. Tozer, *I Talk Back To The Devil* (Camp Hill: Christian Publications 1972) p. 143. Used by permission.

3. Henry Gariepy, *100 Portraits of Christ* (Wheaton Victor Books 1987, 1993) pp. 205-206. Used by permission.

4. A.B. Simpson, *The Christ in the Bible Commentary* (Camp Hill: Christian Publications 1993) pp. 473-474. Used by permission.

5. William Barclay, *Jesus As They Saw Him* (Grand Rapids: Wm. B. Eerdmans Publishing Company 1995) pp. 267-268. Used by permission.

6. Richard Ellsworth Day, *The Shadow of the Broad Brim* (Valley Forge: Judson Press © 1934) p. 168. 800-4-JUDSON. www.judson press.com.

7. Catherine Marshall ed., *The Prayers of Peter Marshall* (Grand Rapids: Chosen Books, a division of Baker Book House Company 1982) p. 35. Used by permission.

8. Henry Gariepy, *100 Portraits of Christ*, pp. 209-210. Used by permission.

9. Hannah Whitall Smith, *The God of all Comfort*, pp. 61-65.

10. Charles Slemming, *He Restoreth My Soul* from The Quiet Hour Series (London: Henry Walter Ltd.)

11. Mrs. Howard Taylor, *The Triumph of John and Betty Stam*, (Philadelphia: China Inland Mission 1935) p. 108.

12. Paul Lee Tan, *Encyclopedia of 7700 Illustrations*, (Rockville: Assurance Publishers 1979) pp. 545-546.

13. Robert Parsons, *Quotes from the Quiet Hour*, p. 81.

14. Arthur Bennett ed., *The Valley of Vision: A Collection of Puritan Prayers and Devotions* (Carlisle: The Banner of Truth Trust, 1975) p. 24. Used by permission.

15. Leon Morris, *The Gospel According to John*, (Grand Rapids: Wm. B. Eerdmans Publishing Company 1971) p. 454. Used by permission.

16. William Barclay, *Jesus As They Saw Him*, (Grand Rapids: Wm. B. Eerdmans Publishing Company 1995) p. 280. Used by permission.

17. Catherine Marshall ed., *The Prayers of Peter Marshall* (Grand Rapids: Chosen Books, a division of Baker Book House Company 1982) p. 67. Used by permission.

18. A.B. Bruce, *The Training of the Twelve*, (Grand Rapids: Kregel Publications 1971) pp. 414-415.

19. Herbert F. Stevenson ed., *Keswick's Authentic Voice*, "Abounding Life" by Rev. W. Graham Scroggie (Holburn: Marshall, Morgan & Scott 1959).

20. Andrew Murray, *Abide in Christ*, (Uhrichsville: Barbour & Company) pp. 30-31.

21. Andrew Murray, *The True Vine* (New Kensington: Whitaker House 1982) pp. 44-45. Used by permission.

22. Andrew Murray, *The Secret of Spiritual Strength* (New Kensington: Whitaker House 1977) pp. 22-23. Used by permission.

WEEK 6

1. Amy Carmichael, *Mountain Breezes* (Fort Washington: Christian Literature Crusade 1999) p. 175. Used by permission.

2. Hannah Whitall Smith, *The Christian's Secret of a Happy Life*, pp. 226-227.

3. Charles Wesley, *Jesus, Lord, We Look To Thee*, 1707-1788.

4. Hannah Whitall Smith, *The God of All Comfort*, pp. 223-224.

5. Charles Slemming, *He Leadeth Me* from The Quiet Hour Series (London: Henry Walter Ltd.)

6. A.B. Simpson, *The Christ Life* (Camp Hill: Christian Publications 1980) pp. 31-32. Used by permission.

7. Ruth Paxson, *Rivers of Living Water* (London: Marshall, Morgan & Scott 1930) pp. 47-49.

8. S.D. Gordon, *Quiet Talks on John's Gospel* (New York: Fleming H. Revell 1915) pp. 252-253.

9. Hannah Whitall Smith, *The Christian's Secret of a Happy Life*, p. 226.

10. Ruth Paxson, *Rivers of Living Water*, pp. 51-53.

11. Zac Poonen, *Beauty for Ashes* (Bombay, India: Gospel Literature Service 1975) p. 100.

12. S.D. Gordon, *Quiet Talks on John's Gospel*, pp. 225-226.

13. Hannah Whitall Smith, *The Christian's Secret of a Happy Life*, pp. 227-228.

14. Ian Thomas, *The Mystery of Godliness* (Grand Rapids: Zondervan Publishing House 1964) p. 23. Permission granted by W. Ian Thomas, Founder of Capernwray Missionary Fellowship of Torchbearers, Inc.) pp. 68-69.

15. Hannah Whitall Smith, *The God of All Comfort*, p. 232.

16. Alan Redpath, *Victorious Christian Living* (Old Tappan: Fleming H. Revell Company 1955) pp. 97-98. Used by permission of Mrs. Marjorie Redpath.

17. Ruth Paxson, *Rivers of Living Water*, p. 55.

WEEK 7

1. F.B. Meyer, *The Way Into The Holiest* (Grand Rapids: Baker Book House 1951) p. 131.

2. F.B. Meyer, *The Way Into The Holiest*, p. 128.

3. F.F. Bruce, *The Epistle to the Hebrews* from The New International Commentary on the New Testament (Grand Rapids: Wm. B. Eerdmans Publishing Company 1990) p. 175. Used by permission.

4. Andrew Murray, *The Holiest Of All* (London: Nisbet & Co.) pp. 180-181.

5. Constance Hudson © 2002 written during the pilot class of *A Heart On Fire*. Used by permission.

6. Alan Redpath, *Victorious Christian Living* (Old Tappan: Fleming H. Revell Company 1955) p. 56. Used by permission of Mrs. Marjorie Redpath.

7. F.B. Meyer, *The Way Into The Holiest*, p. 137.

8. Andrew Murray, *The Holiest Of All*, pp. 176-178.

9. F.B. Meyer, *The Way Into The Holiest*, p. 66.

10. Annie Johnson Flint, *He Giveth More Grace*.

11. F.F. Bruce, *The Epistle to the Hebrews* from The New International Commentary on the New Testament (Grand Rapids: Wm. B. Eerdmans Publishing Company 1990) pp. 206-207. Used by permission.

12. Alfred Edersheim, *The Life and Times of Jesus the Messiah* (Peabody: Henrickson Publishers 1883) p. 611.

13. Spiros Zodhiates, *The Hebrew-Greek Key Study Bible* (Chattanooga: AMG Publishers 1984, 1990) p. 1831. Used by permission.

14. Spiros Zodhiates, *The Hebrew-Greek Key Study Bible*, p. 1886. Used by permission.

15. A.B. Simpson, *The Christ Life* (Camp Hill: Christian Publications 1980) p. 31. Used by permission.

16. Andrew Murray, *Waiting on God* (Chicago: Moody Press 1979) p. 84.

17. An Unknown Christian, *The Kneeling Christian*, p. 23.

18. Mrs. Charles Cowman, *Springs in the Valley* (Los Angeles: The Oriental Missionary Society 1939) p. 54.

19. F.B. Meyer, *The Christ Life for Your Life*, (Chicago: Moody Press 1960) pp. 19-20.

20. Annie Johnson Flint, *Best-Loved Poems*, (Toronto: Evangelical Publishers) p. 13.

21. Amy Carmichael, *Toward Jerusalem*, (Ft. Washington: Christian Literature Crusade 1936) p. 67. Used by permission.

22. A.B. Simpson, *The Holy Spirit or Power From On High Volume 1*, (Camp Hill: Christian Publications Inc.) pp. 242-243. Used by permission.

23. Andrew Murray, *The Holiest Of All*, pp. 273-274.

24. F.B. Meyer, *The Way Into The Holiest*, p. 239.

25. O'Hallesby, *Prayer* (Minneapolis: Augsburg Publishing House 1931) p. 165.

26. Andrew Murray, *The Holiest Of All*, p. 512.

27. Henry Gariepy, *100 Portraits of Christ* (Wheaton Victor Books 1987, 1993) p. 184. Used by permission.

28. Charles Haddon Spurgeon, *The Saint and His Saviour* (Pasadena: Pilgrim Publications 1970) pp. 258-259.

WEEK 8

1. Merrill C. Tenney, *Interpreting Revelation*, (Grand Rapids: Wm. B. Eerdmans Publishing Company 1957) p. vii. Used by permission.

2. Robert H. Mounce, *The Book of Revelation* (Grand Rapids: Wm. B. Eerdmans Publishing Company 1977) p. 145. Used by permission.

3. Charles Haddon Spurgeon, "The Lamb: The Light" in *Spurgeon's Sermons Volume VIII*, (Grand Rapids: Zondervan Publishing House) p. 282.

4. Basilea Schlink, *My All For Him* (Minneapolis: Bethany House 1999) p. 124. Used by permission.

5. William R. Newell, *The Book of Revelation* (Chicago: Moody Press 1935) p. 301.

6. Charles Haddon Spurgeon, *Morning and Evening*, January 10 Evening.

7. Isaac Watts, *The Psalms and Hymns of Isaac Watts* (Morgan: Soli Deo Gloria Publications 1997) pp. 502-503.

8. Arthur Bennett ed., *The Valley of Vision: A Collection of Puritan Prayers and Devotions* (Carlisle: The Banner of Truth Trust, 1975) p. 44. Used by permission.

9. Edward Dennett, *The Name Above Every Name* (Oak Park: Bible Truth Publishers) pp. 107-108. Used by permission.

10. Andrew Murray, *Like Christ* (New York: Bay View Publishing Company) pp. 155-156.

11. Alan Redpath, *Victorious Christian Living* (Old Tappan: Fleming H. Revell Company 1955) pp. 33-34. Used by permission of Mrs. Marjorie Redpath.

12. F.B. Meyer, *The Way Into The Holiest* (Grand Rapids: Baker Book House 1951) pp. 49-50.

13. Charles Haddon Spurgeon, "The Lamb: The Light" in *Spurgeon's Sermons Volume VIII*, p. 285.

14. Amy Carmichael, *Mountain Breezes* (Fort Washington: Christian Literature Crusade 1999) p. 19. Used by permission.

15. G.R. Beasley-Murray, *Revelation in The New Century Bible Commentary* (Grand Rapids: Wm. B. Eerdmans Publishing Company 1983) pp. 278-279.

16. Peter Bayne, *The Testimony of Christ To Christianity* (1862) p. 152.

17. Merrill C. Tenney, *Interpreting Revelation*, p. 120. Used by permission.

18. Robert Parsons, *Quotes From The Quiet Hour* (Chicago: Moody Press 1949) p. 56.

19. Basilea Schlink, *My All For Him,* p. 112. Used by permission.

20. Anne R. Cousin, "In Immanuel's Land" *The Christian Book of Mystical Verse* (Carlisle: Christian Publications 1963) pp. 123-127.

ACKNOWLEDGMENTS

When I write a book it is never written in a vacuum. Life goes on with its many joys and responsibilities. The writing of *A Heart On Fire* would be virtually impossible without the love and support of my beloved husband, David Martin, M.D. He knows when to lean his head in the door and say it's time to drop everything and go have a nice dinner out. He knows when I'm so intensely focused that I forget to eat, and sometimes brings a plate of sliced apples or glass of iced tea and sets it on my desk. The Lord truly knew that you were the one for me, dear husband. Thank you for sharing this journey with me.

And then I want to say that I believe I have the most incredible family in the whole wide world. Mother, thank you for sharing my joys and sorrows in life. You always give me the encouragement to dare to dream big dreams. Dad, I want to thank you for believing in me and telling me to never, ever give up. I have thought of your words countless times just at the point when I thought I might come to a halt. I kept on because of your strong encouragement. Rob, you are the best brother in the whole world. I love it when you call me at five in the morning just to talk. You have been a steadfast rock to me many times in the most difficult places in my life. And then, to my Kayla, my precious niece—you are the apple of my eye. I just cannot get over your enthusiasm for everything. I love your smile, your laugh, and how when you were only two years old you would walk to the door and talk to it even though no one has any idea what you are saying. I do believe that you are going be speaking to thousands someday. You have brought much joy and laughter to my heart in the midst of a very active and challenging ministry. And then to Eloise, the best mother-in-law any girl could have. Though you are with the Lord now face to face, I will never forget all your love and encouragement in my relationship with the Lord. Andy, Keegan, and James—you are such a blessing to me.

Conni Hudson, thank you for asking me to finish my very first book of quiet times, *Pilgrimage of the Heart*. Neither of us had any idea what the Lord had in mind as a result of that! Beverly Trupp, thank you for giving me such wise words at just the right times in my life. Thank you for sharing all my joys in this ministry and showing me how the Lord is truly at work. I understand so many things because you are in my life. I thank the Lord for the gift of you. Cindy Clark, thank you for believing in me and for serving together with me in ministry. I love how ideas and actions are borne in the same moment with you. We sure have fun in ministry! Andy Graybill, I love it when you call me early in the morning to tell me what God is teaching you as you do my books of quiet times. You have been my friend through thick and thin and I thank the Lord for you. Stefanie Kelly Merritt, you are such a bright, shining star in my life. You have been my encouragement as I write and develop in ministry. Your songs minister to my heart and make me cry. Thank you for having such a heart for the Lord. Kelly Abeyratne, thank you for always seeking the face of God and being my comrade in ministry. Connie Sparks, a special thank you for getting excited with me as the Lord has opened the doors in this ministry. Thank you to our Quiet Time team past and present who serve with me and pray fervently for this ministry: Kayla Branscum, Conni Hudson, Myra Murphy, Betty Mann, Cindy Clark, Shirley Peters, Julie Airis Kelly Abeyratne, Elizabeth Sowles, Karen Darras, Paula Zillmer, Sandy Fallon. I thank the Lord for all of you and for your steadfast love and encouragement. Shirley Peters, thank you for your great love for the Word of God. You are such an example to me. Thank you to Johnny Mann, for writing the song "Quiet Time" and dedicating it to Quiet Time Ministries. What an incredible encouragement that song has been in my life many times as I was writing this book. I thank the Lord for both you and Betty, who have been such a steadfast support to me. Thank you to the group who piloted *A Heart On Fire*: Conni Hudson, Michelle Skramstad, Joan Hill, Melissa Brown, Debbie Griffin, Molly Lewis, Kayla Branscum, Cindy Clark, Betty Mann, Myra Murphy, Shirley Peters, Paula Zillmer, Debra Collins, Judy Doyle, Georgeann DeWoody, Sharon Hastings, Sherylyn Yoak, Paula U'Ren, and Jane Lyons. Your sharing and observations were invaluable in the completion of this book. Thank you to the groups who have used these books of quiet times to grow in your relationship with the Lord. Your encouragement has urged me onward in the writing of this book. Thank you to Sharon Hastings and to all the small group discussion leaders who serve with me as we study God's Word together. Thank you to the staff and volunteers at both Quiet Time Ministries and Southwest Community Church.

Kayla Branscum, my assistant: I am amazed at how perfect you are to serve with me in this ministry. You are always ready to do whatever comes up at the moment and can move easily through the doors of ministry that the Lord has opened for us in Quiet Time Ministries. Thank you to the Enriching Your Quiet Time staff for writing and developing the ideas that the Lord gives me.

I am also thankful to my professors at Bethel Theological Seminary who urged me to study hard. I am especially grateful for my Old Testament professor, Dr. Ronald Youngblood, and my New Testament professor, Dr. Walt Wessel, who is now with the Lord. Thank you to Bill and Vonette Bright and Josh and Dottie McDowell. You have been my examples in both my ministry and my relationship with the Lord. Thank you to my agent, Greg Johnson, of WordServe Literary, for all your support and encouragement over the years.

Thank you to the Board of Directors of Quiet Time Ministries: David Martin, Conni Hudson, Shirley Peters, and Jane Lyons, for your faithfulness in this ministry. And finally, a huge thanks to those who give financially to this ministry. I could have never done any of this alone – your gifts have made it possible to launch out in this very exciting ministry; Quiet Time Ministries.

JOURNAL

"Pour out your heart like water in the
presence of the Lord" — Lamentations 2:19 NIV

JOURNAL

"Pour out your heart like water in the presence of the Lord" — Lamentations 2:19 NIV

SIX SECRETS TO A POWERFUL QUIET TIME ©2005

....

....

....

....

....

....

....

....

....

....

....

....

....

....

....

....

Journal

"Pour out your heart like water in the presence of the Lord" — Lamentations 2:19 NIV

SIX SECRETS TO A POWERFUL QUIET TIME ©2005

JOURNAL

"Pour out your heart like water in the
presence of the Lord" — Lamentations 2:19 NIV

....

....

....

....

....

....

....

....

....

....

....

....

....

....

JOURNAL

"Pour out your heart like water in the
presence of the Lord" — Lamentations 2:19 NIV

JOURNAL

"Pour out your heart like water in the
presence of the Lord" — Lamentations 2:19 NIV

SIX SECRETS TO A POWERFUL QUIET TIME ©2005

....

....

....

....

....

....

....

....

....

....

....

....

....

....

ADORE GOD IN PRAYER

"Don't worry about anything;
instead, pray about everything" — Philippians 4:6 NIV

SIX SECRETS TO A POWERFUL QUIET TIME ©2005

*Prayer for*_____

Date: Topic:
Scripture:
Request:

Answer:

_____

Date: Topic:
Scripture:
Request:

Answer:

_____

Date: Topic:
Scripture:
Request:

Answer:

_____

Date: Topic:
Scripture:
Request:

Answer:

_____

Date: Topic:
Scripture:
Request:

Answer:

_____

ADORE GOD IN PRAYER

"Don't worry about anything;
instead, pray about everything" — Philippians 4:6 NIV

SIX SECRETS TO A POWERFUL QUIET TIME ©2005

*Prayer for*_____

Date: Topic:
Scripture:
Request:

Answer:

_____

Date: Topic:
Scripture:
Request:

Answer:

_____

Date: Topic:
Scripture:
Request:

Answer:

_____

Date: Topic:
Scripture:
Request:

Answer:

_____

Date: Topic:
Scripture:
Request:

Answer:

_____

ADORE GOD IN PRAYER

"Don't worry about anything;
instead, pray about everything" — Philippians 4:6 NIV

SIX SECRETS TO A POWERFUL QUIET TIME ©2005

*Prayer for*_____

Date: Topic:

Scripture:

Request:

Answer:

_____

Date: Topic:

Scripture:

Request:

Answer:

_____

Date: Topic:

Scripture:

Request:

Answer:

_____

Date: Topic:

Scripture:

Request:

Answer:

_____

Date: Topic:

Scripture:

Request:

Answer:

_____

Adore God In Prayer

"Don't worry about anything;
instead, pray about everything" — Philippians 4:6 NIV

SIX SECRETS TO A POWERFUL QUIET TIME ©2005

*Prayer for*_____

Date: Topic:
Scripture:
Request:

Answer:
_____

Date: Topic:
Scripture:
Request:

Answer:
_____

Date: Topic:
Scripture:
Request:

Answer:
_____

Date: Topic:
Scripture:
Request:

Answer:
_____

Date: Topic:
Scripture:
Request:

Answer:
_____

ADORE GOD IN PRAYER

"Don't worry about anything;
instead, pray about everything" — Philippians 4:6 NIV

SIX SECRETS TO A POWERFUL QUIET TIME ©2005

*Prayer for*_____

Date: Topic:
Scripture:
Request:

Answer:
_____

Date: Topic:
Scripture:
Request:

Answer:
_____

Date: Topic:
Scripture:
Request:

Answer:
_____

Date: Topic:
Scripture:
Request:

Answer:
_____

Date: Topic:
Scripture:
Request:

Answer:
_____

ADORE GOD IN PRAYER

"Don't worry about anything;
instead, pray about everything" — Philippians 4:6 NIV

SIX SECRETS TO A POWERFUL QUIET TIME ©2005

Prayer for _____

Date: Topic:
Scripture:
Request:

Answer:

Date: Topic:
Scripture:
Request:

Answer:

Date: Topic:
Scripture:
Request:

Answer:

Date: Topic:
Scripture:
Request:

Answer:

Date: Topic:
Scripture:
Request:

Answer:

Made in the USA
San Bernardino, CA
03 December 2017